Our Discovery Island

Film Studio Island

4

TEACHER BOOK

José Luis Morales

PEARSON

ALWAYS LEARNING

Pearson Education Limited
Edinburgh Gate
Harlow
Essex CM20 2JE
England
and Associated Companies throughout the world.

Our Discovery Island ™
www.ourdiscoveryisland.com

First published by Pearson Education do Brasil 2012

Diretor Editorial e de Conteúdo: Roger Trimer
Gerente de Publicação: Sherri Pemberton
Gerente Editorial: Kelly Tavares
Editora de Mídia e Desenvolvimento: Veronica Teodorov
Editora de Desenvolvimento: Viviane Kirmeliene
Adaptação do Manual do Professor: Najin Lima
Adaptação e Tradução do Manual do Professor: Renata Chimim
Supervisora de Produção: Cristina Tavares
Editoração Eletrônica: Figurativa Editorial;

Dados Internacionais de Catalogação na Publicação (CIP)
(Câmara Brasileira do Livro, SP, Brasil)

Morales, José Luis
Our discovery island 4 : teacher book 4 / José Luis Morales. -- São Paulo : Pearson Education do Brasil, 2012.

ISBN 978-85-88318-16-8

1. Inglês (Ensino fundamental) I. Título.

11-07040 CDD-372.6520202

Índices para catálogo sistemático:
1. Inglês : Ensino fundamental 372.6520202

Agradecimentos
A Pearson Brasil agradece aos professores que analisaram Our Discovery Island, contribuindo para aprimorá-lo:
Beatriz de Frias Pereira de Souza, Centro de Línguas e Informática do Cecan-Clic / **Carolina de Castro Nyerges**, Colégio Rainha da Paz / **Daniela Helena Paukovits Teixeira**, Colégio Marista São José / **Daniele Patricia Lages**, Colégio São Judas Tadeu / **Débora Jaroski Barbosa**, Escola Padre José Eichelberger / **Domingos Di Lello**, Casa Thomas Jefferson / **Letícia Santos**, ICBEU Ibiá / **Milena Jatobá Costa Andrade**, Escola Casa do Sol / **Rosana Totti Silveira**, Colégio Nossa Senhora de Sion / **Saula Glovinsky**, Colégio Santa Mônica / **Sonia Aparecida M. N. da Fonseca**, Colégio Santo Agostinho / **Thays Farias Galvão Ladosky**, Colégio Damas da Instrução Cristã / **Vanessa Pegado Ferreira**, Colégio Guilherme Dumont Villares.

Crédito das fotos
Alamy Images: Amazon-Images 51 (Tapir), Arcticphoto 35tl, Bill Bachman 35b, Danita Delimont 65t, idp canal collection 11l, imagebroker 13t, Israel images 41 (Bob), Juniors Bildarchiv 17tl, Christina Kennedy 28t, Vova Pomortzeff 12t, Morley Read 51 (Tarantula), Craig Richardson 68r, Rolf Nussbaumer Photography 51 (Hummingbird), uwesSERENGETI 29b, Visual&Written SL 67l, WorldFoto 41 (4); **Trevor Clifford:** 5, 9b, 15, 17b, 25, 32b, 33, 41b, 43b, 49b, 57b, 63, 64, 65b; **Corbis:** Theo Allofs 49tr, DLILLC 28bl, Randy Faris 11cr, Ina Fassbender / Reuters 19tl, Steve Hix / Somos Images 44bl, JON HRUSA / epa 12bl, Image Source 70b, Herb Schmitz 41 (2), Paul Thompson 60b, Michele Westmorland 67r; **FotoLibra:** Kevin John Myhill 11r; **Getty Images:** AFP / Stringer 19tr, Shaun Botterill 12br, Clive Brunskill 45tr, FilmMagic / Jason LaVeris 4cr, Jose Luis Pelaez / Iconica 41 (Mary), NBAE / Noah Graham 44br, The Image Bank / EIGHTFISH 28cl, Paul Vozdic / Iconica 68l, WireImage / George Pimentel 61b; **Robert Harding World Imagery:** Christian Kober 60tl, Christian Kober 60tl; **Robert Harding World Imagery:** Christian Kober 60tl, Christian Kober 60tl; **iStockphoto:** Jani Bryson 37bl, 41 (Emma), DIGIcal 9tc, Andre Fiedeldey 13b, Daniel Laflor 37tr, Liza McCorkle 11cl, MissHibiscus 29t, ranplett 37tl, Victor Soares 51 (Parrot), Alexey Sokolov 57c, Stefanie Van Der Vinden 49tl, Jason Titzer 43t; **Photolibrary.com:** Asia Images Group 60tr, Corbis 27b, ROM ROM 35tr, rubberball 17tr; **Press Association Images:** AP 27c, John Birdsall / library photo posed by a model 41 (Tim), Rick Bowmer / AP 27t, Charles Sykes / AP 4l; **Rex Features:** 41 (3), Action Press 4cl, Robin Bell 28cr, Alex Coppel / Newspix 19b, Image Source 57tl, 57tr, Jen Lowery 4r, Sonny Meddle 61tl, Alastair Muir 44tr, NBCUPHOTOBANK 41 (1), Newspix 9tr, Sipa Press 4c, Charles Sykes 45c; **Shutterstock.com:** Monkey Business Images 9tl, Monkey Business Images 9, Andere 17 (monkeys), kle555 17 (cat), Dietmar Höpfl 17 (frog), wavebreakmedia ltd 71, L_amica 142 (tree), koya979 142 (presents), paulvg 142 (board game); **Thinkstock:** BananaStock 70t, Brand X Pictures 45tl, Goodshoot 44tl, Photodisc 37br, Photos.com 61tr, Pixland 45b. (b-inferior; c-centro; l-esquerda; r-direita; t-superior)

Crédito das ilustrações
Lee Cosgrove, Anja Boretzki (Good Illustration), Bill Greenhead (Illustration), Marek Jagucki, Mark Ruffle (The Organisation) cut-out mini cards, Humberto Blanco (Sylvie Poggio).

Pearson Education do Brasil
uma empresa do grupo Pearson Education
Rua Nélson Francisco, 26 CEP: 02712-100 São Paulo, SP, Brasil
Tel.: 0800-55-8881 ou 11-2178-8668
e-mail: elt.br@pearson.com
10 9 8 7 6 5 4 3 Set/2013

Our Discovery Island

Film Studio Island 4

TEACHER BOOK

Contents

Introduction

NTRODUCTION

Our Discovery Island is a five-level course for children learning English as a foreign language in primary schools. It offers best practice methodology in the classroom while also offering teachers and students an innovative digital environment. *Our Discovery Island* can be used as a blended learning course. It takes into account the current movement towards using an increased amount of technology in the classroom, and also at home, as more and more families have computers and want safe, effective, educational material for their children.

Our Discovery Island motivates children by introducing them to a group of characters in an Online Island that echoes the island in their book. Students follow the characters through their book while listening to stories, singing songs, communicating and playing games along the way. Most importantly, students will enjoy themselves and make their own discoveries in English. *Our Discovery Island* - where learning is an adventure!

Components

For the Student

The **Student Book** provides materials to effectively present and practice the target language. It introduces new language in lively and engaging contexts. A wide variety of practice tasks lead from controlled language activities to production and personalization activities. Each unit includes listening, speaking, reading and writing activities, ensuring that students develop their skills and are able to practice new language in a broad range of contexts. Additionally, the Student Book contains songs, chants, stories, games, listening and reading texts and communicative activities to ensure lessons are varied, motivating and effective. It is organized as follows:

- a Welcome Unit introducing students to the group of characters and the Island (levels 1 to 4);
- an opening spread with the beginning of the story to engage students in the adventure (levels 3 to 5);
- eight units divided into eight lessons;
- holiday lessons in the back of the book;
- Mini card activities in Lesson 4;
- Four *Wider World* lessons focusing on a real-life topic in other countries, at the end of alternate units.
- Four Review lessons, at the end of alternate units.

The **Access Code** printed at the second cover of the book gives students and parents unique and safe access to the *Online Islands* via the Internet.

The integrated **Workbook** provides reinforcement and consolidation of the language presented in the Student Book. It contains controlled and freer practice plus personalization and further reading texts. It is organized as follows:

- eight units for use after the lessons in the Student Book;
- a picture dictionary in the back of the book to help students remember the target vocabulary.

At the bottom of the Student Book page there is reference to the activities of the Workbook that can be done at the end of the lesson. Full details of the activities are given in the teaching notes.

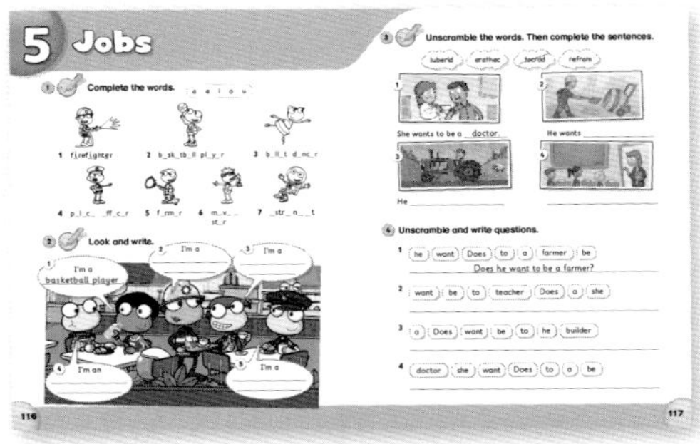

Our Discovery Island includes a unique **Online Island** component (www.ourdiscoveryisland.com). This provides a safe, engaging and highly-motivating environment, where students meet the characters from the Student Book plus a host of other exciting characters, and follow them on an adventure. Students will engage in safe 'closed-chat' dialogues with the characters they meet and will practice target language from the units. They will also follow instructions to help them solve puzzles and play supplementary language games along the way. The Online Island is a great tool to make learning happen in an interactive way, and it further consolidates and extends the language-learning process. Most of all, students will enjoy the experience of learning through play and will absorb English without realizing it! For level 4, students will play on *Film Studio Island*.

The **Multi-ROM** contains interactive activities and games for students to review content. It also includes the songs from the Student Book in karaoke format, as well as flashcards with pictures and audio. All the listening material from the Student Book is also available as mp3 files. It can be used both at school (in the computer lab or in the classroom) and at home.

For the Teacher

The **Teacher Book** is interleaved with the Student Book pages. It provides step-by-step lesson plans covering all the course material. Each lesson is clearly structured into stages:

- starting the lesson;
- presentation;

- practice;
- ending the lesson.

There are also further ideas for extra activities and work with values in every unit. The lesson notes are designed to be flexible support for all teachers, including those who may lack time for planning or who have limited access to resources. For maximum flexibility and variety throughout the teaching year, the following photocopiable materials can be found in the back of the book:

- tests every two units;
- a spinner template.

The following materials can be found online, at www.pearson.com.br/ourdiscoveryisland:

- worksheets for every unit;
- templates for holiday activities.

The **Access Code** printed at the second cover of the book gives the teacher special access to the Online Islands via the Internet.

Teachers have special access to the **Online Island** using the Access code provided in the book. This takes them into any online island and gives access to a user-friendly Progress Review System (PRS), where the teacher can monitor the progress of their students. There are step-by-step help guides detailing all aspects of game play, plus log in and classroom management through the PRS. These are available both on screen and as a download to print. Teachers will also find report cards showing each student's progress, which they can print out for the class and parents.

Teachers also receive the same **Multi-ROM** students have in their Student Books.

Each level of *Our Discovery Island* has a **DVD** with four episodes. Each episode can be used to reinforce and extend the language of the course, focusing on the topics and language of two units. The songs are introduced by three presenters, Sally, Jack and Albert, and there are animated stories, showing further adventures of the Island.

The **Flashcards** present the main target vocabulary in each unit. The teaching notes in the Teacher Book clearly explain how the flashcards can be used to present, practice and consolidate language through games and activities. There are over 200 cards that can be used in levels 1 to 4.

Our Discovery Island **Active Teach** provides software for use on any Interactive Whiteboard (IWB) with integrated tools. It can also be used with a computer and projector. It eases classroom management as it contains direct links to all of the Student Book pages, digitally transformed to create more opportunities for interaction between the student, the teacher and the material. It includes further practice activities and games that recycle the language of the unit and links to audio content, without the need of a separate CD. It has stimulating and engaging **Digital Posters** and flashcards. There are three posters to accompany each level of *Our Discovery Island*. The stories are also presented in an interactive way (see guidelines on how to use stories on page XI).

There is also printable content that can be used in the classroom:

- full version of the Teacher Book tests, in editable format;
- audio script and suggested activities for the DVD;
- suggested activities for the digital posters;
- worksheets for every unit;
- templates for holiday activities;
- end-of-the-year certificate.

Methodology and Organization

Methodology

Our Discovery Island assumes no previous knowledge of English and takes a '5P' approach to communication in order to provide support and encourage production from an early stage. The PPP (Presentation, Practice and Production) is a tried and tested approach which is favored by many teachers in the primary classroom. The lesson sequence is clear and easy to follow and works in a structured way. The *Our Discovery* Island '5Ps' approach adds also Personalization and Pronunciation.

Presentation is the first stage. The teacher demonstrates the key language while providing a model (on audio or Active Teach) for students to hear the correct pronunciation. When using *Our Discovery Island*, teachers can employ the flashcards at this stage of the lesson.

Practice is provided in the form of controlled and more open activities using the presented language. At early levels, this may involve listening to the word and pointing to it in a picture.

Production activities encourage students to use the language either to speak or write something. These activities encourage students to become more autonomous and to manipulate the language in order to communicate.

Personalization activities are also included in the lesson structure to engage students further with the unit language and to help them with language recall.

Pronunciation is a key area in language teaching, and it is addressed in all units. Students practice it through fun and engaging songs and chants that help them acquire the stress, rhythm and intonation of English.

Organization

The eight main teaching units consist of eight lessons, as follows:

Lesson 1

Each unit of *Our Discovery Island* begins with an opening scene with the characters. The target vocabulary of the unit is presented.

Students will:

- practice the new vocabulary with audio support;
- listen to, read and associate the vocabulary with repetitive sounds;
- produce the vocabulary before moving on to a listening comprehension task.

Lesson 2

The new structure is presented in a chant, and the vocabulary from Lesson 1 is fully practiced. A *Look!* box highlights the target language of the lesson.

Students will:

- practice the new structure and review vocabulary in a fun and rhythmic way;
- do a listening comprehension task;
- produce language in a speaking task.

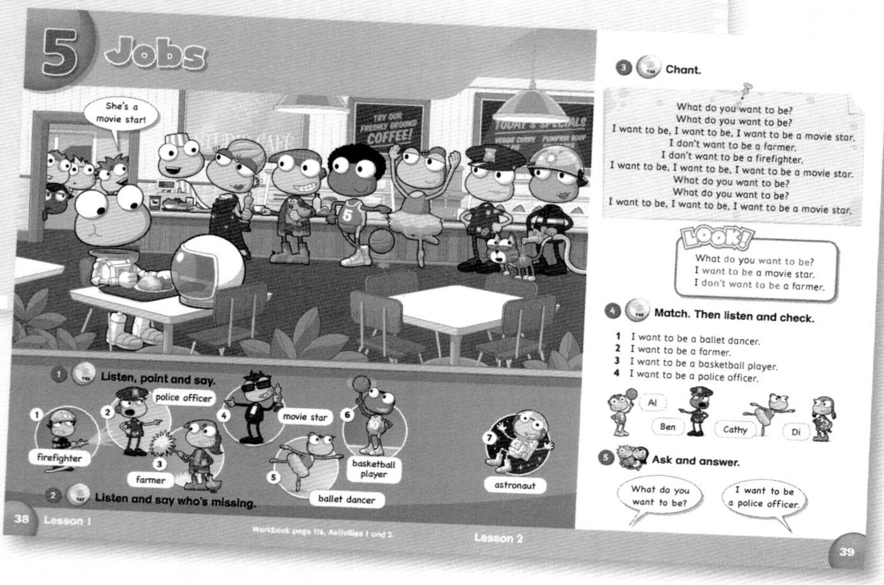

Lesson 3

Language work is extended through a captivating song. There is further practice of vocabulary and structures from Lessons 1 and 2. A karaoke version of the song is available in the Multi-ROM and in the Active Teach. A *Look!* box highlights the target language of the lesson.

Students will:

- practice and extend language in a fun and engaging way;
- produce language in a speaking task, based on the song.

Lesson 4

Speaking, listening, reading and writing skills are practiced in motivating activities. Mini cards are used in games in every unit.

Students will:

- practice the language from previous lessons, while developing the four skills;
- have fun with a game, using the mini cards.

A home-school activity (in the teaching notes) encourages family involvement.

Lesson 5

The story is presented with speech bubbles for reading and with audio support. It consolidates vocabulary and structures from previous lessons, and introduces some new language. The lesson ends with a link to show teachers that students can now do the online activities on *Space Island*.

Students will:

- see how new language is used in conversation;
- have fun with an exciting adventure story.

Lesson 6

New language is presented through a cross-curricular topic in English. The lesson practices new and recycled language from previous lessons. A *Mini project* encourages production of the target language.

Students will:

- learn new concepts from other subjects in English;
- have an opportunity to apply and personalize language.

Cleo, the mascot of *Our Discovery Island 4*, is holding a picture of an item students need to find online on *Film Studio Island*. When they click on it, they are taken to a language game (the mascot appears either in this lesson, in Lesson 3, in Lesson 4 or in the Review/*Wider World* lessons).

12 Listen, read and match.
5
I WANT TO BE A CHAMPION!
1 Naomi Johnson wants to be a champion. She wants to win three medals at the next Olympic Games.
2 At 6 o'clock in the morning Naomi goes swimming. She swims for two hours and then she has a big breakfast. Then she goes running and at 12 o'clock, she has lunch. In the afternoon, she goes swimming again.
3 Sundays are a special day. Naomi doesn't go swimming. She likes watching TV and she goes shopping. She loves shoes!
a
b
c
13 Ask and answer.
1 What/want to be?
2 What time/play/go/do ...?
3 What/eat for breakfast?
4 What/do after lunch?
5 What/do on Sundays?
What do you want to be?
I want to be a firefighter.
MINI PROJECT
Do a class survey. Ask 'What do you want to be?'
Lesson 6
Workbook page 119, Activities 8 and 9.
43

Review / *Wider World*

In alternate units, this lesson is either a Review spread, consolidating the language of the last two units, or a *Wider World* spread, focusing on a real-life topic in other countries. *Wider World* spreads also consolidate the language of the last two units and introduce some new topic-related language.

Students will:

- review vocabulary and structures;
- learn about other cultures;
- have another opportunity to apply and personalize language.

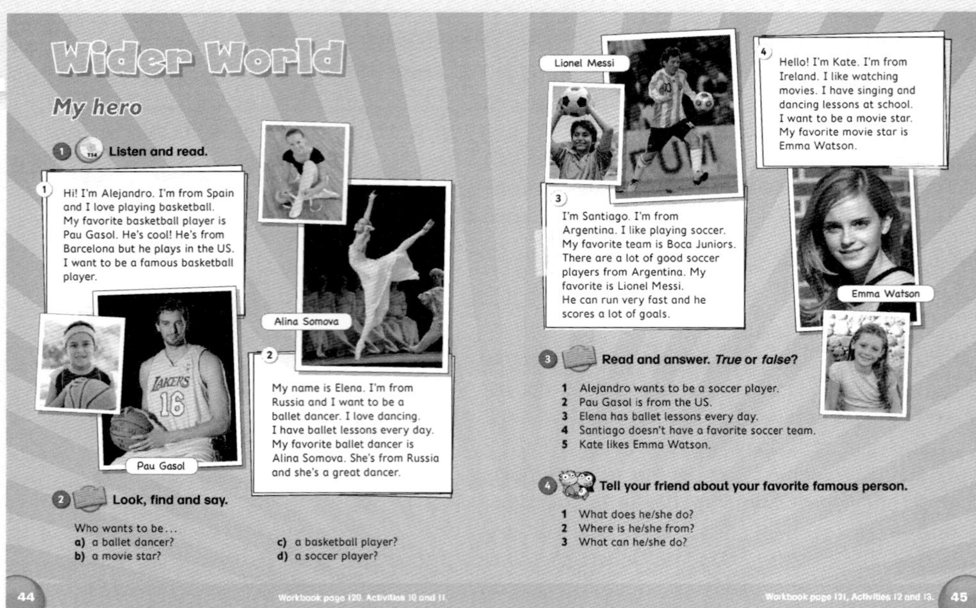
Wider World
My hero
1 Listen and read.
1 Hi! I'm Alejandro. I'm from Spain and I love playing basketball. My favorite basketball player is Pau Gasol. He's cool! He's from Barcelona but he plays in the US. I want to be a famous basketball player.
Pau Gasol
Alina Somova
2 My name is Elena. I'm from Russia and I want to be a ballet dancer. I love dancing. I have ballet lessons every day. My favorite ballet dancer is Alina Somova. She's from Russia and she's a great dancer.
2 Look, find and say.
Who wants to be...
a) a ballet dancer?
b) a movie star?
c) a basketball player?
d) a soccer player?
44
Workbook page 120, Activities 10 and 11.
Lionel Messi
3 I'm Santiago. I'm from Argentina. I like playing soccer. My favorite team is Boca Juniors. There are a lot of good soccer players from Argentina. My favorite is Lionel Messi. He can run very fast and he scores a lot of goals.
4 Hello! I'm Kate. I'm from Ireland. I like watching movies. I have singing and dancing lessons at school. I want to be a movie star. My favorite movie star is Emma Watson.
Emma Watson
3 Read and answer. *True* or *false*?
1 Alejandro wants to be a soccer player.
2 Pau Gasol is from the US.
3 Elena has ballet lessons every day.
4 Santiago doesn't have a favorite soccer team.
5 Kate likes Emma Watson.
4 Tell your friend about your favorite famous person.
1 What does he/she do?
2 Where is he/she from?
3 What can he/she do?
Workbook page 121, Activities 12 and 13.
45

Online Island Introduction

Young Learners and Technology

Research shows that appropriate use of computer technology in education is beneficial for students (Clements and Sarama; Waxman, Connell, and Gray; Byrom and Bingham). Broadly speaking, students can learn *from* computers and *with* computers. Students learn *from* computers when the computer assumes the role of a tutor, with the goal of imparting and increasing basic knowledge and skills. Students learn *with* computers when the computer serves in the role of a facilitating tool, with the goal of developing critical thinking skills, research skills, and the creative imagination (Ringstaff and Kelley).

Computer activities should be age-appropriate and foster instruction in ways that increase learning, motivation, personal productivity, and creativity. Children are naturally curious and willing to interact with computers, and they enjoy their ability to control the type, pace, and repetition of an activity. In some cases, children have even managed to learn how to use a computer with no instruction at all, through their own curiosity, fearlessness, and persistence (Mitra).

Computers in the English Language Classroom

The decision to use computers in the language classroom, including the English language classroom, requires the establishment of both technological goals and language-learning goals. For young children, goals such as the following facilitate a path to focused learning.

Technology Objectives	Language Objectives
• To become familiar with the parts of a computer (CPU, screen, keyboard, mouse, cursor, printer, and so on). • To become familiar with approved software programs for the classroom. • To become familiar with operations (select, drag, save, delete, and so on). • To become familiar with finding, filing, tracking, and organizing information. • To share information and collaborate with others. • To develop learner autonomy.	• To use English to interact in the classroom and to communicate in social situations. • To use English to describe self, family, community, and country. • To use learning strategies to increase communicative competence. • To develop the four skills: listening, speaking, reading, and writing. • To pronounce English words, phrases, and sentences intelligibly. • To use appropriate register.

References

Byrom, E., and Bingham, M., *Factors Influencing the Effective Use of Technology for Teaching and Learning: Lessons Learned from SEIR-TEC Intensive Site Schools,* 2nd ed. Greensboro: SERVE, 2001.

Clements, D. H., and Sarama, J. "Strip Mining for Gold: Research and Policy in Educational Technology – A Response to 'Fool's Gold.'" *Educational Technology Review, 11*(1), (2001): 7–69.

Kneas, K. M., and Perry, B. D. "Using Technology in the Early Childhood Classroom." *Early Childhood Today.* http://www2.scholastic.com/browse/article.jsp?id=4055&FullBreadCrumbs (accessed June 27, 2011)

Mitra, S. "Hole in the wall – can kids learn computer literacy by themselves?" Generation YES Blog. http://blog.genyes.org/index.php/2007/05/24/hole-in-the-wall-can-kids-learn-computer-literacy-by-themselves/ (accessed June 27, 2011)

Ringstaff, C., and Kelley, L. *The Learning Return on Our Educational Technology Investment*. San Francisco: WestEd, 2002. Also available online at http://www.wested.org/online_pubs/learning_return.pdf

The Online Island

The **Online Island** (www.ourdiscoveryisland.com) is an immersive world which accompanies the *Our Discovery Island* series. It is a ground-breaking digital product, combining the methodologies of classroom-based ELT and games-based learning. It is a safe learning environment, suitable for young learners which, via an Internet connection, can be used:

- on individual computers at school or at home;
- in groups at school, in the classroom.

It provides immediate feedback on performance, and contains features that appeal to young learners, such as colorful attractive visuals, clear audio providing pronunciation models, animation, and game-like activities, all of which play a part in student motivation. It is carefully calibrated to appeal to children between the ages of 6 and 11. The target vocabulary and grammar directly reinforce the syllabus of the course. Since tasks are intuitive and clear, and students receive immediate audio and visual feedback on their progress, the program builds learner confidence and independence.

The Online Island was authored by a team of ELT specialists and multimedia games developers. It offers rich and engaging digital worlds, which build on the language and aims contained within the books. The main emphasis is on expanding vocabulary while students learn by playing language games and achieving tasks. New language is introduced gradually and contextualized, so that students feel confident and motivated to complete each level. The key concepts which have guided the design are:

- *Immersion.* The Online Island takes students out of their classroom or home environment and immerses them in a coherent and believable context. Engaging content and beautiful design hold the students' interest and motivate them to continue with the adventure. Research conducted with the Online Island indicates that even very young children are able to maintain concentration and enthusiasm for long periods of time.
- *Stealth learning.* The Online Island is enjoyable and learning takes place almost without students being aware of it. Rather than mirroring the type of tasks in the Student Book, children learn via interactions with characters in the adventure. They are presented with real-world-like tasks, giving them a sense of responsibility and active involvement, which is extremely motivating. Learning takes place through listening and reading comprehension of speech bubbles, and through exposure to the target lexical sets via dialogues, the Picture Dictionary and supplementary language games.
- *Mastery.* Striking the right balance of challenge and achievability is a key component in any game. The *Online Island* has been carefully designed to introduce the key skills needed to complete the task at the start of each level, and then by slowly building the complexity of the language students encounter. It is important that students find the tasks within the adventure sufficiently challenging. Children with prior exposure to digital games expect to fail at complex tasks several times before achieving them. This makes the tasks more, not less, satisfying, once achieved. It also encourages exploration and educational risk-taking. The model of 'try, fail, repeat, succeed' is also important because it gives repeated exposure to the target language, ensuring that students comprehend the language before they move on.
- *Control.* Students love immersive worlds because they feel free within them. They can move their avatar around at their own speed and in their own chosen direction. They are also free to experiment and to fail without censure or observation. This gives them confidence and motivation. The Online Island has been designed to allow children sufficient freedom to enjoy the adventure and games, but at the same time to carefully channel them towards the learning outcomes and to expose them gradually to the target language. A carefully controlled gating system means they must achieve certain tasks before progressing into new parts of the adventure. A starred report card system motivates them to complete all the tasks within a scene, but gives them some freedom to determine when and how they do this.
- *Reward.* The Online Island includes many of the most popular features of existing games, such as collectible items, customization, avatar design and 'hidden' rewards such as new characters who appear once certain tasks are complete as well as audio and visual feedback to a task.

Teacher Support

We recognize that many teachers are likely to be unfamiliar with digital components, so we have developed a series of help guides, both online and as a download to be printed, to help teachers gain confidence in using the Online Island in the classroom, in assisting students with queries about the tasks, or in setting parts of the Online Island for home study.

In conjunction with these resources, there are video walkthroughs of each level, to answer queries about specific sections of the adventure. These videos can also act as an introduction, or provide quick support for teachers who can't spare the time to work through the Online Island themselves.

All teachers will receive an individual Access code to the *Online Island* and, unlike the student version, it will contain a map, allowing them to skip back and forward between scenes.

For ease of classroom management, there is a Progress Review System (PRS) where teachers can register their classes and monitor their progress.

Film Studio Island Online

Film Studio Island Online is set on the fun island of Discovery Film Studios, where students visit a wildlife studio, a special effects studio and a dinosaur studio, among others. They follow the stories of two movie stars: Favolina Jolly and Madley Kool, whom they will recognize from the Student Book.

Students must help Favolina find all the missing charms from her bracelet. They will also have fun helping other characters in all the different movie sets along the way. As they move around Film Studio Island, they will bump into and be able to interact with other characters, such as Jenny, John, Ruby and Sam.

How to Use Stories

Stories are an essential part of language learning because they allow students to absorb information in a fun and stimulating way. Learning outside the normal boundaries of a teacher-based classroom environment creates the opportunity for students to develop their creative and communicative skills. Using stories in the classroom greatly enhances students' ability to listen and to actively respond to target language and structures in a fun and relaxed atmosphere. Stories increase motivation and encourage less confident students to contribute with their ideas and opinions, because they are not confined to the limits of a certain structure. They provide larger chunks of language in a context and provide an opportunity for students to produce language.

There's a story in Lesson 5 of each unit featuring the *Island* characters. These stories serve to review and reinforce the target language and structures of the unit. The artwork is visually stimulating and the audio effects ensure students listen avidly from start to finish. Below is a four-step method for using stories in the classroom that starts with L1 anticipation and ends with (assisted) performance. In order to gather everybody's attention when working with the stories, we suggest you use the Active Teach.

Stage I – Anticipating the Story

The questions to ask before listening to the story provide teachers with the opportunity to introduce any new vocabulary or to review previously learned language and structures. Students can begin to form an idea of the theme of the story and how it might develop. This allows teachers to assess how thoroughly students have absorbed the target language of the unit. At this stage, teachers should ask students questions or carry out a simple discussion in L1 to get them thinking about the story. Teachers shouldn't provide answers at this stage, but rather allow students to think for themselves.

Stage 2 – Hearing and Seeing the Story

The full audio script is given in the Teacher Book, so if access to technology is limited or if it fails during the lesson, teachers can read from the Teacher Book. At this stage, students listen to the story in English and work through it in English to find answers themselves.

Stage 3 – Checking the Story

Questions to be asked after listening to the story are also in the teaching notes. This gives teachers the possibility to further assess the depth of students' comprehension of the story and of the language used. It also sparks students' creativity and imagination by encouraging them to visualize how the story develops.

Stage 4 – Acting the story

After listening to the story several times, students are ready to act it out in groups, providing them with the opportunity to say larger chunks of language. Props can be brought to class and used to make the experience even more stimulating. Teachers may play the recording, or read the audio script from the Teacher Book, while students act out, or students may recite the story from memory.

Below are some suggestions for extra work with the stories.

- While students listen to the story, they perform a specific action for target vocabulary (e.g., students clap when they hear the word *purple,* or stamp their feet when they hear the word *blue*).
- Students draw a new picture for any frame of the story.
- Students create a new ending for the story.
- Students draw their favorite character.
- Students discuss real-life situations with connotations to the story.
- Students comment on how they would feel or how they would behave if they were in a similar situation to one of the story characters.

The **DVDs** give the language of *Our Discovery Island* a new context for students to recycle language of the Student Book. Sally, Jack and Albert provide a song and there is an animated story from each Online Island.

1 Song

Students watch, listen and follow the actions. As they grow more confident, they can join in with the song.

2 Story

Watch the story. Ask students (L1) what happened in the story. Watch again, stopping at key points, and ask them about the language, the images or the story. Ask the students to act out the story. Assign the roles of two of the characters to confident speakers and let other students play the other parts. Encourage them to say as much of the dialogue as they can and prompt them where necessary.

The audio script and suggested activities for the DVD can be found in the Active Teach.

Classroom Management Tips

Our Discovery Island presents different classroom dynamics. It goes from individual work to pairwork, group work and whole class activities. This variety of students grouping in a language learning environment is very important to develop different skills in our students.

When working individually, students have the opportunity to reflect on what they have learned and to put it into practice by themselves, either internalizing the knowledge or realizing what their doubts are.

On the other hand, when working in pairs, groups or in a whole class setting, students are part of a foster cooperative learning, where they learn with and from each other. Students tend to participate more in class when engaged in an activity in which they can express themselves in a situation similar to their real life.

Different class groupings are also positive for the teacher, who is then able to monitor individuals or small groups' performances, instead of having to monitor all the students at the same time.

Assigning individual and whole class work is not considered a difficult task according to most teachers. Therefore we have chosen to explore the instructions on the other kinds of grouping, since they are the ones that have to be more carefully planned and demand more classroom management skills from the teacher, according to the group size and/or profile of the students.

All the activities presented here are suited to any group size and students' age and interests.

Ideas on How to Divide Students into Pairs and Groups

Alphabetical Order: Students are paired or grouped in alphabetical order, according to their first or last name. Alternatively, you can also divide them according to the number of letters in their name.

Animal Sounds: This is a loud, but fun way to divide students into pairs or groups. Have names of animals in slips of paper. Distribute them and ask students not to show their slip to each other. When they are ready, ask them to start making the sound of that animal that they have on the slip of paper. They have to find the other members of their animal family, by grouping themselves according to the sounds they make.

Birthday Order: Students are paired or grouped according to their month or day of birth (e.g., Group 1 from January to June and Group 2 from July to December; odd and even number days, etc.).

Candies: Pass out small colored candies in multiple colors. Students are paired or grouped by same color of candy. Alternatively, you can ask them to form a rainbow with candies and then have a group formed. After the activity, they can eat the candies.

Class Band: Divide students into groups of four anyway you want to or let them choose the students who are going to be part of their group. Each group chooses who is going to be the singer, the drummer, the guitar player or the keyboard player. Then, ask all the drummers to get together, then all singers, and so on. Alternatively, you can do the same with sports category or parts of the house.

Colored Chips: Give a colored chip to each student or have students pick up one from a bag. You can combine colors (e.g., same colors together; different colors together; mix two same color chips and two different ones, etc.).

Colored Pencils: Have some colored pencils in a bag/can. Students who get the same colors are in the same group (or pairs). If you want to form groups of four students, have four pencils of each color. Alternatively, you can form pairs by light and dark colors (e.g., dark blue – light blue; dark green – light green).

Concentric Circles: Students make two circles. The students in the inner circle talk to the ones in the outside circle. Then all students from the outside circle move to the right and talk to different students. This way, they keep meeting different students and have the opportunity to repeat the activity several times. Alternatively, half of the class can stay in their seats and the other half moves around, going from desk to desk in clockwise direction to talk to different students.

Facing Rows: Students in the front row turn to face the second row; the third rows to face the fourth row; and so on. The same procedure can be used with the students on their left/right.

Favorites: Divide students into pairs or groups, according to their favorite leisure activity (e.g., playing sports or dancing. Alternatively, you can choose other categories such as favorite colors, animals, etc.).

Fruit Salad: Have each student choose their favorite fruit or give out pictures of fruit to each of them. Then, they form groups according to kinds of fruit. A fruit salad must have at least four different ingredients.

Horseshoe Setting: This setting focuses on the board, but there's still space for pairwork and group work. It's possible to have single desks (pairwork) or double desks (group work).

Matching: Students take a picture of an animal out of a bag and then group accordingly (e.g., all dogs together, all birds together, etc.).

Numbered Flowers: Prepare small flowers made with popsicle sticks and colored paper. Write a number at the end of each stick and place them in a small vase or container, filled with sand or dirt. Each student picks up a flower, then they get together in pairs or groups according to their number (e.g., same numbers, sequential numbers, odd or even numbers, etc.).

Numbered Heads: Assign a number for each student, according to the number of students per group (e.g., in a class with twenty students you may want to have six groups with four students in each, so assign numbers from 1-4). Then, ask all equal numbers to work together.

Opposites Attract: Students get together with someone different from them anyway (e.g., different color hair; boy – girl; tall – short; black eyes – green eyes, etc.).

Picture Puzzle: Have different sets of pictures or drawings cut into puzzle pieces (prepared beforehand). Each student receives a piece. They have to find a match to their puzzle. All the students who have a piece of the same puzzle are grouped together. Have in mind the number of students you want to have per group before cutting out the puzzle pieces.

Question & Answer: Half of the class receives a question and the other half has the answers. Students have to find their partner by finding the corresponding question/answer.

Rock, Paper, Scissors (or any other similar game): Students are paired or grouped after the game is played (e.g., all first winners can be grouped together, and so on). Any lucky game can be used to divide students into pairs or groups, but avoid games that require skills or any kind of strategy.

Similarities: Students get together according to something they have in common (e.g., same hair color, same shirt color, shoe size, height, clothing size, same favorite color, etc.).

Stand and Sit: Half of the class stands up and the other half remains seated. This way you have two groups. You can split them into smaller groups, by assigning a different action to part of each group.

Strategic Grouping: Depending on the purpose of the activity, you may want to group them using one of these combinations: stronger and weaker students together, stronger students together, weaker students together, talkers and listeners together. Whatever you choose, do not let students know what the grouping combination is.

Signalizing that the Activity Has Finished

Some teachers are reluctant to use different kinds of grouping or even to assign speaking activities and play games in large classes because of class disruption and the difficulty they have to grab students' attention. With this in mind, we bring you some suggestions to help you deal with this situation.

With children, especially younger ones, it is advisable to be consistent in the activity you choose to grab their attention. Therefore, use the same one for a long period of time, so that students get used to it. Whenever you decide to change the activity, let students know about it and practice with them beforehand.

Attention Grabbers

Can You Hear Me? Start talking to them in a very low voice and say, *If you can hear me raise your hand*. Students who hear you raise their hand, which will call the other ones' attention and they will do the same.

Clapping: Clap your hands in different patterns and speed. Students have to join you in clapping. Say, *Clap once if you can hear me*. Some students join you. Then say, *Clap twice if you can hear me*. And finally, *Clap three times if you can hear me*. At this point, students will notice that the activity has finished.

Eyes on Me: Count to three saying, *One, two, three... eyes on me!* Students stop the activity and say, *One, two three...eyes on you!* This way, if the other students have not heard you, they will hear the students and then notice that the activity is finished.

Give Me Five: Raise your hand and say, *Give me five*. Students put their hands up and say, *Five*. Then they start to count from 1 – 5. If that does not call everyone's attention, say *Give me five again*. Students repeat the count.

Lights Off: Turn the lights off and on again to call their attention.

Raising Hands: Raise your hands until students notice them and gradually stop talking.

Ring a Bell: Set a timer for the amount of time you would like the activity to last or ring a bell. When students hear the sound, they stop the activity.

Silent Request: Create a signal for silence. Then practice the signal with your students until they know that every time you make that signal it is time to stop the activity.

Singing: Play or sing an *Our Discovery Island* song or chant. Have students join you.

Stop Light: Make a stop light with removable color circles. When in green, students can talk in pairs or in groups. When in yellow, they must be ready to end the conversation. When in red, it is time to stop talking. If they are too loud, you can quickly go from green to red. If they are quieter again, go back to green.

Voices: When you say *Voices*, students say a quiet *Shhh...* Repeat the procedure until you have everyone's attention.

Critical Thinking

Think!

In levels 3 to 5, *Our Discovery Island* provides an extension *Think!* task (either in Lesson 6 or in the *Wider World* lesson). These tasks are designed to give students an extra challenge and motivation to solve a problem or answer a question, in order to help develop their critical thinking skills. The tasks and teaching suggestions are fully explained in the teaching notes.

If you decide to do a *Think!* task, start by writing it on the board. Then explain it in L1 and encourage some brainstorming in pairs or small groups. Elicit possible answers as hypotheses and place special emphasis on the need to support their answers. If the issue or question can be researched, invite students to check their hypotheses by looking up information in the school library or online, either in class or at home

There are certain questions you can ask in class that can foster students' ability for analysis and logical thinking. They can be asked during the *Think!* task and also during other activities in the book. See some examples below:

- What do you already know about this topic?
- What would happen if _________________________?
- What connections do you see between ________ and ________?
- Where could you look to verify this information?
- What clues in the text tell you ______________________?
- What do you think (character in a story) will do next?
- How do you picture ____________________ in your mind?

If students need to carry out any kind of research to complete the *Think!* task, it is important that everyone's contributions (text, images, videos, etc.) be displayed or somehow shared with the whole class. Take advantage of these moments to discuss the relevance and the reliability of the sources students quote. You can also take this opportunity to invite an 'expert' on the topic (another teacher, a parent or a student who is particularly fond of the topic and has studied it in depth) to visit your class at a later date - or use a software application for chats over the Internet, if the technology is available – to expand on the topic.

Scope and Sequence

Unit	Vocabulary	Structures
WELCOME	50–100 / Months jungle, movie star, make (a movie), shark, studio	
1 FREE TIME	cooking, playing computer games/the guitar, riding a scooter, skateboarding, skiing, watching TV help, find, lying in the sun, detective, listening, looking for / climbing the stairs, lighthouse / slide stadium, water park	Does (he) like (reading)? / Yes, (he) does./ No, (he) doesn't. / What do you like doing? Do you like (playing the guitar)? Yes, I do./No, I don't. / I'm from (Canada).
2 ANIMALS	crocodile, elephant, giraffe,hippo, lion, monkey Africa, leaves, live tongue, trunk	Do (lions/they) eat meat? Yes, they do./No, they don't (Lions/They) live in (Africa). (My cat/He/She/It) lives (with me).
3 WEATHER	cloud, rain, snow, storm, the sun, wind stormy, wet fall, spring, summer, winter, season, year blow, fly my kite, laugh, shine, sky, splash	What's the weather like (today)? It's (cold) and (snowy). It's (spring). It (snows) in the (winter).
4 MY WEEK	do gymnastics, do karate, go skateboarding, go swimming, have ballet lessons, have music lessons bus, car, train far, singing lessons, work children, plane, radio, rivers, roads, snowmobile	What do you do on (Saturdays)? / I (do gymnastics) at (ten o'clock). / (He) has (music lessons) at (four o'clock) / What time do you (do karate)? / I (do karate) at (two thirty) / How do you go to (school)? / I go to (school) by (bus). / How does (he) go to (the park)? / (He) goes to (the park) by (bike). / (He) walks to (the park). / Does (he) walk to work? / He goes to work by (car)
5 JOBS	ballet dancer, builder, doctor, farmer, movie star, teacher champion, medals, Olympic Games, go shopping famous, goals, score	What do you want to be? I want/don't want to be a (farmer). Does (he) want to be a (builder)? Yes, (he) does./No, (he) doesn't. I love (dancing/animals).
6 RAINFOREST	bridge, mountain, valley, waterfall / behind, in front of, next to / claws, jaws / curly, pretty, tiny / hippo, jaws, river bed / swing / hippo, hummingbird, spider, tapir	(It) is (behind/in front of/next to) the (box). They have (curly tails).
7 FEELINGS	thrilled crying, laughing, shouting, smiling naughty, long goodbyes, make faces, always, diver choir, fireworks, lantern, traditional	Why is (he) (crying)? / Because (he)'s (sad). / It's funny. / What makes you feel (happy)? / (Sunny days) make me feel (happy). / What makes you (cry)? / (Sad films) make me (cry). / How does it make you feel? / It makes me feel (happy).
8 BY THE SEA	beach, fishing, horseback riding, sailing, snorkeling, surfing crazy about, really, scene butterfly fish, coral reefs, dead, global warming, parrotfish, save, seahorse, sea snakes, starfish	What's everyone doing? What are you (scared of)? I'm scared/not scared of (sharks). I'm bored with (toy cars). I'm fond of (fishing). I'm terrified of (sharks).
Holiday • Mother's day	Mother's Day, toast, tea, rose, box of chocolates, care, know, treat,	
Holiday • Christmas	dessert, ham, potatoes, snow balls, snowman, turkey, vegetables, yard / special, turkey, sprouts, pudding, crackers / snowball, snowman, hanging	

Recycled Language	Cross-Curricular	Values
Appearance, Clothes / Hello. My name's (Ruby). / 'm (John). / This is my (sister), (Jenny). / (She) likes (movies). / Do you like (Daniel Radcliffe)? / Yes, I do./No, I don't. / I love (Madley Kool). / cool, favorite, monster		
cleaning, eating, playing soccer, reading, riding a bike, sleeping, swimming snowy, sunny boat, favorite food	Social science: special houses	Spending time with friends and family
They're (crocodiles) ./They're (big). (Elephants) can (play with a ball), but they can't (jump). They don't (sleep very much). big, drink, ears, eat, feet, fruit, grass, insects, jump, meat, play, sleep, stand up, strong, swim	Science: amazing animals	Respecting animal life
Actions, Feelings cold, hot, cloudy, rainy, snowy, sunny, windy apples, birds, flowers, park, sing, trees circle, houses long (arms), zoo	Geography: hurricanes	The importance of preserving wildlife
bike, boat, park, school busy He can't swim.	Social science: how children go to school	The importance of study and education.
Actions astronaut, basketball player, firefighter, police officer, soccer player breakfast, lunch, shoes I'm from (Russia).	PE: I want to be a champion!	The importance of goals and aims
Animals, Actions, Food, Prepositions, Weather / rainforest, river, sea / (long) arms, eyes, feet, legs, (sharp) tails, wings small	Geography: the Amazon rainforest	The importance of respecting small animals and plants
Animals, Clothes, Free-time activities, Weather angry, funny, happy, hungry, sad, scared, thirsty, tired, eating, drinking, movies sharp claws, teeth bus, dragon, train	Music: movie posters and music	The importance of caring for others
Actions, Animals, Free-time activities, Weather cheese, pasta, sea, toy cars What's (Cleo) doing? How does (this coral reef) make you feel?	Science: save the reefs	The importance of protecting the seas and sea life
Feelings always , breakfast present		
Weather board games, dinner, lunch lights		

DISCOVERY STUDIOS
Wow!
FILM STUDIO ISLAND TOURS
1
2
Welcome to Discovery Studios.
3
STAGE 23
Do you like jungles?
Whoa! Sorry!
4
Hey! I **like** jungles. Look at **me**!
5
Aarrgh! I don't like monsters!
Miaoooow!
15
T02

STORY
6
Look! It's Madley Kool! I **love** Madley Kool.
7
He's tall **and** strong **and** he's **really** cool.
8
He's making a movie here.
9
Madley Kool? Really? Here?
He's my favorite movie star.
10
It's a movie about . . .
11
SHARKS!

Discovery Studios

Lesson aims
To introduce the characters; to present the story.

Target language
jungle; movie, movie star, studios; shark; He's tall and strong.

Recycled language
cool, favorite; Do you like (jungles)? I like (jungles). I don't like (monsters); I love (Madley Kool).

Materials
Multi-ROM

Starting the class

- Greet student saying *Hello/Welcome* as they come into the classroom. Introduce yourself; say, for instance, *I'm (name)* or *I'm Miss/Mrs./Mr. (last name)*, depending on school culture.
- Point to a student and ask, *What's your name?* Continue with other students, until all students have introduced themselves. If there are new students in the class, introduce them in a special way, e.g., *Children, this is (name), a new friend. Say hello to (name).*

SB pages 2-3

Presentation

- Focus students' attention on the story and encourage them to guess what it is about (L1). They can look at other pages in the book to get ideas. Write students' predictions on the board.
- Point to the characters and say their names – they are, from left to right in frame 1, Sam, Jenny, John and Ruby. Point to frame 5 and introduce Cleopatra, the cat. Write the names on the board and say them in turn.
- Ask, *Where are the children?* Point to the sign for Discovery Studios in frame 1 and explain (L1) they make movies at studios.
- To introduce *movies*, give some examples of famous movies that students probably like. Then ask several students, *What's your favorite movie?* To introduce movie star, use some famous actors and actresses. Point to Madley Kool in frame 6 and say, *He's a movie star*. Introduce other vocabulary items students need in order to understand the story.

1 Listen.

- Say, *Now, we're going to listen to the story. Listen and look at the pictures*. If necessary, mime to make meaning clear.
- Play T02. Students listen and check if their predictions were correct. Play the recording again. Students listen and follow in their books.
- Divide the class into groups (see ideas for group formation on pp. XII and XIII) and assign a character to each. Play T02 again, and students repeat their character's lines from their seats. You might invite some students to roleplay the story.

Ending the lesson

- Divide the class into two teams and ask students to close their books. Retell the story, making some intentional mistakes. Every time students spot a mistake, they put up their hands and correct it. Groups get points for each correction made by a group member.
- Encourage teams to predict what is going to happen in the story in later units.

OPTIONAL ACTIVITY

Game

Play *Pass the secret* (see p. T88) with a line from the story.

Welcome

1 T03 **Listen and say.**

2 T04 **Listen and answer.**

1 Sam, 2 Jenny, 3 Ruby, 4 John

3 **Ask and answer.**

Do you like . . . ?

Yes, I do.

No, I don't.

Workbook page 90, Activity 1.

4 T05 Listen and say.

5 T06 Listen and sing.

January, February,
March, April,
May or June.
What's your favorite?
What's your favorite?
What's your favorite month?
July, August,
September, October,
November or December.
What's your favorite?
What's your favorite?
What's your favorite month?

6 T07 Listen and say.

7 T08 Listen and point.

53 77 54
81 75 89
98 66

Workbook page 91, Activities 2 and 3.

Welcome

Lesson 1

Lesson aims
To understand a description and identify oneself and others; to talk about likes and dislikes.
Recycled language
Appearance, Clothes, Colors; *movie star, movies; What's your name? I'm (John) / My name's (Ruby); Do you like (Jim Carrey)? Yes, I do. / No, I don't.*
Materials
Multi-ROM, soft ball or bean toss, pictures of famous people

Starting the lesson

- Play *Ball/Bean toss* (see p. T89) to review language from previous levels. It is also an opportunity for students to get to know each other better, introducing themselves and telling a little about their likes and dislikes, for example.

SB page 4

Presentation

- Point to the characters and ask, *Who's this?* If you have not worked with the Discovery Studios story, introduce the characters. Then point to the skateboard and ask, *What is it?*
- Use the characters' appearance and clothes to review language. Point to (Ruby) and ask, *Does (she) have (a long dress)? Does (she) have (long hair)?*
- Invite some students to describe the characters.

1 Listen and say

- Focus students' attention on the picture again. Ask, *Where are they? (At Discovery Studios).*
- Tell students (L1) that the characters are introducing themselves. Then play T03 for students to follow in their books.
- Ask students to close the books. Play T03 a second time and ask the class to guess who is speaking.
- Now divide the class into groups of four and assign a character to each member of the group. They repeat their characters' lines from their seats.

2 Listen and answer.

- Point to the different characters and ask students to say something about him/her (e.g., for Jenny, they can say, *She likes Madley Kool*). Then tell students they are going to listen to descriptions of the characters, and that they need to guess who is being described.
- Play T04 as students look at the picture carefully. You can ask them to write down their guesses in their notebooks.
- Play it again, pausing after each question so that students can say the correct name.

T04

1 He has blond hair. He likes skateboards. He's 8. What's his name?
2 She likes music, movies and Madley Kool. She has a brother. She's 11. What's her name?
3 She has pink glasses. She's wearing a skirt. She's 9. What's her name?
4 He has a sister. He has red hair. He's 8. What's his name?

Group work

- Divide the class into small groups (see ideas for group formation on pp. XII and XIII). Ask them (L1) to choose a character and write one more question for the rest of the class, e.g. *She has white sneakers and a purple T-shirt. What's her name?* (*Jenny*)

3 Ask and answer

- Stick the pictures of famous people on the board and ask students to name them. Then ask, *Do you like...?* (*Yes, I do. / No, I don't.*)
  Note: choose pictures of famous people students are familiar with.
- Then focus students' attention on the pictures of famous people on the page. Ask them if they know who they are (they are movie stars) and if they can remember any movies they are in.
- Now divide the class into pairs (see ideas for dividing students on pp. XII and XIII). Students ask and answer questions about these people, using the language in the speech bubbles. Monitor pairs to help with pronunciation, if necessary.

Game

- Divide the class into two teams. A student from Team A chooses one of the famous people from Activity 3 and describes him/her, without saying the name. Team B guesses who it is. Then they switch roles. You can also use the pictures of famous people you brought to class to make the activity more challenging.

Ending the lesson

- Play *Bingo* (see p. T89). Have students choose the topic for the game.

OPTIONAL ACTIVITY
Game
Play *Conversation relay* (see p. T89)

WB page 90

1 Read and write. Then match.

- Students read the descriptions and complete them with the character's name. Then they match them to the correct pictures.

Lesson 2

Lesson aims
To learn numbers 50 – 100; to learn the months.
Target language
Months, Numbers 50 – 100
Recycled language
Days of the week, Numbers 1 – 50
Materials
Multi-ROM, calendar, homemade word cards with the months, masking tape

Starting the lesson

- Play *Bingo* (see p. T89) to review numbers 1 – 50.
- Review the days of the week with a calendar. Point to it and ask, *What day is today?* Write the days of the week on the board, say the words and students repeat. Then ask each student to choose a day of the week. Chant the days of the week in order. Each time students hear the day they have chosen, they stand up and sit down quickly.

SB page 5

Presentation

- Show the current month on the calendar and say it aloud (*February*). Then ask students (L1) which month comes before it (*January*) and which comes after (*March*). Write the months in chronological order on the board. Continue until all the months are written on the board.

4 Listen and say.

- Play T05 once, showing the pages of the calendar in turn, or pointing to the words on the board.
- Play it again, pausing after each month. Students repeat. Then each student says a month in chronological order. Continue until all students in class have said a word.
- Draw students' attention to the use of initial capitals when writing the months.

> January, February, March, April, May, June, July, August, September, October, November, December — **T05**

5 Listen and sing.

- Play T06 once. Students follow in their books. Then play it again a few times until students are confident enough to sing along.
- Give students the homemade word cards for the months. They stand up when their month is mentioned in the song.

Extra!

- Place the word cards around the classroom. Play the song (T06) again and students walk to their favorite month word card when they hear the question *What's your favorite month?* Ask some volunteers to explain their preferences (L1).

Presentation

- Review numbers 10 – 50 with the homemade number cards, by counting the numbers with the class. When you get to 50, ask students to predict what comes next, then elicit the other numbers.

6 Listen and say.

- Play T07. Students listen and point to the numbers on the page. Play it again, pausing after each number for students to repeat.

7 Listen and point.

- Write some numbers between 50 – 100 on the board, then invite a student to come to the front. Call out a number and the student circles it on the board. Continue with other students.
- Play T08. Students listen, repeat and point to the correct number on the page.
- Ask students to close their books. Then play T08 again, pausing after each number. Invite students to write the number they hear on the board.

> 89, 77, 98, 54, 66, 81, 75, 53 — **T08**

Ending the lesson

- Divide students into two teams (see ideas for group formation on pp. XII and XIII) and ask students to stand up. Tell the teams (L1) to line up according to the chronological order of the months students were born in. Explain that, they should only say their month (they are not allowed to use L1, or any other words in English). The first team to line up in the correct order is the winner.

OPTIONAL ACTIVITY
Game
Play *Jumping the line* (see p. T88) to review numbers 50 – 100, using the concept of odd and even numbers.

WB page 91

2 Read and complete. Then draw yourself.

- Students complete their description. Then, they draw themselves picture.

3 Look and number.

- Students look at the months listed randomly and number them in the correct order.

1 Free time

1 T09 **Listen, point and say.**

2 T10 **Listen and point.**

Workbook page 92, Activity 1.

3 Chant.

Madley Kool, Madley Kool,
He likes playing soccer,
and swimming in the pool.
Does he like skiing and watching TV?
Yes, he does. Just like me!

Does he like cooking?
Does he like cooking?
No, he doesn't.
And he doesn't like cleaning.

LOOK!

Does he **like playing** soccer?
Yes, he **does**./No, he **doesn't**.

4 What do Jenny and Sam like? Listen and circle.

5 Ask and answer.

Does Sam like cleaning?

No, he doesn't.

1 Free time

Lesson 1

Lesson aims
To present and practice new vocabulary; to present the new structure.
Target language
cooking, skiing, watching TV; I like (cooking). (He) likes (playing soccer).
Recycled language
Actions
Materials
Multi-ROM, Flashcards (Actions, Free time), homemade word cards with the months, A4 paper, colored pencils and markers

Starting the lesson

- Invite a student to come to the board and pick a month word card. He/she draws or mimes something to represent the month (e.g., a Brazilian flag for September, or fireworks for January). The class guesses the month.

SB page 6

Presentation

- Present the free-time activities using the flashcards. Explain (L1) that these are things people can do when they are not at school/work. Hold them up in turn and say the words/phrases for students to repeat. Hold up the flashcards again, asking individual students to say the words.

1 Listen, point and say.

- Draw students' attention to the free-time activities at the bottom of the page. Then play T09, pausing after each word/phrase to give students time to find the picture. Play it again, pausing after each word/phrase, and students repeat them.
- Ask students, *What's number (three)?* They look at the images and answer. If you want to make the activity more challenging, ask students to close their books and try to say the free-time activities from memory.

Presentation

- Mime a sport or an activity. Say, e.g., *I like playing tennis.* Give some more examples using flashcards from previous levels. Then ask some individual students, *And you? What do you like doing?* Students answer.
- Next, say, *I don't like swimming*, and ask other students to come up with other examples. Make sure students use verb + *-ing* in their answers
- Shuffle the flashcards of free-time activities and actions and ask a student to choose one. He/She shows it to the class and makes a sentence (e.g., *I like watching TV*). Use the student's sentence to give an example in the third person singular (e.g., *He likes watching TV*). Continue with other students.
- If you want students to keep a written register of the structure, write their examples on the board and ask students to copy the sentences into their notebooks.

2 Listen and point.

- Draw students' attention to the main illustration. Point to the characters and ask, *Who's this?* Then ask, *Where are the children?* Students look at the picture and search for clues (e.g., the photographs on the wall). Explain (L1) that Ruby, John, Jenny and Sam are at Madley Kool's trailer at the film studio.
- Next, tell students that they are going to listen to the characters talk about Madley Kool's trailer. Play T10, and they point to the activities as they are mentioned.
- Focus on the picture. Say, for instance, *He likes playing soccer*. Students point to the object that represents the activity (the soccer ball). Continue with other items in the main illustration.
- Ask (L1) if they think Madley Kool's trailer is clean and organized. You can use the main illustration to discuss the importance of cleanliness.

T10

Jenny	Where's Madley Kool? Is he here?
John	No, he isn't.
Jenny	Look at his room!
John	He likes playing soccer.
Sam	Look at the photos! He likes skiing. Hmm, does he like swimming?
John	Yes, he does. And he likes watching TV.
Jenny	But he doesn't like cooking.
Ruby	Ugh! He doesn't like cleaning!

Ending the lesson

- Play *I spy* (see p. T90) with the items in the main illustration.

OPTIONAL ACTIVITY
Make a poster
Give students paper and tell them (L1) to draw themselves and things they like doing. They then write a few sentences describing the picture (e.g., they draw a racket and write, *I like playing tennis*). Display the mini posters.

WB page 92

1 Match.

- Students read the words and match them to the correct picture.

Lesson 2

Lesson aims
To review the vocabulary of Lesson 1 with a chant; to present the new structure.
Target language
Does (he) like (skiing)? Yes, (he) does./No, (he) doesn't.
Recycled language
Actions, Free-time activities
Materials
Multi-ROM, Flashcards (Actions, Free time), paper ball

Starting the lesson

- Invite a student to the board and give him/her a flashcard. He/she holds it up and then smiles or frowns. The class says the correct sentence, e.g., *(He) likes (cooking).* Continue with other students.

SB page 7

Presentation

- Focus students' attention on the main illustration. Ask, *Does Madley Kool like (cooking)?* Students just answer *Yes* or *No*. Echo the answers and say, *Yes, he does./No, he doesn't.* Continue with other free-time activities.

3 Chant.

- Draw students' attention to the chant. Play T11, and students listen and follow the words. Play it again, pausing after each line for students to repeat.
- Play it a third time for students to sing along. To help students, stick the flashcards (Free time) on the board and point to them as the words are mentioned.
- Now divide the class into two groups (see ideas for group formation on pp. XII and XIII). Play the chant again, with the groups chanting alternate lines.

Presentation

- Draw students' attention to the question and short answers in the *Look!* box. Write them on the board (so that all students can follow your explanation) and point out the highlighted words. Explain (L1) that they need to use an action ending in *–ing* after *like* and that they need to use *does* in questions and short answers with *he* and *she*. Use different colors (or underline/circle items in the sentences) to help students understand the structures and the rule.
- Elicit other questions about Madley Kool and write them on the board, with the corresponding answer. Ask students to copy the examples into their notebooks.

Extra!

- Stick the flashcards (Free time and Actions) on the board. Ask students to choose among the flashcards another thing that Madley Kool likes doing and to draw an object that represents this activity.
- When they have finished, divide the class into pairs to play a guessing game (see ideas for dividing students on p. 00). Student A asks questions to guess what Madley Kool likes doing in Student B's picture (e.g., *Does he like reading?*). Student B can only answer, *Yes, he does* or *No, he doesn't*. When Student A guesses correctly, they switch roles.

4 What do Jenny and Sam like? Listen and circle.

- Point to the characters and ask, *Who's this?* Then point to the objects and elicit which activities they represent.
- Next, tell students (L1) that they are going to listen to Ruby and John talking about things that Jenny and Sam like doing.
- Play T12. Students circle the objects that show what each character likes.
- Check as a class. Ask, *What does Jenny/Sam like?* Students answer.

T12

Ruby	What does Jenny like? Does she like skiing?
John	No, she doesn't.
Ruby	Does she like playing soccer?
John	Yes, she likes playing soccer. And she likes watching TV.
Ruby	How about Sam? Does he like cooking?
John	Yes, he does. But he doesn't like cleaning.
Ruby	Does he like reading?
John	No, he doesn't.
Ruby	Oh, no! That's not good!

5 Ask and answer.

- Divide the class into pairs (see ideas for dividing students on pp. XII and XIII). When you have their full attention, focus on the language in the speech bubbles (you can read the dialogue with another student). Then students take turns asking questions about Sam and Jenny in Activity 4.
- Monitor pairs to help with intonation in the question and with language use. If necessary, refer students to the language in Activity 1.

Ending the lesson

- Play *Aye, aye, Captain!* (see p. T89) with the free-time activities.

OPTIONAL ACTIVITY
Game
Play *Basketball* (see p. T89) with characters' likes and dislikes in Lessons 1 and 2.

WB page 92

2 Read and circle.

- Students read the sentences and look at the pictures. Then they circle *like* or *don't like*.

6 T13 Listen and sing.

SONG

1

2

What do you, do you like doing?
What do you, do you like doing?

Do you like riding your bike?
Yes, I do. I like riding my bike.
Do you like playing the guitar?
Yes, I do. Look! Look! I'm a pop star.
Chorus
Do you like playing computer games?
No, I don't. I like riding my scooter.
Do you like skateboarding, too?
Yes, I like skateboarding! How about you?
Chorus

3

4

5

LOOK!

What **do** you **like doing**?
Do you **like playing** the guitar?
Yes, I **do**./No, I **don't**.

Workbook page 92, Activity 2.

Lesson 3

Lesson aims
To extend the unit vocabulary set; to practice the vocabulary with a song.
Target language
What do you like doing?; playing computer games, playing the guitar, riding my scooter, skateboarding
Recycled language
Free-time activities; *Do you like (playing thw guitar)? Yes, I do. / No, I don't. riding my bike*
Materials
Multi-ROM, Flashcards (Action and Free time)

Starting the lesson

- Divide the class into two groups (see ideas for group formation on pp. XII and XIII), then play the chant from Lesson 2 (T11). One group asks the questions, the other answers. They change lines and chant again.

SB page 8

Presentation

- Present the new vocabulary using flashcards and the pictures in the book. Point to the pictures and say, *I like playing the guitar*. Then ask students, *Do you like playing the guitar?* Continue with the other pictures.

6 Listen and sing.

- Play the song (T13) with books closed. The class performs the actions while listening, adding nodding for *Yes, I do* and shaking the head for *No, I don't*.
- Then ask students to open their books. Play T13 again for students to follow the lines. Play it a third time, and students sing along.
- Divide the class into boys and girls. They sing their lines in turn and do the chorus as a class.

Extra!

- Divide the class into small groups. Students write a new verse for the song using different activities they have learned (e.g., *Do you like cleaning your room?*). If necessary, monitor groups to help with language.
- Sing the song again, adding the new verses created by the groups.

Presentation

- Focus on the questions and answers in the *Look!* box and write them on the board. Ask students (L1) to pay attention to the highlighted words and to the use of *do* in questions and short answers. Help students create a simple rule (e.g., *In questions, use do with you; in answers, use do and don't*). Write the rule on the board, and students then copy it into their notebooks.
- Ask several students, *What do you like doing?* Write their answers on the board. Use different colors (or underline/circle items in the sentences) to help students understand the structure. You can ask students to copy the examples into their notebooks

Pairwork

- Divide students into pairs (see ideas for dividing the class on pp. XII and XIII). When you have their full attention, explain (L1) the activity. In their notebooks, students write three things they like doing, but one of the sentences must be false. Then Student A asks, *What do you like doing?* Student B answers using his/her three sentences.
- Next, Student A decides which sentence is false and asks Student B, *Do you like (playing computer games?)* to confirm his/her guess. If Student B's answer is *No, I don't*, the guess is correct. Then it is Student B's turn to ask questions.
- Demonstrate the activity with a student before they start working in pairs. If necessary, write some key language on the board for students to use as prompts. Monitor pairs to help with language use.

Ending the lesson

- Divide the class into two groups. They take turns choosing a character from the pictures in Activity 6. They mime what he/she likes doing (e.g., playing the guitar). The other group guesses what it is (e.g., *He likes playing the guitar*).

OPTIONAL ACTIVITY
Flashcard game
Play *Race to touch* (see p. T88) with the flashcards.

Lesson 4

Lesson aims
To develop reading, writing and speaking skills.
Values
Spending time with friends and family.
Recycled language
Actions, Free-time activities
Materials
Multi-ROM, A4 paper, Unit 4 mini cards, scissors

Starting the lesson

- Sing the song from Lesson 3 (T13) again.

SB page 9

7 Look at Activity 6. Ask and answer.

- Divide the class into pairs (see ideas for dividing students into pairs on pp. XII and XIII). When you have their full attention, explain (L1) the activity. Student A chooses one of the pictures from the song in Activity 6. Student B asks, *What do you like doing?* Student A answers. Next, Student B identifies the picture and says its number. Then they switch roles.
- Monitor pairs to check their performance and pronunciation. As a follow-up, you can ask students to write the exchanges in their notebooks.

8 Listen and ✓ or ✗.

- Draw students' attention to the girl in the picture. Say, *This is Fiona.* Ask students to imagine what she likes doing. Write their predictions on the board.
- Play T14 and students confirm their guesses. Then focus on the chart. Play the recording again, and students check or cross the activities according to what they hear.

Fiona	Hi, I'm Fiona. I like skateboarding and I like swimming. I don't like watching TV. I like riding my bike.	**T14**

Writing practice

- Give each student an A4 sheet of paper. Ask them to write a text about themselves that is similar to the recording in Activity 8. Write a model on the board, using your own information.
- Students work individually on their texts. Monitor them to help with language use.
- If time allows, students finish their writing in class (alternatively, you can assign it as homework). They can also decorate their texts with drawings, or even stick pictures of themselves. Display students' work on the classroom walls.

Values

- Talk about (L1) what you like doing with your friends and family. Say, for instance, *I like playing computer games with my dad.* Write some examples on the board.
- Ask several students, *Do you like (playing soccer with your friends)? What do you like doing with your family/friends?* Then discuss with the class (L1) the importance of spending time with friends and family.

9 Go to p. 73 and play the game.

- Divide the class into pairs. Ask them to cut out the mini cards on p. 73. When they have cut all the cards, say a free-time activity represented in the cards (e.g., *playing the guitar*), and students hold it up. Continue with the other images.
- Focus on the illustration and the language in the speech bubbles. Tell students (L1) that the children are playing a game and that the class will do the same with their cards. They put them face down on their desks. Explain the activity: Student A picks a card from the table and, without looking at the card, shows it to Student B. Then Student A asks a question to guess the activity on the card, e.g., *Does (she) like (cooking)?* If the question corresponds to the image on the card, Student B answers, *Yes, (she) does*; if it doesn't, he/she answers, *No, (she) doesn't*. Student A keeps the card if he/she guessed correctly. They switch roles.

At home, students discuss with their family members what they like doing together. Then students write a few sentences (e.g., *I like skateboarding with my brother*). Invite some students to share their sentences with the class in the following lesson.

Ending the lesson

- Students play *What's missing?* (see p. T88) with the mini cards.

OPTIONAL ACTIVITY
Game
Play *The ball II* (see p. T89) to ask questions about the characters, e.g., *Does (Madley Kool) like (cleaning)? What does (Madley Kool) like doing?* Use a paper ball or soft ball.

WB page 93

3 Read and ✓ or ✗.

- Students read the sentences and check or cross the pictures to show what Ruby and John like or don't like doing.

7 Look at Activity 6. Ask and answer.

What do you like doing?

Number 3.

I like playing the guitar.

8 T14 Listen and ✓ or ✗.

	✓	✗
skateboarding	✓	
swimming	✓	
watching TV		✗
riding my bike	✓	

9 Go to page 73 and play the game.

Workbook page 93, Activity 3.

10 T15 Listen and read. Then act.

STORY

NOW GO TO FILM STUDIO ISLAND.

Workbook page 94, Activities 4 and 5.

Lesson 5

Lesson aims
To consolidate the unit language with a story.
Recycled language
Actions, Free-time activities; *Where's (Madley)? I like (watching); She likes (sleeping).*
Receptive language
actually, detective, find, help, listening, looking for, lying in the sun
Materials
Multi-ROM, speech bubbles with the lines of the story

Starting the lesson

- Describe the main illustration in Lesson 1 making some deliberate mistakes (e.g., *Madley Kool likes cleaning the house*). Point to Jenny and say, for instance, *This is Ruby.* Students say *False*! when they spot the mistake. They then correct the information.

SB page 10

Presentation

- Introduce any new vocabulary items you consider relevant for the comprehension of the story. If necessary, use mime or L1.
- Point to the cat and ask students (L1) if they remember who she is (she is Cleopatra, and students saw her for the first time in the Discovery Studios story).

10 Listen and read. Then act.

- Ask students (L1) what they remember about the characters' adventures so far. Before listening to the story, ask the following questions for the corresponding frames. Try to ask and discuss them in English:
  1 Where are the children? [In the Studio.]
  2 *(Pointing to Cleopatra.)* Is she a pretty cat? [Open discussion.]
  3 Who are they talking about? [Open discussion.]
  4 Where are the children going? [Open discussion.]
  5 What's the cat thinking about? [Open discussion.]
  6 *(Pointing to the thought bubble.)* Why is the cat dressed like this? [Open discussion.]
- Play T15, and students follow the story in their books. Play it again, pausing after each line for students to repeat.
- Next, to check students' understanding of the story, ask the following questions:
  1 What are the children doing? [They're looking for Madley Kool.]
  2 What's the cat's name? [Cleopatra.]
  3 What does Cleo like doing? [She likes sleeping, eating and lying in the sun.]
  4 Where are the children going? [They're going to look for Madley Kool.]
  5 Can Cleo help the children find Madley Kool? [Yes, she can.]
  6 What does she like doing? [She likes watching, looking and listening.]
  What is she? [She's a detective.]
- Ask the class (L1) to predict what is going to happen in the next episode of the story.
- Divide students into five groups and assign a character to each. Students read their parts as a class from their seats. This may encourage shyer students to take part in the acting later on.
- Invite five students to take the parts of John, Ruby, Sam, Cleo and the man. Ask the volunteers to go to the front of the class to act out the story. Encourage tone of voice and expressions to match those in the pictures. Alternatively, you could have other students read the lines while those five students act it out.

Ending the lesson

- Prepare speech bubbles with the lines of the story and hand them out to different students. Play T15 again. When their line is playing, students jump up and go to the front of the classroom. They arrange themselves in order and hold up their speech bubbles.

Students can now go online to Film Studio Island and enjoy the fun and games, at home or at the school computer lab. Ask them to find the 'horse' that Cleo is holding in one of the pages of the unit (p. 9). Then tell students they should find the horse on Film Studio Island (it is between the first and second buildings, immediately inside Discovery Film Studios). When students click on the horse, they are taken to a supplementary language game based on the vocabulary in Unit 1.

OPTIONAL ACTIVITY
Mini card game
Play *Quick peek* (see p. T88).

WB page 94

4 Look and write. Use the words in the box.

- Students complete the sentences using the words in the box.

5 Look at the code and write a message.

- Students look at the code wheel and use (a) the alphabet that is on the larger circle outside of the wheel and (b) the code letters that are on the smaller circle inside. Then they replace the letters and write the sentence.

Lesson 6

Lesson aims
To integrate other areas of the curriculum into the English class; to develop the cross-curricular topic through a short project.
Cross-curricular focus
Social science – special houses
Target language
boat, lighthouse, sea, climbing the stairs
Recycled language
Rooms; *(She) likes (reading and playing the guitar). (He) doesn't like (climbing the stairs).*
Materials
Multi-ROM, poster board, colored pencils and markers, pictures of an igloo, a trailer and a windmill

Starting the lesson
- Play *Give me one* (see p. T89) to review the rooms in the house.

SB page II

Presentation
- On the board, draw a cross-section of a house with four rooms and label them *kitchen*, *bedroom*, *bathroom* and *living room*.
- Ask students questions about what they like doing in each room (e.g., *What do you like doing in the living room? Do you like playing computer games in your bedroom?*).
- Next, draw a boat slowly and ask the class to guess. Introduce *boat*. Repeat with *lighthouse*.
- Ask the class what a lighthouse is for (L1) and if they would like to live in one.

11 Listen and read.
- Draw students' attention to the children. Say, *This is Rosa, and this is Will.* Ask students (L1) to predict where they live. Write students' ideas on the board.
- Play T16 once. Students confirm their guesses.
- Play Rosa's part again. Ask a few questions: *Does she like living in a boat? What does she like doing in the boat house?*
- Before playing Will's part again, ask, *Does Will like climbing stairs?* Mime to make the meaning of *stairs* clear to the class. Then play the recording.

12 Read and say *Rosa* or *Will*.
- Focus students' attention on the sentences. They read them and decide if they refer to Rosa or Will. Do the first sentence with the class.
- Ask individual students to read the sentences. The class says the correct name.

Think!
Note: Some lessons (Lesson 6 or Wider World) have an extension Think! task. These tasks are designed to help develop students' critical thinking skills by motivating them to solve a problem or answer a question.

- Write the sentences on the board: *I don't like the cold. I don't like big houses. I don't want to stay in the same place all the time.*
- Stick the pictures of the windmill, the igloo and the trailer on the board. Then divide students into small groups. Encourage them to discuss and choose the best house for the person in the sentences. Write students' ideas on the board, and ask them to explain their choices (the best house for the person is the trailer)

Mini project
- Divide the class into small groups (see ideas for group formation on pp. XII and XIII). Brainstorm with students (L1) what an unusual house would look like. Draw a cross-section or a floor plan for students to use as a model, and then write their ideas for rooms and features on the board.
- Give each group a sheet of poster board. Students design a house and label the rooms (if necessary, help them with additional vocabulary). Encorage them to be criative. At the bottom of the sheet, they write some sentences describing what they like doing in the different rooms (e.g., *I like swimming in the pool*).
- When they have finished, invite some groups to describe their posters and favorite free-time activities. Display the projects around the classroom.

Ending the lesson
- Divide the class into two groups (see ideas for group formation on pp. XII and XIII). Say a word (e.g., *lighthouse*, *guitar*, etc.). Groups say *Rosa* or *Will*. Alternatively, say some incorrect sentences. Groups take turns correcting the sentences. You may turn this into a competition by awarding points for correct answers.
- Students play *Memory buzz* (see p. T88) with the mini cards.

OPTIONAL ACTIVITY
Mini card game
Play *Memory buzz* (see p. T88) with the mini cards.

WB page 95

6 Find out about Megan. Then write *T* (true) or *F* (false).
- Students read about Megan and write *T* or *F* according to the information in the text.

7 Read the text in Activity 6 again and complete.
- Students read about Megan again and complete the chart.

11 T16 **Listen and read.**

Special Houses

This is Rosa. Look at her house. It's a boat. Rosa likes her boat. She doesn't like watching TV. She likes reading and playing the guitar. She also likes riding her bike, but not on the boat!

This is Will. This is his house. It's a lighthouse! There are a lot of stairs. Will likes living in the lighthouse, but he doesn't like climbing the stairs. He likes playing computer games and watching TV. He likes cooking, too. His favorite food is fish.

12 **Read and say *Rosa* or *Will*.**

1 I don't like climbing the stairs. Will
2 I don't like watching TV. Rosa
3 I like reading. Rosa
4 I like playing computer games. Will
5 I like cooking. Will

MINI **PROJECT**

Design an unusual house. Write about things you like doing in it.

Workbook page 95, Activities 6 and 7.

Wider World

On the weekend

1 T17 **Listen and read.**

1

Hi, I'm Kelly. I'm from Canada. It's snowy here. I like skiing. It's fun. I can go very fast. Do you like skiing?

2

Hi, I'm Tumelo. I'm from South Africa. I like playing soccer at school with my friends. I can see the Soccer City stadium from my house. It's really big. My favorite team is the Mamelodi Sundowns.

2 T18 **Listen and say the name.**

1 Javier, 2 Anne, 3 Kelly, 4 Tumelo

Workbook page 96, Activities 8 and 9.

3

Hi, I'm Anne. I'm from France. I like riding my bike with my mom and dad. It's good exercise. I like riding my bike on sunny days. My little brother likes riding, too!

4

Hi, I'm Javier. I'm from Spain. I like swimming. Look! I'm at the water park with my friends. I like going down the slides. It's great!

3 Read and answer. *True* or *false*?

1 Kelly can't go very fast. False
2 Tumelo likes playing soccer at school. True
3 Anne likes riding her bike with her family. True
4 Javier is at the water park with his family. False

4 Ask your friend about his/her free-time activities.

Do you like playing soccer?

Yes, I do.

5 Talk about one of these free-time activities.

flying a kite | drawing | rock climbing | playing board games | juggling

Workbook page 97, Activities 10 and 11.

Wider World

Lesson aims
To review the language of Unit 1; to personalize the unit language; to learn about other cultures; to provide an opportunity for self-evaluation.

Target language
drawing, flying a kite, juggling, playing board games, rock climbing

Recycled language
Actions, Free-time activities, Weather; *Do you like (playing soccer)? Yes, I do./No, I don't.*

Receptive language
slides, stadium, water park

Materials
Multi-ROM, a world map or globe, mini cards, pictures of the new free-time activities in Activity 5, poster board, colored pencils and markers, Flashcards (Actions and Free time), Worksheet 1

Special note: The activities from the *Wider World* lesson can be done in one or two classes, depending on the use of the *Pairwork, Extra!, Game* and *Optional activities* sections. The Workbook activities can also be assigned for homework in different classes.

Starting the lesson

- Play *Teacher says* (see p. T89). Instead of saying, for instance, *Teacher says, Sleep!*, say, *Teacher says, I like (playing the guitar).* Students then mime the activity.

SB pages 12-13

Presentation

- Bring a map of the world. Say, *I'm from (Brazil).* Point out your country on the map. Then point out Brazil to students. Ask, *And you?* Students answer.
- Focus students' attention on the photographs of the children. Then ask, *What's her/his name?* Students look for the answers in the texts.
- Ask questions about the weather and clothes the children are wearing. If necessary, you can use the pictures to introduce new vocabulary. Ask students to guess where the children are from. Help them find the countries on the map.
- Next, name the things the children are doing. Ask students if they like doing the same things. Can they do all those activities in their country? Why? Why not? (L1)
- Elicit other free-time activities that are common in Brazil. List them on the board. If necessary, help with vocabulary.

1 Listen and read.

- Tell students (L1) they are going to listen to and read a text about four children and their free-time activities. Students follow the text as they listen to the recording. Play T17 once, giving them their a first contact with the text. Then play it again.
- Next, play each part separately and ask some questions to check comprehension:
  - *What does (Tumelo) like doing?*
  - *Does Anne like riding her bike with her friends?*
  - *Does (Javier) like (swimming)?*
- As a follow-up, you can invite individual students to read parts of the text. (Alternatively, you can work with shadow reading. Play T17. Students read the words while trying to stay at the same speed and rhythm as the recording. As students keep reading, you can turn the sound down occasionally.)

Game

- Say and mime, e.g. *I like reading.* Ask a student to repeat the sentence adding another element and the mime (e.g., *I like reading and drinking*).
- Continue in the same way and, after three turns, say, *BUT I don't…!* The next student says a negative sentence about an action that hasn't been mentioned before (e.g., *I like reading and drinking and eating, BUT I don't like playing tennis*).
- If he/she doesn't repeat an action that has been used in the game before, he/she starts the new round. If he/she repeats, he/she misses the next turn.

2 Listen and say the name.

- Students listen to T18 and say who is speaking. Play the recording once through, then play it a second time, pausing after each sentence. Students say the names.

T18

1	**Javier**	I like going down the slides.
2	**Anne**	I like riding my bike on sunny days.
3	**Kelly**	I like skiing.
4	**Tumelo**	I like playing soccer at school with my friends.

3 Read and answer. True or false?

- Students read the sentences. They reread the information about the children and decide if the sentences are true or false. They correct the false ones. If necessary, clarify vocabulary.
- As a follow-up, you can ask students to correct the false statements in their notebooks.

Pairwork

- Divide the class into pairs (see ideas for dividing the class into pairs on pp. XII and XIII). Students lay two sets of mini cards face down in a line.
- Student A turns a card over and says, for instance, *I like cooking.* Then he/she points to another card and asks, *What do you like doing?* Student B turns the card over and says, for instance, e.g., *I like...* If it is a match, he/she keeps both cards and asks the next question; if it is not, he/she turns the card face down again. Students continue taking turns until they have used all the cards.

Game

- Divide the class into two groups (see ideas for group formation on pp. XII and XIII). Ask one student from Group A to act out a free-time activity. Ask, *What does he/she like doing?* The student's group guesses the activity. If they guess correctly, they get a point; if they don't, Group B has the chance to answer. Then it is Group B's turn.

4 Ask your friend about his/her free-time activities.

- Divide the class into pairs. When you have their full attention, elicit from students different free-time activities they enjoy doing. Write their ideas on the board, helping them with additional vocabulary if necessary.
- Draw students' attention to the language in the speech bubbles. Demonstrate the activity with two or three students, using the activities on the board. Next, students take turns asking and answering about their favorite free-time activities. Monitor pairs to help with language use.
- As a follow-up, you can ask students to report on their partner's favorite free-time activities (e.g., *Lucas likes playing soccer. He doesn't like cooking*). Alternatively, they can write the sentences in their notebooks.

5 Talk about one of these free-time activities.

- Focus students' attention on the free-time activities. Use the pictures to introduce new vocabulary and have students repeat the words/phrases several times. Stick the pictures on the board and ask students which activities they like doing/would like to do.
- Divide the class into five groups (depending on the number of students you have, you can divide them into ten groups) and assign an activity to each. Then give groups sheets of poster board. Groups draw a scene with children performing the activity and write sentences to describe it. Students can refer to colors, weather, what the children are doing, etc. Walk around the classroom to help students with language.
- When groups have finished, invite some to describe their posters. Display students' work on the classroom walls.

Picture Dictionary

- Focus students' attention on p. 140 and show students the images for 'Free-time'.
- Divide the class into pairs. Students read the words under the pictures. Then they take turns challenging each other to spell the words.

Now students can do Worksheet I.

Ending the lesson

- Play *Draw it relay* (see p. T89).

OPTIONAL ACTIVITIES

Game

Play *Bingo* (see p. T89) to review vocabulary.

Make a sentence

Show flashcards and pictures of free-time activities that students know. Divide the class into two teams. One student from each team in turn chooses an image and says a sentence (e.g., *He likes skiing*). Give a point for each correct sentence. Teams can use pictures that have been described before, but they can't use the same sentences.

WB pages 96-97

8 Complete the puzzle.

- Students use the pictures as clues to complete the crossword puzzle.

9 Read, think and complete.

- Students use the lists of likes and dislikes to complete the sentences.

10 What do you like doing? Draw a picture.

- Students draw their favorite activity in the frame and color it.

11 What do you like doing? Use the words in the box.

- Students write a description of their picture, using the words in the box.

Self-assessment

- Students choose and color the appropriate number of stars depending on how well they think they have complete the unit. Discuss with students what they have learned, what they can do now, which activities they liked best and which ones were difficult.

2 Animals

1 T19 **Listen, point and say.**

2 T20 **Listen and say the missing word.**
Crocodile.

Workbook page 98, Activity 1.

3 Chant.

Do hippos eat insects?
No, they don't. Hippos eat grass.
Do monkeys eat grass?
No, they don't. Monkeys eat fruit.
Do lions eat meat?
Yes, they do. Lions eat meat.
Do giraffes eat leaves?
Yes, they do. Giraffes eat leaves.

LOOK!

Do lions **eat** meat?
Yes, they **do**./No, they **don't**.

4 Listen and circle the correct word.

1 Crocodiles eat *meat* / *insects*, too.
2 Giraffes eat *fruit* / *leaves*.
3 What do hippos *eat* / *do*?
4 Elephants eat leaves and *fruit* / *grass*, too.

5 Ask and answer.

Workbook pages 98 and 99, Activities 2 and 3.

Lesson 1

Lesson aims
To present and practice new vocabulary.
Target language
crocodile, elephant, giraffe, hippo, lion; leaves; (Lions) eat (meat).
Recycled language
Animals, Food, Body parts
Materials
Multi-ROM, Flashcards (Animals and others)

Starting the lesson

- Brainstorm animals that students have learned so far. Write their ideas on the board.
- Next, write the headings *Pets*, *Farm*, *Forest* and *Insects*. Then point to one of the headings. Students say the animals from the list on the board that go in that category.

SB page 14

Presentation

- Focus students' attention on the main illustration. Remind them (L1) of what happened in Unit 1 (the children are looking for Madley Kool and they meet Cleo, the cat detective).
- Ask questions to help the class describe the main illustration, e.g., *Are they in the jungle? (No, they're in a movie set.) Who's this? How many birds are there?*
- Present the vocabulary using the flashcards. Hold up each flashcard in turn and say the words for students to repeat. Hold up the flashcards again, this time asking individual students to say the words.
- Stick the flashcards on the board. Invite a student to come to the front and point to the flashcards randomly. The class says the words he/she points to.

1 Listen, point and say.

- Draw students' attention to the pictures of animals at the bottom of the page. Play T19, and students point to the pictures in their books. Play it again, pausing after each word, and students repeat them. Ask some individual students to say the words.

2 Listen and say the missing word.

- Tell students (L1) that they are going to listen to the characters talking about the animals in the main illustration, but that one of the animals from Activity 1 will be missing.
- Instruct them to pay close attention to the main illustration. Play T20 once up to *What's missing?*. Give students time to locate the animals in the illustration and find out which item is missing (*crocodile*). Play it again to the end.
- Play T20 again, pausing after each line for students to repeat. Encourage tone of voice and expressions to match those in the pictures.
- You can ask questions to check students' comprehension, e.g., *Does Ruby like (the lion)?*

T20

Sam	Where's Madley Kool? Is he here?
Jenny	No, he isn't. But look at all the animals! What's your favorite animal? I like the giraffe. Look at his long neck!
John	I like the monkeys. They're funny.
Ruby	I like the elephant. It's big! And I like the hippo. It's cool.
Sam	Look! It's a lion! What do lions eat?
Ruby	They eat meat. Quick, Run!
Narrator	What's missing?
Children	Crocodile!

Presentation

- Direct students' attention to the food words labeled in the main illustration – *meat, fruit, insects, grass* and *leaves.* Check the meaning.
- Point to the lion and the meat and say, *Lions eat meat.* Then point to the elephant and to the leaves. Ask, *And elephants? Do elephants eat meat?* Students answer *Yes* or *No*. Say, *Elephants eat leaves.* Continue with the other animals.
- As a follow-up, you can ask students to write the sentences in their notebooks.

Ending the lesson

- Play a guessing game. Ask students to think of an animal. Ask questions to guess what animal it is, e.g., *Is it big/small? Does it have four legs?* Use this activity to review a variety of questions, e.g., *Is it (big)? Is it (brown)? Can it (swim)?*
- When students have understood the activity, think of an animal and tell them to ask the questions.

OPTIONAL ACTIVITY
Flashcard game
Play *Flashcard act out* (see p. T88).

WB page 98

1 Match.

- Students match each animal to the correct word and section of the animal park.

Lesson 2

Lesson aims
To review the vocabulary of Lesson 1 with a chant; to present the new structure.
Target language
Do (lions) eat (meat)? Yes, they do./No, they don't.
Recycled language
Animals; *fruit, grass, insects, leaves, meat*
Materials
Multi-ROM, Flashcards (Animals), kraft paper, pictures of animals, markers, glue

Starting the lesson

- Play *Charades* (see p. T88) to review animal vocabulary.

SB page 15

3 Chant.

- Focus students' attention on the chant. Then play T21 for students to listen and follow the words. Play it again, pausing after each line for students to repeat.
- Play the chant once more for students to join in. If necessary, use the flashcards to help prompt the words.

Presentation

- Draw students' attention to the question and short answers in the *Look!* box. Write them on the board (so that all students can follow your explanation) and point out the highlighted words. Explain that *they* is the plural form of *he* and *she*. Then focus on the use of *do*. Help them create a simple rule (e.g., *Use* do *in questions with* they*; use* do/don't *in short answers*).
- Elicit other questions about the animals in the main illustration and write them on the board, with the corresponding answer. Use different colors (or underline/circle items in the sentences) to help students understand the structures and the rule. Ask students to copy the examples into their notebooks.

Extra!

- Write on the board *meat*, *insects*, *fruit*, *leaves* and *grass*. Brainstorm with students other animals they know that like to eat these things, (e.g., *Dogs eat meat. Frogs eat insects*).
- You may wish to explain that animals that like meat are *carnivores*; that those that eat fruit, grass and vegetables are *herbivores*; and that those that eat both are *omnivores* (e.g., rats, bears and humans).

4 Listen and circle the correct word.

- Focus students' attention on the sentences. Tell them (L1) that Sam, Ruby, Jenny and John are talking about different animals and the food they eat. According to what has been said, students circle the correct word.
- Play T22 once. Students just listen. Then play the recording again. They circle the correct word.
- You may wish to ask a few questions to check comprehension, e.g., *Do crocodiles eat insects? What do hippos eat?*

T22

Sam What do lions eat?
Ruby They eat meat. Crocodiles eat meat too. Quick, where's the meat?
Jenny And giraffes eat leaves from trees. Look at them!
John What do hippos eat?
Ruby They eat grass. Elephants eat leaves and grass too. What do frogs eat?
John They eat insects... and monkeys eat fruit! Hey, you! Monkey, come back! That's my fruit!

5 Ask and answer.

- Divide the class into pairs (see ideas for dividing students on p. 00). When you have their full attention, focus on the language in the speech bubbles (you can read the dialogue with another student). Then students take turns asking questions about the animals in the main illustration and the food they eat.
- Monitor pairs to help with the intonation in the question and with language use. At the end of the activity, you can ask some pairs to perform the dialogues for the class.

Ending the lesson

- Play *Hot seat* (see p. T88).

OPTIONAL ACTIVITY
Animal poster
Make a poster with the class. Give students cut-out pictures of animals. Write *Herbivores/Carnivores/Omnivores* on top of a large sheet of kraft paper and ask students to stick in the corresponding pictures.

SB pages 98-99

2 Look and write.

- Students guess what animal it is by looking at the parts of the body. They then write sentences as in the examples.

3 Read and write.

- Students look at the table with pictures of animals and the things they eat. They then complete the sentences with the missing information.

6 T23 **Listen and sing.**

SONG

Lions live in Africa.
They're big and strong.
They like sleeping all day long.
They run very fast
To catch their lunch.
What do they eat?
They eat meat.
Crunch, crunch, crunch!

Oscar lives with me.
He's a very small mouse.
He likes sleeping in my house.
He runs very fast
To get his lunch.
What does he eat?
He eats cheese.
Munch, munch, munch!

LOOK!

Lions **live** in Africa.
They **live** in Africa.
My cat **lives** with me.
He/She/It **lives** with me.

Lesson 3

Lesson aims
To extend the unit vocabulary set; to practice the vocabulary with a song.
Values
Respecting animal life.
Target language
Africa, catch; (Lions) live (in Africa). (Oscar) lives (with me).
Recycled language
Animals, Food
Materials
Multi-ROM, Flashcards (Animals), a map of the world, pictures of endangered animals, A4 paper, colored pencils

Starting the lesson

- Play *Make a sentence* (see p. T88) to review questions and short answers.

SB page 16

Presentation

- Show the map of the world and ask, *Where's Africa?* Invite students to answer. Point to the map and say, *Here, this is Africa.* Ask, for instance, *Are there (monkeys) in Africa?* Students answer.
- Introduce new vocabulary using mime and L1 if necessary. Say, *I live in (city/town/neighborhood).* Then ask students, *Where do you live?* Use students' answers to introduce the third person singular *(Beatriz) lives in (city/town/neighborhood).*

6 Listen and sing.

- Play T23. Students listen and follow the words in their books. Create mime and gestures to go with the actions in the song, then play the song again for students to join in with the words and mime.
- Divide the class into two groups (see ideas for group formation on pp. XII and XIII). Play T23 again. Group A sings the lines for the lions, and Group B sings the lines about Oscar. Then they switch and sing again.

Presentation

- Draw students' attention to the sentences in the *Look!* box and write them on the board. Point out the use of the pronouns to replace *Lions* and *My cat* in the sentences. Then ask students about the difference between *live* and *lives* in the sentences. Help them come up with a simple rule, reminding students of the use with other pronouns (e.g., *Add an* s *to the action with* he, she *and* it). You can ask students to copy the rule into their notebooks.
- Elicit other examples from students, using other verbs and animals, both in the singular and plural form. Write the examples on the board. Use different colors (or underline/circle items in the sentences) to help students understand the rule. Ask students to copy the examples into their notebooks.

Values

- Talk with students (L1) about the importance of respecting animal life. Ask their opinion about hunting animals for their fur or skin. Mention, for instance, crocodiles, which are hunted to make bags and shoes.
- Ask students (L1) what they know about endangered species in Brazil (golden lion tamarins, jaguars and hyacinth macaws, among others) and in the world (giant pandas, sea turtles, tigers, polar bears, monarch butterflies and mountain gorillas, among others). You can introduce *endangered species, extinction* and *illegal hunting.* Show students some pictures of the endangered animals and teach their names in English.

Tell the class to discuss the threat to wildlife with a family member. Students can teach their relatives the words in English for the endangered animals they saw in class.

Ending the lesson

- Play *Draw it relay* (see p. T89).

OPTIONAL ACTIVITY

Drawing activity
On an A4 sheet of paper, students draw and color a picture of an endangered animal. When they have finished, they write a short description of the animal, e.g., *Pandas are endangered animals. They live in China. They're black and white and they're big. They eat bamboo. They don't usually eat meat, but sometimes they eat birds or rodents.* Help students with new vocabulary, writing any new words on the board for the class to see and use.

Lesson 4

Lesson aims
To develop speaking, listening and writing skills.
Recycled language
Animals; *They eat meat*; *He eats cheese*; *Giraffes live in Africa*
Materials
Multi-ROM, Unit 2 mini cards, scissors, A4 paper

Starting the lesson

- Say some true or false sentences about the song from Lesson 3. (e.g., *Lions live in Brazil*; *Oscar eats cheese*, and so on). Students stand up and clap their hands if the sentence is incorrect.

SB page 17

7 Look at Activity 6. Ask and answer.

- Divide the class into pairs (see ideas for dividing students on pp. XII and XIII). Draw students' attention to the speech bubbles and explain the activity. Student A looks at the song in Activity 6 and says a sentence about lions or Oscar, e.g., *They run fast*. Student B answers, for instance, *Lions*. Then Students A and B switch roles.
- Monitor pairs to help students with the correct use of the verb forms.

8 Listen and number.

- Focus students' attention on the pictures. Ask them to name the animals. Then ask students what they know about those animals. Ask, *Are they zoo animals? Are they pets? What do they eat? Where do they live? Can they swim?* Write students' ideas on the board.
- Tell students that you are going to play a recording about those animals. Play T24, pausing after each sentence for students to identify the animals.
- Play it again. This time, students listen and number the animals in the pictures.

T24

They live in Africa, they eat meat and they can swim.
It lives in a house, it eats meat and it likes sleeping.
They live in Africa, they eat leaves and they're tall.
They live in Africa, they eat fruit and they can climb trees.

9 Go to p. 75 and play the game.

- Divide students into pairs. Ask students to go to p. 75 and cut out the mini cards. When they have cut out all the cards, say a word represented in the card (*hippo*), and students then hold up the card. Continue with the other cards.
- Students put their sets of cards in two piles, face down on a desk. Student A turns over a card from his/her pile. Then he/she turns over a card from Student B's pile. When Student A turns over a card in Student B's pile that matches the card already face up in his/her pile, both students race to be the first to call *Snap!*.
- The student who calls *Snap!* first names the animals on the cards (e.g., *They're giraffes*) and says a sentence about them (*Giraffes live in Africa*). He/she keeps both cards. Then students switch roles and start playing again. The winner is the student with the most cards when the game ends.
- Demonstrate the game with two or three students before they start playing. If necessary, monitor pairs to help with language use.

Writing practice

- Give each student an A4 sheet of paper. Ask them to choose three animals from their mini cards set and to write sentences about them, similar to the ones in the lesson.
- Students work individually on their texts. Help them with language use. They can also decorate their texts with drawings. Display students' work on the classroom walls.

Ending the lesson

- Students play *What's missing?* (see p. T88) with their mini cards.

OPTIONAL ACTIVITY
Game
Play *Spelling bee* (see p. T89) with the animal words.

WB page 100

4 Read and circle.

- Students look at the example and then circle the correct word.

5 Find, think and write the questions.

- Students look at words and use them to write questions

7 Look at Activity 6. Ask and answer.

They eat meat.

Lions.

He eats cheese.

Oscar.

8 T24 Listen and number.

9 Go to page 75 and play the game.

Snap! They're crocodiles.

Crocodiles eat meat.

10 T25 Listen and read. Then act.

STORY

NOW GO TO FILM STUDIO ISLAND.

Workbook pages 100 and 101, Activities 6 and 7.

Lesson 5

Lesson aims
To consolidate the unit language with a story.
Recycled language
Animals; *They're (big).They eat (grass and leaves). They like (eating meat).*
Materials
Multi-ROM, Flashcards (Animals), Unit 2 mini cards

Starting the lesson

- Play a guessing game with the animals that appear in the new episode – elephant, crocodile, hippo. Begin drawing one of the animals very slowly and invite students to guess which one it is.

SB page 18

10 Listen and read. Then act.

- Remind students of the story in Unit 1 and ask, for instance, *Where are the children? (On a movie set.) Are there animals?* Students answer and name the animals.
- Before listening to the story, ask the following questions for the corresponding frames. Try to ask and discuss them in English:

1 *(Pointing to the elephants.)* What are these? [Elephants.]
2 What's the elephant doing? [It's eating.]
3 Do elephants eat cats? [Open discussion.]
4 Where's John? [Open discussion.]
5 *(Pointing to the hippo.)* What's this? [It's a hippo.]
6 Where are the crocodiles? [They're in the water.]

- Play T25, and students follow the story in their books. Play it again, pausing after each line for students to repeat.
- Next, to check students' understanding of the story, ask the following questions:

1 What's the name of the movie? [*Jim of the Jungle*.]
2 What do elephants eat? [Grass and leaves.]
3 Do elephants eat cats? [No, they don't.].
4 Are there any hippos in the water? [Yes, there are.]
5 Can John see the crocodiles? Where are they? [No./They're in the water.]
6 What do crocodiles eat? [They eat meat/boys.]

- Ask the class (L1) to predict what is going to happen in the next episode of the story.
- Divide students into five groups and assign a character to each. Students read their parts as a class from their seats. This may encourage shyer students to take part in the acting later on.
- Invite five students to take the parts of John, Ruby, Sam, Cleo and Jenny. Ask the volunteers to go to the front of the class to act out the story. Encourage tone of voice and expressions to match those in the pictures. Alternatively, you could have other students read the lines while those five students act it out.

Extra!

- Describe the frames in the story making some deliberate mistakes, e.g., *Elephants are small./There are two elephants in picture 1.*
- Every time students spot a mistake, they stand up and correct it.

FOR THE NEXT LESSON

- Ask students to look for interesting facts about an animal they like. They can use the Internet or reference books for their research. They can also bring pictures of the animals. Students will use the information for the mini project in Lesson 6.

Ending the lesson

- Play *The ball* (see p. T88) with the Animal flashcards. You can divide the class into two or three groups to play the game.

Students can now go online to Film Studio Island and enjoy the fun and games, at home or at the school computer lab. Ask them to find the 'light' that Cleo is holding in one of the pages of the unit (it is on p. 19). Then tell students they should find the light on Film Studio Island (it is inside the Wildlife Studio, at the very top of the tree where Jungle Man's tree house is). When students click on the light, they are taken to a supplementary language game based on the vocabulary in Unit 2.

OPTIONAL ACTIVITY
Mini card game
Play *Memory buzz* (see p. T88) with the mini cards.

WB pages 100-101

6 Write the animals in the correct columns. Add four more.

- Students look at the pictures of animals and classify them into big or small. They write the animals in the correct bubble and add more names.

7 Look at the code on p. 94 and write the messages.

- Students replace the letters with the correct letters in the wheel on p. 94 and write the sentence.

Lesson 6

Lesson aims
To integrate other areas of the curriculum into the English class; to develop the cross-curricular topic through a short project.
Cross-curricular focus
Science – amazing animals
Target language
every day, standing up, tongue, trunk
Recycled language
Animals; *They can (play with a ball), but they (can't jump).*
Materials
Multi-ROM, A3 paper, Unit 2 mini cards, colored pencils, glue

Starting the lesson

- Review the use of *can/can't* and *have*. Say some sentences about different animals (e.g., *Birds can fly. Elephants can't jump*). Elicit other sentences from students.

SB page 19

Presentation

- Ask students (L1) if they know any amazing facts about animals. Ask, for instance, *Which birds have wings, but can't fly? (Penguins and hens, among others.) Which animals sleep for months when it's cold? (Bears and squirrels, among others.)*

11 Listen and read.

- Direct students' attention to the article. Explore the pictures and use them to introduce new vocabulary.
- Tell the class they are going to read and listen to a text about amazing animals. Students follow the text in their books. If necessary, clarify vocabulary. Then ask students which animal is the most amazing, the elephant or the giraffe.

12 Listen and answer. *True* or *false*?

- Tell students that now they are going to listen to some sentences about the animals in Activity 11. They need to listen to the sentences and decide if they are true or false.
- Play T27 once through. Then play it again, pausing after each sentence, so that students have time to answer.

T27

1 Elephants can swim.
2 Giraffes don't sleep very much.
3 Elephants can play tennis.
4 Giraffes have pink tongues.
5 Giraffes clean their ears with their tongues.

13 Ask and answer.

- Divide the class into pairs (see ideas for dividing students on pp. XII and XIII). Draw students' attention to the speech bubbles and explain the activity. Student A looks at the text in Activity 11 and says a sentence about one of the animals. Student B guesses which animal it is. Then they switch roles.

Think!

Note: Some lessons (Lesson 6 or Wider World) have an extension Think! task. These tasks are designed to help develop students' critical thinking skills by motivating them to solve a problem or answer a question.

- Write the task on the board: *Can gorillas survive in the desert? Explain your answer. Give two reasons.*
- Divide students into small groups. Encourage them to discuss the question and think of possible explanations for their answer. Write students' ideas on the board, and ask them to explain their choices.
- Take students to the school library or to the computer lab to look up information on books or online to confirm their hypotheses. They can also do this as homework. If students search online, take the opportunity to discuss the relevance/reliability of the sources they quote. Encourage students to suggest several possible sources and how to judge their reliability.

Mini project

- Ask students (L1) what interesting facts they discovered about the animals they like. If some students forgot to bring the information, ask them to work with others who have brought material.
- Give students A3 sheets of paper. They write sentences about the animals and illustrate the text with pictures or drawings. Help students with language use and additional vocabulary.
- When they have finished, invite some students to describe their posters. Display the projects around the classroom.

Ending the lesson

- Play *Lexical groups* (see p. T90) using the vocabulary of the unit.

OPTIONAL ACTIVITY
Mini card game
Play *Memory game* (see p. T88) with the mini cards

WB page 102

8 Read the text on p. 19 again. Then complete the crossword.

- Students refer to the text and complete the sentences. Then they complete the crossword.

9 Find and write the words.

- Students look at the silhouettes of the animals and unscramble the words. Then they write the words under each animal.

10 Write about monkeys. Use the words in the box.

- Students follow the example and use the words in the box to write sentences about monkeys.

11 T26 **Listen and read.**

Amazing Animals!

Elephants

Elephants say hello with their trunks.
They can play with a ball!
They can swim, but they can't jump.

Giraffes

Giraffes can sleep standing up.
They don't sleep very much.
They have long, black tongues.
They clean their ears with their tongues!
They don't drink every day.

12 T27 **Listen and answer. *True* or *false*?**

1 True, 2 True, 3 False, 4 False, 5 True

13 **Ask and answer.**

They sleep standing up.

Giraffes!

MINI **PROJECT**
Choose an animal.
Find and write five amazing facts.

Review Units 1 and 2

How to play

Giraffes eat leaves.

Cats like watching TV.

Review Units 1 and 2

Lesson aims
To review the language of units 1 and 2; to personalize language; to provide an opportunity for self-evaluation.
Recycled language
Vocabulary and structures from Units 1 and 2.
Materials
Spinners and counters, A3 paper, colored pencils, Flashcards (Animals and Free time), pictures of famous animals from the movies/cartoons, a bag or a box, a paper ball or soft ball, masking tape
Special note: The activities from the *Review* lesson can be done in one or two classes, depending on the use of the *Pairwork*, *Extra!*, *Game* and *Optional activities* sections. The Workbook activities can also be assigned for homework in different classes.

Starting the lesson

- Play *Question chain* (see p. T90) to review the questions learned in Units 1 and 2 and a variety of other questions related to animals and free-time activities. In order to help less confident students, write prompt words on the board and point to them during the activity.
- Play *Letter mess* (see p. T90) to review animal vocabulary.

SB pages 20-21

Group work

- Divide the class into two or more groups (see ideas for group formation on pp. XII and XIII). Ask students to close their books. Then assign the role of 'secretary' to a student in each group and give them an A4 sheet of paper.
- Say some true or false sentences about what happened to the characters in Unit 1 (e.g., *Madley Kool likes playing soccer*; *Jenny doesn't like watching TV*; *Cleo likes sleeping, eating and lying in the sun*, and so on).
- Students listen quietly and then discuss with their 'secretaries' if the sentences are true or false. The 'secretaries' write the groups' answers.
- When you have finished, ask the secretaries to report their answers. The group with the most correct answers is the winner.

Game

- Say a sentence about the eating habits of one of the animals in Unit 2 (e.g., *Lions eat meat*). Ask a student to repeat the sentence and to add another element (e.g., *Lions eat meat*; *monkeys eat fruit*).
- Continue the activity with another student, but then say, *BUT they...* The student says a negative sentence (e.g., *But they don't eat pizza!*).
- After a few rounds, invite a student to take over as teacher.

Pairwork

- Divide students into pairs (see ideas for dividing the class on pp. XII and XIII) and give each pair an A3 sheet of paper.
- Ask students (L1) to imagine an animal that does not exist. They draw and color the picture of the invented animal. Next, students write sentences to describe what color it is, if it is big or small, where it lives, what it likes doing, what it eats, etc. You can write a model (or prompts) on the board to help students. If necessary, help students with vocabulary and sentence organization.
- When students have finished, they describe their animal to other pairs. Display their work on the classroom walls.

Board Game

- Point to the animals on the board game, and students say their names.
- Divide the class into pairs again, or use the same pairs from the previous activity. Give each pair counters (use buttons or erasers), a paper clip and a spinner (you can find a template for a spinner at www.pearson.com.br/ourdiscoveryisland). Show the class how to use the spinner with a pencil and a paper clip (place the paper clip in the center of the spinner, then place the pencil point inside the paper clip and spin it).
- Explain (L1) the rules of the board game. Students put their counters on the *Start* square. Student A spins the spinner and moves the correct amount of squares. If he/she lands on a square in which an animal is eating, he/she says (e.g., for square 4), *Giraffes eat grass.*
- If he/she lands on a square in which an animal is doing something, he/she says (e.g., for square 14), *Parrots can fly.* Or (e.g., for square 15), *Cats like watching TV.*
- If the sentence is incorrect, Student A moves back to the square he/she was on before spinning. Then it is Student B's turn.
- Demonstrate the activity with a student before they start working in pairs. Monitor pairs to help with pronunciation and accuracy.

Writing practice

- Ask students to write five sentences about the squares on the board games in their notebooks. Check students' work for grammar and spelling, then correct any mistakes. Alternatively, you can ask partners to exchange notebooks and correct their classmate's work.

Game

- Divide the class into two teams. Invite a student from each team to come to the board. The student from Team A whispers a word from Units 1 or 2 to the student from Team B.
- The student from Team B draws a picture of the word on the board for his/her team to guess. Then they switch roles. Have other students come to the board and continue playing the game.

Group work

- Divide students into small groups and give each a picture of a famous animal. You can use characters from movies and cartoons that students are familiar with. Ask groups to keep their pictures secret. Keep one of the pictures to demonstrate the activity.
- Students ask you questions to find out who your animal is (e.g., *Is it a fish? Is it big? Can it swim? Does it eat insects? Does it like (jumping)? Does it have (legs)?*). You can only answer *Yes* or *No*.
- When students guess the animal, it is their turn to play. Invite a group to come to the board and choose an animal. The class then asks them questions to guess the animal. If necessary, help students come up with the questions. To make the activity more challenging, you can limit the number of questions.

Ending the lesson

- Play *Basketball* (see p. T89) to review vocabulary (e.g., animals, food, free-time activities and language of Units 1 and 2).
- Put the flashcards (Animals and Free time) in a bag or box. Take one and begin to take it out very slowly. The class guesses what picture it is. The first student to make a correct guess takes your role.

OPTIONAL ACTIVITIES

Games

Play *Jumping the line* (see p. T88) using the vocabulary of Units 1 and 2.

Play *Stop the bus* (see p. T90) to review actions, food and animal vocabulary.

Play *Aye, aye, Captain!* (see p. T89) to review actions animals can do.

WB page 103

11 Draw your favorite animal.

- Students draw a picture of an animal they like. Then they color it.

12 Write about your favorite animal.

- Students write a description of their animal by completing the sentences.

Self-assessment

- Tell students (L1) that they have to choose and color the appropriate number of stars depending on how well they think they have completed the unit. Discuss with students what they have learned, what they can do now, which activities they liked best and which ones were difficult.

3 Weather

1 T28 **Listen, point and say.**

2 T29 **Listen and say the missing word.**

Cloud.

Workbook page 104, Activities 1 and 2.

3 Chant.

What's the weather like today?
It's cloudy and rainy. We're sad, we can't play.
What's the weather like today?
It's snowy and windy. We're sad, we can't play.
What's the weather like today?
It's cold, wet and stormy. We're scared, we can't play.
What's the weather like today?
It's hot and sunny. We're happy, let's play!

LOOK!

rain rain**y** cloud cloud**y** storm storm**y**

4 Listen and check the sentences you hear.

1 It's cold and snowy. ✓
2 It's wet and rainy. ✓
3 It's cloudy and rainy.
4 It's stormy. ✓
5 It's snowy and windy.
6 It's hot and sunny. ✓

5 Ask and answer.

Number 4. What's the weather like?

It's windy.

Weather

Lesson 1

Lesson aims
To present and practice new vocabulary.
Target language
cloud, rain, snow, storm, the sun, wind
Recycled language
Clothes; *cold, hot*
Materials
Multi-ROM, Flashcards (Weather and Clothes), clothes, a map of Brazil, sticky notes, colored pencils

Starting the lesson

- Display some pictures and flashcards of clothes students learned in previous levels (e.g., *T-shirt, pants, skirt, socks, shoes, dress, boots, sweat suit* and others). To make the activity more interesting, bring real clothes if possible.
- Review *hot/cold.* Show a clothes item and ask, *Is it for hot weather or cold weather?* Continue with the other items.

SB page 22

Presentation

- Present the weather vocabulary using the flashcards. Hold them up in turn and say the words/phrases for students to repeat. Hold up the flashcards again, asking individual students to say the words.

1 Listen, point and say.

- Draw students' attention to the pictures at the bottom of the page. Then play T28, pausing after each word/phrase to give students time to find the picture. Play it again, pausing after each word, and students repeat them.
- Ask students, *What's number (three)?* They look at the images and answer. If you want to make the activity more challenging, ask students to close their books and try to say the weather vocabulary from memory. Students can continue in pairs.

2 Listen and say the missing word.

- Now focus on the main illustration. Point to the characters and ask, *Who's this?* Then ask, *Where are the children? (In the film studio.)* Ask students to name the different weather vocabulary in the illustration. Point to Sam and ask, *What's he doing?* Write students' predictions on the board.
- Instruct them to pay close attention to the main illustration. Play T29 once up to *What's missing?*. Give students time to locate the different weather in the illustration and find out which item is missing (*cloud*). Play it again to the end.
- Play T29 again, pausing after each line for students to repeat. Encourage tone of voice and expressions to match those in the pictures.
- Check students' predictions about Sam (He's playing with the special effects at the studio).

T29

Sam	Wow! Look at this!
Jenny	Don't touch, Sam!... Where's Madley Kool?
Sam	Look at this big, red button!
Jenny	Sam! Don't touch!
Sam	What does this do?
All	Aaaarrgghh!!! Ooooh!!!
Sam	Oh! Wow! ... Rain! ...Wind! ... A storm! ... Snow!
Ruby	It's cold! Brr... Quick, Sam! Press the button again. Ah! There's the sun again! It's hot.
Narrator	What's missing?
Children	Cloud!

Group work

- Divide students into small groups (see ideas for group formation on pp. XII and XIII) and give each a blank sticky note (try to use large ones).
- Display a big map of Brazil on the board. Ask students (L1) to locate the place where they live, as well as other relevant cities, on the map. Ask what they know about the weather in different parts of the country. You can write their ideas on the board.
- Next, groups choose a weather word. They draw a picture of the word (e.g., a cloud or rain) on the note. Then they choose where to put it on the map. Invite groups to come to the board and stick their drawings around the country.
- When all groups have done this, they say what the weather is like in each region, e.g., *There's a lot of rain in (place), It's hot/cold here in (place).* Help students with language.

Ending the lesson

- Play *Hangman* (see p. T89) using weather words.

OPTIONAL ACTIVITY
Game
Play *What's missing?* (see p. T88) with the flashcards.

WB pages 104

1 Match.

- Students look at the map and the pictures. Then they match the weather words to the pictures.

2 Look, read and complete.

- Students read the weather forecast and use the words in Activity 1 to complete it.

Lesson 2

Lesson aims
To review the vocabulary of Lesson 1 with a chant; to present the new structure.
Target language
rainy, snowy, stormy, wet, windy; What's the weather like today? It's (cloudy) and (rainy).
Recycled language
cloud, rain, snow, storm, the sun, wind; cold, hot; happy, sad
Materials
Multi-ROM, Flashcards (Weather), A4 paper

Starting the lesson

- Use the flashcards to review the vocabulary from Lesson 1. Hold up the flashcards and elicit the words. Alternatively, ask individual students to come to the front and write the words on the board.

SB page 23

Presentation

- Show a flashcard (e.g., rain) and ask, *What's the weather like?* Then say, *It's rainy.* Ask the class to repeat the answer after you. Continue with the other cards to introduce *cloudy, windy, snowy* and *sunny*. Introduce *stormy* and *wet* with drawings on the board.

3 Chant.

- Focus students' attention on the chant. Then play T30 for students to listen and follow the words. Play it again, pausing after each line for students to repeat.
- Play the chant once more for students to join in. If necessary, use the flashcards to help prompt the words.

Presentation

- Draw students' attention to the words in the *Look!* box. Write them on the board, so that all students can follow your explanation. Ask them what they notice about each pair. Explain (L1) that we call the weather *rain*, but that we say *It's rainy* or *It's a rainy day*.
- Write some example sentences on the board (e.g., *Look at the rain. It's rainy today*). Students copy the sentences into their notebooks.

4 Listen and check the sentences you hear.

- Point to the characters in the main illustration and ask, *Who's this? What's his/her name?* Then tell students (L1) that the characters are still playing with the weather machine.
- Focus on the six sentences and explain that students have to check the ones they hear (only four sentences will be mentioned). Say the sentences, and then students repeat.
- Play T31 once. Students check the sentences as they hear them.

T31

1
Sam I like this weather machine. Let's play again. What's the weather like now, Ruby?
Ruby Oh, no! Now it's cold and snowy. Brrrr, I don't like the snow. Stop, Sam!
2
John And now it's wet and rainy. Where's my umbrella? I'm wet!
3
Ruby Oh, no! It's stormy now. Look at Cleo. She's scared. She doesn't like storms.
4
Sam What's the weather like now, Jenny?
Jenny Ah, it's a lovely day. It's hot and sunny. I'm happy.
Man Oh, no! My hat!

5 Ask and answer.

- Divide the class into pairs (see ideas for dividing students on p. 00). When you have their full attention, focus on the language in the speech bubbles (you can read the dialogue with another student). Then students take turns asking questions about the weather in the pictures.
- Monitor pairs to help with the pronunciation and language use. At the end of the activity, you can ask some pairs to perform the dialogues for the class.
- As a follow-up, students can write the dialogues in their notebooks.

Ending the lesson

- Students play *Picture guess* (see p. T88).

OPTIONAL ACTIVITY
Picture dictation
Play *Picture dictation* (see p. T90) using the unit vocabulary.

WB page 105

3 Look and write.

- Students use the weather words in the word box to complete the sentences below the pictures.

4 Complete.

- Students complete the sentence to answer about the current weather condition.

6 Listen and sing.

SONG

Spring, summer, fall, winter.
Four seasons in the year.

It's spring! It's spring!
It rains in the spring.
I jump and splash in the rain.
Chorus
It's summer! It's summer!
The sun shines in the summer.
I splash and swim in the sea.
Chorus

It's fall! It's fall!
The wind blows in the fall.
I fly my kite in the sky.
Chorus
It's winter! It's winter!
It snows in the winter.
I laugh and play in the snow.

LOOK!

It rains in the spring.
I splash in the rain.

7 Look at Activity 6. Ask and answer.

It snows. I play in the snow.

It's winter.

Workbook page 106, Activities 5 and 6.

Lesson 3

Lesson aims
To extend the unit vocabulary set; to practice the vocabulary with a song.
Target language
fall, spring, summer, winter, year; blow, kite; shine, splash; It (rains) in the (spring).
Recycled language
fly, play, swim; months of the year
Materials
Multi-ROM, Flashcards (Weather), a calendar, homemade word cards with the months

Starting the lesson

- Show the weather flashcards in turn and ask, *What's the weather like?* Students answer, for instance, *It's windy*. Then ask students, *What's the weather like today?* You can write the answer on the board (and then repeat the question and write the answer on the board at the beginning of every class).

SB page 24

Presentation

- Show a calendar to the class. Review the months. Ask, *When is (Christmas)? When is (Mother's Day)?*
- Then ask, *How many months are there in a year?* Ask, e.g., *Is it cold/hot in July? Is it windy in January?*
- Write the dates for the seasons on the board and ask students what is special about the dates. Then introduce the seasons. Students repeat the words.
- Ask questions about the weather in different seasons, e.g, *Is it (hot) in the (winter)? What's the weather like in the (winter)?*
- Use the pictures to introduce the other relevant vocabulary in the song.

6 Listen and sing.

- Play T32. Students listen and follow the words in their books. Create mime to go with the actions in the song. Then play the song again for students to join in with the words and mime.
- Divide the class into four groups and assign each group a season. Play T32 again, and groups sing the lines for their season.

Presentation

- Draw students' attention to the sentences in the *Look!* box and write them on the board. Ask students to find the difference between both sentences (in the first sentence, beginning with *it*, the word *rain* takes an *s*; in the second, which begins with *I*, it doesn't). Help students create a simple rule, based on structures they have seen before. They can copy the rule into their notebooks.
- Elicit other examples from students, using other verbs (e.g., *I play tennis. He plays football*). Use different colors (or underline/circle items in the sentences) to help students understand the rule. Students copy the examples into their notebooks.

7 Look at Activity 6. Ask and answer.

- Divide the class into pairs (see ideas for dividing students on pp. XII and XIII). Draw students' attention to the activities in Activity 6. Elicit other things we can do in the different seasons. Write students' ideas on the board.
- Then explain the activity. Student A looks at the song in Activity 6 and chooses a season (*spring*). Then he/she says a sentence that describes the weather and an activity he/she does in the (spring), or that refer to the activities in the song. Student B guesses the season. They switch roles.

At home, students think about the activities they do in summer or winter with their family. Then they make a mini poster showing the activities. When they have finished, they write a few sentences describing it.

- Invite some students to describe their posters the following class. Display their work on the classroom walls.

Ending the lesson

- Write the seasons at the top of the board. Then show a month word card and say, *It's (October). It's (winter)*. Students correct your sentence and come to the board to stick the word card under the correct season. Continue with the other months.

OPTIONAL ACTIVITY
Game
Play *Bingo* (see p. T89) to review vocabulary.

WB page 22

5 Look and write. Use the words in the box.

- Students write the correct season under each picture, using the words from the word box.

6 Look and write. Then match.

- Students look at pictures 1 to 4 and complete the sentences using the words in the box. Then they match a season (1 to 4) to the correct picture of a child doing something.

Lesson 4

Lesson aims
To develop reading, writing and speaking skills.
Recycled language
Actions, Seasons, Weather; *favorite, kite; I like (flowers).*
Materials
Multi-ROM, A4 paper, colored pencils, Unit 3 mini cards, scissors, Flashcards (Weather)

Starting the lesson
- Write the day and date on the board. Ask, *What's the weather like today?* Then draw the appropriate weather symbol from p. 23. Write a short sentence too (e.g., *It's cold and cloudy*). You can repeat this procedure every class, and students then copy into their notebooks.

SB page 25

8 Read and match.
- Focus students' attention on the texts and pictures. Tell them to read each text silently. Then they match the texts and seasons. If necessary, help individual students with vocabulary.
- Check students' answers. Ask (L1) what helped them get the right answer. As a follow-up, you can invite some students to read the texts aloud.

Extra!
- Students vote for their favorite season. You can draw a pie chart or another graph on the board with the results. Invite some students to explain their choices.

Writing practice
- Give each student an A4 sheet of paper. Ask them to write a short paragraph about their favorite season, including information about the weather and what they do in that season. You can write a model with students on the board and also ask them to refer to Activity 8.
- Students work individually on their texts. If necessary, monitor them to help with language use. They can decorate their texts with drawings. Display students' work on the classroom walls.

9 Go to p. 77 and play the game.
- Students cut out the mini cards. When they have finished, say a word represented in the card (e.g., *windy*), and students hold up the card. Continue with the other cards.
- Students choose three cards and put them face up on the table. Say the weather words. If you say a word from the cards students have chosen, they turn it over.
- The winner is the student who turns over three cards first. Play it again, with a student taking your role.

Game
- Divide the class into two groups. Call a student from Group A and give him/her a weather flashcard (any one except *cloud* and *wind*).
- The student mimes getting dressed to go out in the type of weather in the flashcard. Then Group A guesses the weather (e.g., *Rain!*). If the answer is correct, they get a point. Then it is Group B's turn.

Ending the lesson
- Students play *Memory game* (see p. T88) with their mini cards.

OPTIONAL ACTIVITIES

Game
Play *Category writing* (see p. T89) to review the language of Units 1, 2 and 3.

Weatherman
Divide the class into small groups. Explain (L1) what a weatherman is. Tell students to imagine they are the weather kids on TV. Write some expressions on the board: *Good morning./Good afternoon. The weather today is (hot and sunny). There is (wind) here. Goodbye.*
Groups choose the expressions they like and then write their forecast for their town/city/region and draw the weather symbols. Then they come to the front and act it out like a TV weather report.

WB page 107

7 Think and write the words.
- Students look at the word boxes. Then they guess which season each box represents and classify the words in the correct season.

8 Look at the code on p. 94 and write the message.
- Students replace the letters with the correct letters in the wheel on p. 94 and write the sentence.

8 Read and match.

a It's windy and I can fly my kite. There are a lot of apples on the tree!

b It's hot and I go to the park. It's my favorite season.

c I like flowers. The birds sing in the trees.

d It snows and it's cold. I play in the snow.

9 Go to page 77 and play the game.

10 T33 Listen and read. Then act.

STORY

NOW GO TO FILM STUDIO ISLAND.

Workbook page 108, Activity 9.

Lesson 5

Lesson aims
To consolidate the unit language with a story.
Target language
lie on the beach, quiet
Recycled language
Weather; *We can (lie on the beach).*
Materials
Multi-ROM, pictures of a beach and of a person with his/her index finger over the lips, speech bubbles with the lines of the story, kraft paper, pieces of construction paper, markers, glue

Starting the lesson

- Play *Memory buzz* (see p. T88) with the mini cards.

SB page 26

10 Listen and read. Then act.

- Use the pictures to introduce *lie on the beach* and *quiet*.
- Remind students of the story in the previous units and ask, for instance, *Where are the children? (On a movie set.)* Then draw their attention to the frames and ask, *What's the weather like?*
- Before listening to the story, ask the following questions for the corresponding frames. Try to ask and discuss them in English:
  1 What are they doing? [Making a movie.]
  2 Are the children happy? [No.]
  3 Why is Sam's face green? [Open discussion.]
  4 What are the children looking for? [Open discussion.]
  5 Where are the children? [On the beach.]
  6 Where is Cleo? [In the spotlights.]
- Play T25, and students follow the story in their books. Play it again, pausing after each line for students to repeat.
- Next, to check students' understanding of the story, ask the following questions:
  1 Ask students if they know why the director says *Action!*. (Explain if necessary.)
  2 Why does Ruby say *Quiet!*? (L1) [They can't make any noise in the movie set.]
  3 What's the weather like? [It's stormy.]
  4 What can they see? [A beach.]
  5 What can the children do on the beach? [They can read, lie on the beach, climb trees, jump and swim.]
  6 Is Cleo happy? Why? [Yes, because she likes sleeping.]
- Ask the class (L1) to predict what is going to happen in the next episode of the story.
- Divide students into six groups and assign a character to each. Students read their parts as a class from their seats. This may encourage shyer students to take part in the acting later on.
- Invite five students to take the parts of the characters in the story. Ask the volunteers to go to the front of the class to act out the story. Encourage tone of voice and expressions to match those in the pictures. Alternatively, you could have other students read the lines while those five students act it out.

Ending the lesson

- Prepare speech bubbles with the lines of the story and hand them out to different students. Play T25 again. When their line is playing, students jump up and go to the front of the classroom. They arrange themselves in order and hold up their speech bubbles.

Students can now go online to Film Studio Island and enjoy the fun and games, at home or at the school computer lab. Ask them to find the 'computer' that Cleo is holding in one of the pages of the unit (p. 9). Then tell students they should find the computer on Film Studio Island (it is on the top floor of the Special Effects studio, on the extreme left). When students click on the computer, they are taken to a supplementary language game based on the vocabulary in Unit 3.

OPTIONAL ACTIVITY
Weather chart
Divide the class into small groups. Each group draws a symbol for a weather word on a piece of construction paper and writes the corresponding word on it. When they have finished, they show it and say what it is (e.g., *It's snowy*).
Next, draw a grid with the days of the week on a large sheet of kraft paper. Leave four blank lines, so that students can keep track of the weather for a month. Ask students to write the days of the week on the chart. At the beginning of every class, children say, for instance, *Today's (Monday). It's (sunny).* Then they put the weather symbol on the corresponding day and week.

WB page 108

9 Complete the crossword.

- Students look at the pictures and complete the crossword.

Lesson 6

Lesson aims
To integrate other areas of the curriculum into the English class; to develop the cross-curricular topic through a short project.
Cross-curricular focus
Geography – hurricanes
Target language
camera, hurricane, round, waves, knock down
Recycled language
Weather; *scared, sea*
Materials
Multi-ROM, Flashcards (Weather), A3 paper, colored pencils, glue, scissors, a map of the world, reference books, sticky notes, Unit 3 mini cards

Starting the lesson

- Divide the class into two teams. They stand up. Show flashcards of weather words and say a sentence (e.g., *It's sunny*). Make some intentional mistakes. If the sentence is correct, students say *Yes* and turn around. If you make a mistake, they say *No* and sit down. Model a few times. Ask individual students to take your role.

SB page 27

11 Listen and read.

- Direct students' attention to the text. Explore the pictures and use them to introduce new vocabulary. Explain (L1) what a hurricane is.
- Tell the class they are going to read and listen to a text about hurricanes. Students follow the text in their books. If necessary, clarify vocabulary.
- Discuss with students why hurricanes are dangerous and what people can do to keep safe during one.

12 Read and answer. *True* or *false*?

- Students read the sentences individually and decide if they are true or false. You can play T34 again while the class is reading the text.
- Then ask individual students to read the answers and correct the false ones.

Think!

- Write the task on the board: *Is a hurricane the same as a typhoon or a cyclone? What's the same about them? What's different? How can you find out?*
- Divide students into small groups. Encourage them to discuss the question and think of possible explanations for their answer. Write students' ideas on the board, and ask them to explain their choices.
- Take students to the school library or to the computer lab to look up information on books or online to confirm their hypotheses. They can also do this as homework. If students search online, take the opportunity to discuss the relevance/ reliability of the sources they quote. Encourage them to suggest several possible sources and how to judge their reliability.

Pairwork

- Ask students to close their books. Then divide the class into pairs (see ideas for dividing the class on pp. XII and XIII).
- Write the first half of some sentences from the text on one side of the board (e.g., *A hurricane is…*; *It can knock down…*; *There are big waves…*). Write the endings in jumbled order on the other side of the board. Students copy into their notebooks, then work with their partner to match the halves. When they have finished, they open their books and check their answers.

Mini Project

- Bring reference books to the classroom. If conditions permit, students can use the Internet at the school computer lab.
- Ask (L1) students what they know about other extreme weather conditions. Elicit words such as *earthquake*, *tsunami*, *heat cold waves*, *floods* and *cyclones.*
- Divide the class into small groups. Each group chooses one situation of extreme weather and look for information about it. Give groups A3 sheets of paper. Students write a few sentences about their choice. They can illustrate their text with pictures copied from books, or printed from the web. If necessary, help them with language.
- Display the projects around the room. Students describe their projects to the class.

Ending the lesson

- Play *What's missing?* (see p. T88) with the mini cards.

OPTIONAL ACTIVITY
Where are hurricanes?
Display a map of the world. Bring reference books or, if conditions permit, use the Internet.
Divide the class into pairs and ask them to look for information about where in the world hurricanes are more likely to occur. Students write a list of places. Give them sticky notes and ask them to write the names of the countries / regions on them. Then they locate the places on the map and stick their notes.

11 T34 **Listen and read.**

HURRICANE!

What is a hurricane?

A hurricane is a big storm. There's a lot of wind and a lot of rain. The hurricane goes round in a big circle. It can knock down trees and houses. There are big waves on the sea, too.

What's the eye of a hurricane?

The eye is the center of the hurricane. It isn't windy and rainy there. Can you see the eye of the hurricane in the picture?

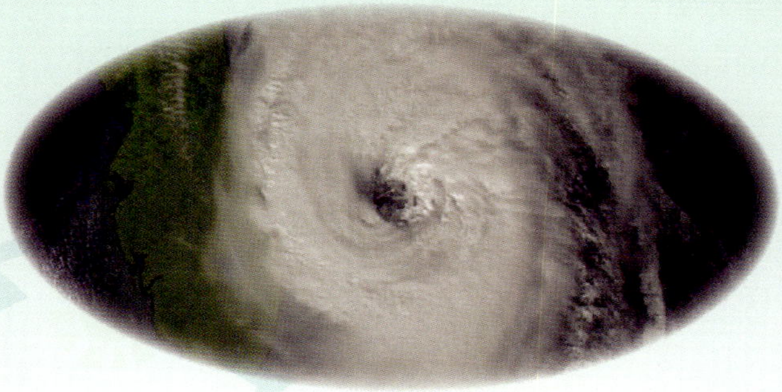

When are there hurricanes?

There are hurricanes in the summer and the fall.

12 **Read and answer. *True* or *false*?**

1 A hurricane is a big storm. True
2 It's hot and sunny during a hurricane. False
3 The eye isn't in the center of the hurricane. False

Wider World

Wildlife parks

1 **Listen and read.** T35

1

I'm Surian. I live in Borneo. There is an orangutan center near my house. Baby orangutans are cute. They eat bananas every day. Orangutans have long red hair and long arms. They like climbing trees.

2

I'm James. I live in London. I like going to the zoo to see animals. My favorite animals are lions. There are some cute lion cubs, too.

2 **Read and answer.**

1 What do baby orangutans eat? Bananas.
2 Where do orangutans live?
3 What does James like doing?
4 Where does Akeyo live?
5 What's the weather like in Kenya?
6 Which animals does Akeyo like?

2 In an orangutan center. / 3 He likes going to the zoo. / 4 In the Serengeti National Park. / 5 It's very hot. / 6 He likes giraffes.

Workbook page 108, Activity 10.

3

I'm Akeyo. I live in the Serengeti National Park in Kenya. It's very hot here. There are a lot of different animals in the park. I like the giraffes. They're tall and they have long necks.

3  **Read and say the name.**

1 He lives in London. James
2 They eat bananas. Orangutans
3 They are tall and have long necks. Giraffes
4 They have long arms. Orangutans
5 His house is near an orangutan center. Surian

4  **Ask and answer.** Answers will vary.

1 Is there a zoo near you? Which animals can you see there?
2 Do you go to the zoo with your family?
3 Are there national parks in your country? Where are they?
4 What's your favorite animal? Does it live in your country?

5  **Write about wild animals in Brazil.**

Workbook page 109, Activities 11 and 12.

Wider World

Lesson aims
To personalize the unit language; to learn about other wild animals and their habits; to provide an opportunity for self-evaluation.
Values
The importance of preserving wildlife.
Target language
National Parks; lion cubs, orangutan
Recycled language
Body parts, Food, Seasons, Weather; *They like (climbing trees).*
Materials
Multi-ROM, Flashcards (Weather), Unit 3 mini cards, a map of the world or a globe, reference books, A4 paper, a bag or box, pictures of animals, magazines, Worksheet 3
Special note: The activities from the *Wider World* lesson can be done in one or two classes, depending on the use of the *Pairwork, Extra!* and *Optional activities* sections. The Workbook activities can also be assigned for homework in different classes.

Starting the lesson

- Play *Question chain* (see p. T90) to review questions related to the weather, e.g., *Do you like (swimming) in the (summer)? Is it cold/hot in the winter? What's the weather like today?*
- Next, brainstorm names of wild animals, providing the words in English if necessary. Then draw an animal very slowly on the board for the class to guess. Ask students to describe it (e.g., *It's big. It eats meat. It has four legs*).

SB pages 28-29

Presentation

- Draw students' attention to the pictures. Ask them to name the animals: *orangutan, lion, giraffes, zebras*. Repeat the words several times. Explain *lion cub.* Say, *Look, these are baby lions, they're lion cubs*. Then discuss (L1) what kind of weather condition is more suitable for those animals.
- Ask students to look at the texts, find the names of the countries/cities and locate them on the map or globe.
- Focus on the third text and explain (L1) what a wildlife park is.

1 Listen and read.

- Tell students (L1) they are going to listen to and read a text about three children and the wild animals they like. Ask students to follow the text as they listen to the recording and to tell you the names of the children. Play T35 once for students to have a first contact with the text. Then play it again.
- Next, play each part separately and ask some questions to check comprehension. Clarify vocabulary.
  - *What do baby orangutans eat?*
  - *What are James' favorite animals?*
  - *What's the weather like in the Serengeti National Park?*
- As a follow-up, you can invite individual students to read parts of the text. (Alternatively, you can work with shadow reading. Play T35. Students read the words while trying to stay at the same speed and rhythm as the recording. As students keep reading, you can turn the sound down some times.)

2 Read and answer.

Focus students' attention on the questions. They read the texts again carefully and answer the questions in their notebooks. Check the answers as a class.

3 Read and say the name.

- Draw students' attention to the sentences. They read the texts again and write the correct name in their notebooks.
- When they have finished, divide the class into pairs (see ideas for dividing students on pp. XII and XIII). Student A says a sentence, and Student B says the name. Then they change roles.

Extra!

- Ask students to close their books. Divide the class into two teams (see ideas for group formation on pp. XII and XIII) and choose a 'captain' for each team. The two captains stand some meters from the board.
- Read the texts from Activity 1, making some intentional mistakes. When students spot a mistake, the captains go to the board and write the correct word. The student who writes the correction first gets a point for his/her team.

Values

- Focus on the map of the world or globe. Ask students if they know where there are wild animals (in Africa, in South America, in Australia...). Next, ask what they know about national parks in Brazil (where they are, what kind of animals can be found in these places). Why are there national parks? Why are they so important?
- You can bring reference books or, if conditions permit, take students to the school computer lab to look for information on wild animals and national parks on the Internet. Ask students to share their findings with the class.

4 Ask and answer.

- Students discuss the questions in small group. Some suggestions on how to carry out the activity successfully:
  - Have students sit in a circle, so that they can face each other. They can sit on the floor or move their chairs.
  - Provide any additional vocabulary students need to express their ideas. If a vocabulary item is relevant for all the students in class, write it on the board.
  - Encourage different students to express their ideas, but respect quieter ones.
  - Encourage students to express their ideas in English as much as possible. You can rephrase students' sentences in L1 in English.
- As a follow-up, you can ask students to write the answers in their notebooks.

5 Write about wild animals in your country.

- Brainstorm names of wild animals that can be found in Brazil. Then divide the class into pairs and give each an A3 sheet of paper.
- Tell students to choose one or two wild animals and write a description. They can include information about where these animals live, what they eat and what they look like. Students can use the reference books you brought to look for information. Help them with additional vocabulary and sentence structure.
- They can also draw pictures to illustrate their work. When they have finished, invite some pairs to share their texts with the class. Display the pictures around the room.

Picture dictionary

- Focus students' attention on p. 140 and show students the images for *Animals*.
- Divide the class into pairs. Students read the words under the pictures. Then they cover the words and take turns saying the words.

Now students can do Worksheet 3.

Ending the lesson

- Divide the class into two groups. One student from Group A mimes an animal. Group B guesses what animal it is. If they guess correctly, they get a point. Then they switch roles.

OPTIONAL ACTIVITIES

Game

Play *Quick Peek* (see p. T88) using the mini cards from Unit 3.

Coded message

Write a coded message on the board and ask students to decode it using the wheel from p. 94. Then divide the class into pairs for them to write their own coded messages. Ask pairs to exchange messages and decode them. Then they read the messages to the class.

WB pages 108-109

10 Read the email. Then complete the answer.

- Students read the email, then complete the sentences with the correct information.

11 Draw your favorite season.

- Students draw and color a scene related to their favorite season in the picture frame.

12 Write about your favorite season.

- Students write a description of their picture by completing the sentences (e.g., *My favorite season is summer/I like swimming/I go to the beach.*

Self-assessment.

- Students choose and color the appropriate number of stars depending on how well they think they have completed the unit. Discuss with students what they have learned, what they can do now, which activities they liked best and which ones were difficult.

4 My week

1 Listen, point and say. T36

1

go skateboarding

2

go swimming

3

do karate

4

do gymnastics

5

have ballet lessons

2 Listen and say the missing phrase. T37

Do gymnastics.

Workbook page 110, Activities 1 and 2.

3 Chant.

What do you do on Saturdays?
What do you do on Saturdays?
I do gymnastics at 10 o'clock.
She does gymnastics at 10 o'clock.
I go swimming at 11 o'clock.
He goes swimming at 11 o'clock.
I have ballet lessons at two thirty.
She has ballet lessons at two thirty.
I go skateboarding at 4 o'clock.
He goes skateboarding at 4 o'clock.

LOOK!

I go swimming at 11 o'clock.
He goes swimming at 11 o'clock.

4 Listen and answer. *True* or *false*?

1 John has music lessons at 3 o'clock. False
2 Ruby does karate at six thirty. False
3 Jenny does gymnastics at 10 o'clock. True
4 Sam goes skateboarding at 4 o'clock. True

5 Look and make sentences.

1 Ruby/ballet lessons
Ruby has ballet lessons at two thirty.

2 John/swimming
John goes swimming at eleven o'clock.

3 Madley Kool/music lessons
Madley Kool has music lessons at eleven thirty.

4 Madley Kool/karate
Madley Kool does karate at three thirty.

Workbook page 111, Activity 3.

4 My week

Lesson 1

Lesson aims
To present and practice new vocabulary.
Target language
do gymnastics, do karate, go skateboarding, go swimming, have ballet, have music lessons
Recycled language
What's your name? I'm John.
Materials
Multi-ROM, Flashcards (My week)

Starting the lesson

- Play *Teacher says* (see p. T89) to review sports and actions. Say, for instance, *Teacher says, Move your legs.*

SB page 30

Presentation

- Focus students' attention on the picture. Remind them (L1) of the movie sets in the previous units.
- Point to the karate clothes. Ask (L1) what kind of movie set this is (e.g., karate or martial arts). Then ask, *Can you see Madley Kool? Where is he?* Students point to Madley Kool in the picture.
- Present the vocabulary using the flashcards. Hold up each flashcard in turn and say the activities for students to repeat. Hold up the flashcards again, this time asking individual students to say the phrases.
- Stick the flashcards on the board. Invite a student to come to the front and point to the flashcards randomly. The class says the words he/she points to.

1 Listen, point and say.

- Draw students' attention to the pictures of the activities at the bottom of the page. Play T36, and students point to the pictures in their books. Play it again, pausing after each phrase, and students repeat them. Ask some individual students to say the words.

Pairwork

- Divide students into pairs (see ideas for dividing the class on p. 00). They take turns asking questions about the pictures in Activity 1, e.g., *What's number (three)? (Do karate.)*

2 Listen and say the missing phrase.

- Now focus on the main illustration again. Point to the characters and ask, *Who's this?* Ask students to name the different activities in the illustration. Then point to the characters, and students say the corresponding activity in the speech bubble. Ask students (L1) what is happening. Write their predictions on the board.
- Tell students (L1) that they are going to listen to the characters talking about the activities in the main illustration, but that one of the items from Activity 1 will be missing.
- Instruct them to pay close attention to the main illustration. Play T37 once up to *What's missing?*. Give students time to compare the dialogue to the pictures in Activity 1. Play it again to the end.
- Play T37 again, pausing after each line for students to repeat. Encourage tone of voice and expressions to match those in the pictures.
- Check students' predictions about the story (the chidren are being interviewed about their activities).

T37

Tina Hi. I'm Tina from *Star* magazine. I'm here to talk to Madley. Madley Kool. Where is he?
John I don't know. You can talk to me.
Tina You? Erm... What's your name?
John I'm John.
Tina OK. Hi, John,
John Hi.
Tina John, what do you do on Saturdays?
John I go swimming in the morning and I have music lessons in the afternoon.
Ruby Hello, I'm Ruby. I do karate in the morning and I have ballet lessons in the afternoon.
Sam I'm Sam. I go skateboarding in the afternoon.
Jenny And I...
Tina What's that?
Narrator What's missing?
Children Do gymnastics!

Ending the lesson

- Divide the class into pairs. They take turns choosing a character from the thought bubbles in the picture. One student mime what the characters are doing. The other student then guesses who it is.

OPTIONAL ACTIVITY
Game
Play *Charades* (see p. T89) to review the actions learned in this Lesson and in Unit 1

WB page 110

1 Look and write.

- Students write the phrases for the corresponding pictures.

2 Look, think and complete.

- Students complete the sentences with the correct word from the box.

Lesson 2

Lesson aims
To review the vocabulary of Lesson 1 with a chant; to present new structure.
Target language
Telling the time; *at*, *on*
Recycled language
Activities
Materials
Multi-ROM, Flashcards (My week), a toy clock, A4 paper

Starting the lesson

- Play *Aye, aye, Captain!* (see p. T89) to review the vocabulary of Lesson 1.

SB page 31

Presentation

- Bring a toy clock to the class or draw one on the board. Show ten o'clock and say, *It's ten o'clock.* Students repeat. Give more examples. Encourage students to tell the time.
- Show ten thirty. Say *It's ten thirty*. Practice telling other times. You can ask a student to come to the board and move the hands of the clock.

3 Chant.

- Focus students' attention on the chant. Then play T38 for them to listen and follow the words. Play it again, pausing after each line for students to repeat.
- Play the chant once more for students to join in. If necessary, use the flashcards to help prompt the words.

Extra!

- Draw blank clock faces on the board and write, for instance, *It's nine o'clock* and *It's two thirty* next to each. Ask students to say what time it is and to draw the clock hands. Students copy into their notebooks.
- Keep practicing with other times.

Presentation

- Draw students' attention to the sentences in the *Look!* box. Write them on the board, so that all students can follow your explanation. Ask them to pay attention to the differences between both sentences. Help them come up with a simple rule (e.g., *Use* go *with* I *and* goes *with* he *and* she*)*.
- Then point out the use of *at* with times. Use the sentences in the chant to show students the use of *on* with days of the week.
- Elicit examples from students, using the first and third verb forms. Write them on the board. Students copy the sentences into their notebooks.

4 Listen and answer. *True* or *false*?

- Ask students to look at the main illustration. Remind them that a journalist is interviewing the children. Tell them (L1) that they will listen to the rest of the conversation.
- Draw students' attention to the true or false statements. Then play T39. If necessary, you can play it again two or three times. Check answers by asking individual students to read the sentences.
- Play the recording again. Ask (L1) what lesson the children do not have (*acting lessons*). Explain (L1) the meaning of *acting lessons*. Then ask students why the journalist suddenly left (she is disappointed that the children are not actors).

T39

Tina	Hello again. So, John, what time do you have music lessons?
John	At three thirty.
Tina	And Ruby... What time do you do karate?
Ruby	At nine thirty.
Tina	Jenny, what time do you do gymnastics?
Jenny	At ten o'clock.
Tina	Sam, what time do you go skateboarding?
Sam	At four o'clock.
Tina	So... John has music lessons at three thirty, and Ruby does karate at nine thirty. Jenny does gymnastics at ten o' clock, and Sam goes skateboarding at four o'clock. And when do you have acting lessons?
Sam	Acting lessons? We don't have acting lessons.
Tina	What?! Aren't you actors?
Ruby	Actors? No, we aren't!
Tina	Oh... well, thank you for talking to me. Goodbye.

5 Look and make sentences.

- Divide the class into pairs (see ideas for dividing students on pp. XII and XIII). Students take turns looking at the clocks and saying what the children do at different times. Do the first one as an example. Monitor pairs to check language use.
- As a follow-up, they write the sentences in their notebooks.

Ending the lesson

- Play *The ball* (see p. T89). Students say sentences including the time they do the activities (e.g., *I go swimming at two thirty*).

OPTIONAL ACTIVITY
Flashcard game
Play *Hot seat* (see p. T88).

WB page III

3 Look at the calendar and write.

- Students look at the calendar entries and write sentences about each activity.

6 Listen and sing.

SONG

How does she go to school?
Does she go by bike or car?
Does she go by bus or does she walk?
Is it very far? Is it very far?
She goes to school by bus.
Yes, she goes to school by bus.
She doesn't go by bike or car.
She goes to school by bus.

How does he go to the park?
Does he go by bike or car?
Does he go by bus or does he walk?
Is it very far? Is it very far?
He goes to the park by bike.
Yes, he goes to the park by bike.
He doesn't walk or go by bus.
He goes to the park by bike.

LOOK!

How **does** she **go** to school?
She **goes** to school **by bus**.
He **walks** to the park.

7 Play the game.

Workbook pages 111 and 112, Activities 4 and 5.

Lesson 3

Lesson aims
To extend the unit vocabulary set; to practice the vocabulary with a song.

Target language
boat, far, walk; How does (she) go to (school)? Does (she) go by (bike) or (car)? (She) goes to (school) by (bus).

Recycled language
bike, bus, car, park, school, train

Materials
Multi-ROM, Flashcards (My week), map of the town/city, spinners or dice

Starting the lesson

- Play *Bingo!* (see p. T89) to review telling the time.

SB page 32

Presentation

- Focus on the picture. Point to the three vehicles in turn and review the words.
- Say, *I go to (the park) by (car), and you?* Ask several students. Then point to a student who answered the question and ask, *How does (he) go to school? The* class tries to remember his/her answer. Rephrase it by saying, *(He) goes to school by (car).*
- Introduce *walk* by giving some examples and using mime. Then use a map of your town/city to explain the meaning of *far*.

6 Listen and sing.

- Play T32. Students listen and follow the words in their books. Create mime to go with the different ways of going to school/ the park in the song. Then play the song again for students to join in with the words and mime.
- Divide the class into two groups – boys and girls. The boys sing the lines about the girl; the girls sing the lines about the boy. Play T40 again, and the groups sing the song.

Presentation

- Focus students' attention on the question and answers in the *Look!* box and write them on the board. Point out the use of *does* in questions and the use of *by* with means of transport. Then draw their attention to the use of *walk*.
- Elicit other examples from students, writing the sentences in the third person singular. Use different colors (or underline/ circle items in the sentences) to help students understand the structure. Students copy the examples into their notebooks.

7 Play the game.

- Divide the class into pairs (see ideas for dividing students on pp. XII and XIII). Focus on the pictures and students repeat the means of transport. Introduce/review words.
- Draw students' attention to the language in the speech bubbles and explain (L1) the activity. Student A asks, *How does he go to school?* Student B spins the spinner (or casts the die) and answers according to the number he/she gets, e.g., *Five! He goes to school by train.* Then they switch roles.
- If necessary, monitor pairs to help with language use. As a follow-up, students can write the sentences in their notebooks.

Tell the class to teach their parents the song and sing it at home together. They can also sing it on their way to and from school.

Ending the lesson

- Students sing the song again. Divide the class into two groups. One group sings the questions, and the other sings the answers.

OPTIONAL ACTIVITY

Sentence building chain

Students build sentences by adding one word each. Student 1 says, for instance, *Sam...* Then Student 2 says, *Sam goes...* And Student 3 says... *Sam goes to.* They continue until they have made the sentence. Then another student begins a new chain. If a student forgets a word or makes an incorrect addition, the group misses their turn and another group starts. They can't repeat places or means of transport. You may divide the class into two groups and turn the game into a competition.

WB pages 111-112

4 How does he/she go to the park? Look, think and write.

- Students look at items 1 to 4, find the corresponding match in the big picture and complete the sentences as in the example.

5 Follow and write.

- Students find the means of transport each child uses to go to school by tracing their way through the maze. Then they complete the sentences.

Lesson 4

Lesson aims
To develop reading, listening and speaking skills.

Target language
afternoon, evening, morning; go to a party; What do you do on (Saturdays)? What does (Fifi) do on (Saturdays)? What time does (she) have (ballet lessons)?

Recycled language
Activities, Days of the week, Telling the time; *busy; How does (she) go to (her ballet lesson)? Does (she) walk? (She) loves (dancing). (She) doesn't like (walking).*

Materials
Multi-ROM, Unit 4 mini cards, scissors, toy clock, A4 paper, masking tape

Starting the lesson

- Bring a toy clock to the class. Move the hands and show different times, and students then say, *It's (three thirty).* Then move the hands to, for instance, and say, *It's five thirty*. Students clap their hands if the time right or wave their arms and correct you if it's wrong.

SB page 33

Presentation

- Draw a page of a calendar on the board. Write the day and date at the top of the page, then divide it into three parts. Label the parts *morning*, *afternoon* and *evening*. Then write some appointments for each part of the day and say sentences about what you do, e.g., *I (go swimming) in the (morning)*. Ask students questions about what they do during the day.
- Use the picture to introduce *go to a party*.

8 Look and read.

- Focus on the four pictures. Ask questions about what Fifi is doing in each one. Then students read about Fifi's day.
- Ask a few comprehension questions (e.g., *What does she do in the morning? Does she like ballet lessons?*).

9 Listen and answer. *True* or *false*?

- Tell students (L1) they will listen to some sentences about the text and decide if they are true or false. Play T41 once. Students just listen.
- Then play each sentence in turn, pausing to allow time for students to decide and write *true* or *false* in the boxes. Play it again and check answers.
- As a follow-up, ask the class to correct the false sentences in their notebooks.

T41
1 Fifi has ballet lessons at ten o'clock.
2 She walks to her ballet lesson.
3 She has ballet lessons in the afternoon.
4 She goes skateboarding in the afternoon.
5 She likes Saturdays.

Writing Practice

- Give each student an A4 sheet of paper. Ask them to write a text about an imaginary character (or about a friend) similar to the text in Activity 8. Students can use the text as a model.
- Students work individually on their texts. Monitor them to help with language use. If time allows, students finish their writing in class, otherwise they finish it at home. They can decorate their texts with drawings. Display students' work on the classroom walls.

10 Go to p. 79 and play the game.

- Divide the class into pairs (see ideas for dividing students on pp. XII and XIII). Ask them to cut out the mini cards on p. 79. When they have cut all the cards, say an activity represented in the cards (*have ballet lessons*), and students then hold it up. Continue with the other images.
- Focus on the illustration and the language in the speech bubbles. Tell students (L1) that the children are playing a game and that the class will do the same with their cards. Students put them face down on their desks. Explain the activity: Student A asks, *What do you do on Saturdays?* Then Student B picks a card from the table, looks at it, but doesn't show it to Student A. Then he/she mimes the activity in the card. Student A guesses the activity and says, for instance, *You (have music lessons).* If the sentence is correct, Student A keeps the card. Then they switch roles.

Ending the lesson

- Write different times on the board in random order. Then divide the class into two teams (see ideas for group formation on pp. XII and XIII). Students line up in front of the board.
- Call out a time that is listed on the board. One student from each group runs to the board and circles the time mentioned. The first one to circle the correct time gets a point for his/her team.

OPTIONAL ACTIVITY
Game
Play *Jumping the line* (see p. T88) u°sing the text in Activity 8.

WB page 112

6 Unscramble and write sentences.

- Students unscramble the words and write the sentences.

8 Look and read.

What does Fifi do on Saturdays?

She has ballet lessons in the morning. She loves dancing!

How does she go to her ballet lesson? Does she walk?

No, she goes by car! She doesn't like walking.

What time does she have her ballet lesson?

At 10 o'clock.

What does she do in the afternoon?

She goes skateboarding in the park at 2 o'clock. Then she goes to a party with her friends. She has a lot of fun on Saturdays!

9 Listen and answer. *True* or *false*?

T41

1. True
2. False
3. False
4. True
5. True

10 Go to page 79 and play the game.

Workbook page 112, Activity 6.

11 T42 **Listen and read. Then act.**

STORY

NOW GO TO FILM STUDIO ISLAND.

Lesson 5

Lesson aims
To consolidate the unit language with a story.
Target language
singing lessons, work
Recycled language
Activities; *Does he walk to work? He goes to work by car. On (Mondays) he (does karate). He can't swim.*
Materials
Multi-ROM, A4 paper

Starting the lesson

- Students play *Quick peek* (see p. T88) using the mini cards.

SB page 34

11 Listen and read. Then act.

- Using mimes and examples, introduce *work* and *singing lessons.*
- Remind students of the story in the previous units and ask, for instance, *Where are the children? (On a movie set.)*
- Before listening to the story, ask the following questions for the corresponding frames. Try to ask and discuss them in English:

1 Who are the children talking to? [Open discussion,]
2 *(Pointing to Madley Kool.)* Who's this? [Madley Kool.]
3 What is Madley Kool doing? [Open discussion.]
4 What is he doing? [Open discussion.]
5 What's the weather like? [It's hot and sunny.]
6 Is Madley Kool happy? [No, he isn't. He's scared.]

- Play T42, and students follow the story in their books. Play it again, pausing after each line for students to repeat.
- Next, to check students' understanding of the story, ask the following questions:

1 Who are the children asking about? [Madley Kool.]
2 How does he go to work? [By car.]
3 What does he do on Mondays? [He does karate.]
4 Is the teacher happy? Why? [No, she isn't, because Madley can't sing.]
5 When does he go swimming? [On Saturdays.]
6 Can Madley swim? [No, he can't.]

- Ask the class (L1) to predict what is going to happen in the next episode of the story.
- Divide students into four groups and assign a character to each. Students read their parts as a class from their seats. This may encourage shyer students to take part in the acting later on.
- Invite five students to take the parts of the characters in the story. Ask the volunteers to go to the front of the class to act out the story (one of the students performs Madley Kool's activities). Encourage tone of voice and expressions to match those in the pictures. Alternatively, you could have other students read the lines while those five students act it out.

Game

- Divide the class into two groups (see ideas for group formation on pp. XII and XIII). Retell the story making some deliberate mistakes. Every time groups spot a mistake, students put up their hands and correct it.

Game

- Tell students (L1) to pretend that they are spies and that they have to send secret messages to other spies of their organization.
- Divide the class into pairs and tell them to write secret messages to their classmates, using the code on p. 94. They exchange messages and decode them. Invite some pairs to read the messages to the class.

Ending the lesson

- Review what happens in the story. Write some incomplete sentences about Madley Kool on the board (e.g., *He goes to work... On Mondays he...*, etc.). Ask students to complete them.
- You may turn this activity into a competition by dividing the class into two teams and asking one student from each team to complete each sentence.

Students can now go online to Film Studio Island and enjoy the fun and games, at home or at the school computer lab. Ask them to find the 'umbrella' that Cleo is holding in one of the pages of the unit (p. 32). Then tell students they should find the umbrella on Film Studio Island (it is to the left of the swimming pool in the recreation area). When students click on the umbrella, they are taken to a supplementary language game based on the vocabulary in Unit 4.

OPTIONAL ACTIVITY
Game
Play *Category writing* (see p. T89) using the vocabulary of this unit.

Lesson 6

Lesson aims
To integrate other areas of the curriculum into the English class; to develop the cross-curricular topic through a short project.
Cross-curricular focus
Social science – how children go to school
Target language
plane, radio, rivers, roads, snowmobile
Recycled language
boat, cold, cool, home; How do you go to school?
Materials
Multi-ROM, a map of the world or a globe, A4 paper, Flashcards (My week)

Starting the lesson

- Divide the class into two groups (see ideas for group formation on pp. XII and XIII). Group A writes a means of transport on a piece of paper and gives it to a student from Group B. This student comes to the board and mimes it (e.g., a car). Group B guesses what it is.

SB page 35

12 Listen, read and match.

- Direct students' attention to the the title of the article. Tell them to cover the text with a piece of paper and predict (L1) what the text is about.
- With books closed, play T43 once. Students check their predictions.
- Then tell students to open their books. They read and match the texts to the pictures. Explain (L1) that they don't need to understand every word in the text to match it to the pictures.
- Now play T43 again, pausing after each text to check answers.
- Ask a few comprehension questions (e.g., *How do Lanau and his friends go to school? Where is Ricky's school?*).

13 Find the words.

- Students look at the pictures and guess where in the world these children may live. Ask, *Where are they from?* Students guess (e.g., Alaska, Canada, China). Display the map and ask students to locate the countries.
- Focus on the words. Tell students to find them in the texts. Call on individual students to read the sentence with the word in. Clarify vocabulary.
- Ask students (L1) if they would like to go to school by boat or snowmobile, or have classes at home like Ricky.

Extra!

- Work with shadow reading. Play T43. Students read the words while trying to stay at the same speed and rhythm as the recording. As students keep reading, you can turn the sound down some times.

14 Look at Activity 12. Ask and answer.

- Divide the class into pairs (see ideas for dividing the class on pp. XII and XIII) and draw their attention to the speech bubbles. Brainstorm questions that students could ask about the children in the text. Write the questions on the board.
- Next, students take turns asking and answering questions about the children in the text. Encourage students to use the ideas on the board, but also to come up with new questions.
- As a follow-up, students can write the questions and answers in their notebooks.

Think!

- Write the task on the board: *Make a list of different ways children can get to school in your town. Which is the fastest? Which is the safest? Which is the 'greenest'?*
- Divide students into small groups. Encourage some brainstorming and elicit possible answers as hypotheses. Place special emphasis on the need to support their answers (in L1 if necessary).Write students' ideas on the board, and ask them to explain their ideas.

Mini project

- Take students to the computer lab, so they can use the Internet for their research. In order to save time, you can select some websites in advance.
- Divide the class into pairs. Ask (L1) students if they know about how children go to school in other places in the world. Tell them to look for information and to write a few sentences about their findings. They may illustrate their texts with drawings or pictures printed from the web.
- When they have finished, invite some pairs to share their work with the class. Display the projects on the classroom walls.

Ending the lesson

- Students play *Make a sentence* (see p. T88) using the vocabulary of the unit.

OPTIONAL ACTIVITY
Game
Play *Conversation relay* (see p. T89).

WB page 113

7 Look and write.

- Students look at the pictures of the children and match them with the means of transport. Then students complete the sentences.

8 Look at the code on p. 94 and write the message.

- Students replace the letters with the correct letters in the wheel on p. 94 and write the sentence.

12 T43 **Listen, read and match.**

How do you go to school?

Do you go by car or bus? Or do you walk?
Read about how these children go to school.

1

2

3

a

2 Lanau doesn't go to school by car. There aren't many roads where he lives, but there are a lot of rivers. So Lanau and his friends go to school by boat.

b

3 Ricky's school is far away, so he has his lessons at home. His lessons are on the radio and on the Internet. On Fridays, his teacher goes to his house by plane.

c

1 Susanna lives in a cold place. She doesn't walk to school. She goes to school by snowmobile. She likes riding her snowmobile. It's cool!

13 **Find the words.**

cold | boat | home | snowmobile | teacher | car

14 **Look at Activity 12. Ask and answer.**

Does Susanna go to school by boat?

No, she doesn't.

MINI PROJECT

Find out how other children go to school.

Workbook page 113, Activities 7 and 8.

Review Units 3 and 4

1 T44 **Listen, point and say the number(s).**

6, 4 and 5, 2 and 8, 1 and 7

2 **Look at Activity 1. Ask and answer.**

Workbook page 114, Activities 9 and 10.

3 Ask and answer. What's the weather like?

4 Listen and say the number. 4, 1, 6, 3, 5, 2

T45

5 Read and find.

On Saturdays he does karate at 10 o'clock. He likes computer games. He walks to school.

1

Name: Adam
Goes to school: car
Likes: soccer
Doesn't like: computer games
On Saturdays: swimming 10 o'clock

2

Name: Ben
Goes to school: walks
Likes: computer games
Doesn't like: cleaning
On Saturdays: karate 10 o'clock

Workbook page 115, Activities 11 and 12.

Review Units 3 and 4

Lesson aims
To review the language of units 3 and 4; to personalize language; to provide an opportunity for self-evaluation.
Values
The importance of study and education.
Recycled language
Vocabulary and structures from Units 1 and 2
Materials
Multi-ROM, pictures of children going to school, Flashcards (Weather and My week), a box, A4 paper, Worksheet 4
Special note: The activities from the *Review* lesson can be done in one or two classes, depending on the use of the *Pairwork*, *Extra!*, *Game* and *Optional activities* sections. The Workbook activities can also be assigned for homework in different classes.

Starting the lesson

- Put all the weather flashcards face down on your table or in a box. One student picks a card and says the first letter of the word. The class guesses what the word is. Model the activity before students do it. If the first guess is wrong, the student says another letter. Continue until the other students guess or the first student says the word.
- Divide the class into two teams (see ideas for group formation on pp. XII and XIII) and play *Spelling bee* (see p. T89).

SB pages 36-37

1 Listen, point and say the number(s).

- Focus students' attention on the picture. Ask them, *Where are they? What are they wearing? Do boys and girls wear the same clothes?*
- Ask students to describe the weather. Ask, *What's the weather like? (It's fall. It's cloudy and windy.)* Then tell the class that the students are leaving school. Ask, *How do they go home?* Have students list the means of transport they see in the picture.
- Now tell students that they are going to listen to a recording and that they need to identify the correct person in the picture.
- Play T44 once. Students just listen.
- Play the recording again. Students point to the correct person and say the correct number.

T44

I walk home.
I go home by bus.
I go home by bike.
I go home by car.

Values

- Discuss with students different ways children go to school (e.g., by bus, by boat, etc.). If you brought pictures, show them to the class.
- Talk (L1) about how children go to school in their country or area. Focus on the difficulties some children face to attend classes and on the efforts they and their families make.
- Talk (L1) about the role of education in students' lives. Highlight the importance of studying to create a better future for them.

2 Look at Activity 1. Ask and answer.

- Divide the class into pairs, then draw students' attention to the language in the speech bubbles. Student A says a sentence about the picture, then Student B identifies the correct number in the picture. They switch roles.
- Monitor pairs to help with language use. As a follow-up, you can ask students to write the questions and answers in their notebooks.

3 Ask and answer. What's the weather like?

- Review weather vocabulary using the pictures. Then say a number (*Five!*), and students describe it (*It's snowy*).
- Students work in pairs. Demonstrate the activity with a student. Ask, *What's the weather like in number (four)?* The student looks at the picture and answers, *It's (stormy).*
- If necessary, write the question on the board to help students,. Monitor pairs to help with language use. As a follow-up, you can ask students to write the questions and answers in their notebooks.

Extra!

- Write the seasons at the top of the board. Then elicit different activities students do in each season. They copy the list into their notebooks.

Game

- Ask students to choose three weather words and write them in their notebooks. Next, start showing the flashcards, without saying the words. The first student to cross out all his/her three words is the winner.

4 Listen and say the number.

- Focus students' attention on the clocks. Tell them that they are going to listen to a recording and to say which clock it refers to.
- Play T45 once. Students just listen. Then play it again, pausing after each line to allow students time to look and say the number.
- As a follow-up, students can write the sentences in their notebooks.

T45

It's nine thirty.
It's six o'clock.
It's twelve o'clock.
It's six thirty.
It's three thirty.
It's one o'clock.

5 Read and find.

- Draw students' attention to the files of the boys. Ask what their names are.
- Then explain the task. Students read the first text, on the note. Then they read the texts about Adam and Ben and decide which one the note refers to (Ben).
- As a follow-up, students can write a similar note about Adam in their notebooks.

Extra!

- Write the words *go*, *have* and *do* on the board, inside circles. Then ask students which activities go with each verb. Draw lines from the circles and write the activities. Students copy into their notebooks.
- As a follow-up, students can write sentences using the collocations in their notebooks.

Now students can do Worksheet 4.

Ending the lesson

- Put the flashcards (My week) in a bag or box. Pick one and begin to take it out very slowly. The class guesses what picture it is. The first student to make a correct guess takes your role.
- Alternatively, students make a sentence using that activity (e.g., *I have music lessons in the morning*).

OPTIONAL ACTIVITY

Guess the action

Draw an object (e.g., a bus). The class has to make a sentence using that object. Students say, *I go to school by bus.* Ask individual students to take your role.
You can turn this into a competition by dividing the class into two teams.

WB page 114-115

9 Complete the words and find the answer.

- Students complete the words with the missing letters, then arrange the letters correctly to write the day of the week.

10 Write about what you do on Mondays.

- Students look at the activities listed on the diary and write sentences about each one.

11 What do you do on Saturdays? Draw a picture.

- Students draw and color a picture about what they do on Saturdays.

12 Write about what you do on Saturdays.

- Students write a description of their picture by completing the sentences.
- Write about what you do on Monday.

Self-assessment.

- Students choose and color the appropriate number of stars depending on how well they think they have completed the unit. Discuss with students what they have learned, what they can do now, which activities they liked best and which ones were difficult.

5 Jobs

1 Listen, point and say. T46

2 Listen and say who's missing. T47

The police officer.

Workbook page 116, Activities 1 and 2.

3 Chant.

What do you want to be?
What do you want to be?
I want to be, I want to be, I want to be a movie star.
I don't want to be a farmer.
I don't want to be a firefighter.
I want to be, I want to be, I want to be a movie star.
What do you want to be?
What do you want to be?
I want to be, I want to be, I want to be a movie star.

LOOK!

What **do** you **want to be**?
I **want to be** a movie star.
I **don't want to be** a farmer.

4 Match. Then listen and check.

1 I want to be a ballet dancer. Cathy
2 I want to be a farmer. Di
3 I want to be a basketball player. Al
4 I want to be a police officer. Ben

5 Ask and answer.

What do you want to be?

I want to be a police officer.

5 Jobs

Lesson 1

Lesson aims
To present and practice new vocabulary.
Target language
ballet dancer, basketball player, farmer
Recycled language
astronaut, firefighter, movie star, police officer
Materials
Multi-ROM, Flashcards (Jobs), A4 paper

Starting the lesson

- Start drawing part of a vehicle from Unit 4 very slowly. Students guess what it is, asking, for instance, *Does he go to school by (train)?* Limit the number of attempts (e.g., four) to make the game more exciting.

SB page 38

Presentation

- Use the flashcards to teach the vocabulary. Hold them up in turn and say the words. Students repeat. Then hold up the flashcards again, asking individual students to say the words.
- Point to the characters in the main illustration and say their jobs. Students repeat.

1 Listen, point and say.

- Draw students' attention to the pictures at the bottom of the page. Then play T46, pausing after each word to give students time to find the picture. Play it again, pausing after each word, and students repeat them.
- Ask students, *What's number (three)?* They look at the images and answer. If you want to make the activity more challenging, ask students to close their books and try to say the job words from memory.

2 Listen and say who's missing.

- Now focus on the main illustration. Point to the characters and ask, *Where are the children now?* Introduce *cafeteria.*
- Tell students (L1) that they are going to listen to the characters talking about the different people in the main illustration, but that one of the jobs from Activity 1 will be missing.
- Instruct them to pay close attention to the main illustration. Play T46 once up to *What's missing?*. Give students time to locate the people in the illustration and find out which job is missing (*police officer*). Play it again to the end.
- Play T46 again, pausing after each line for students to repeat. Encourage tone of voice and expressions to match those in the pictures.

Sam	Wow! Look! Where's Madley Kool? Is he here?	T47
Jenny	No, I can't see him. But look at her. She's very pretty.	
Movie star	Thank you. Thank you so much. Thank you, darling.	
Jenny	She's a movie star!	
Sam	Look! She can dance. She's a ballet dancer.	
Ruby	Look! He's a farmer! He has a hen!	
John	Look! A basketball player! Wow, cool ball!	
Ruby	Look at him, at the table. He's wearing big boots. He's an astronaut.	
Jenny	Oh! A firefighter! Cleo, watch out!	
Narrator	Who's missing?	
Children	The police officer!	

Pairwork

- Divide the class into pairs (see ideas for dividing the class on pp. XII and XIII). Student A makes a sentence about one of the people in the main illustration, e.g., *He's wearing big boots.* Student B then answers, *Astronaut*. Demonstrate the activity with some students before they start working in pairs.
- Encourage students to make sentences that are different from those on the recording (e.g., *She has a pink dress*; *He likes basketball*).

Extra!

- Give students a piece of paper. They draw an object (e.g., a baskteball) that identifies a job of their choice. Brainstorm items for each job (basketball, cow, etc.) and draw them on the board, so that students can choose which one to copy if they wish.
- Point to the (cow) on the board and say, *I'm (a farmer).* Then invite students to introduce themselves and say their occupations, e.g., *I'm (name) and I'm a (basketball player).* **Note:** Point out that we say *I'm* an *astronaut*. Students will learn about *a*/*an* in Lesson 2.

Ending the lesson

- Shuffle the flashcards and pick one. Hold it up. Students say and mime the job (e.g., for *basketball player*, they pretend to bounce a ball).

OPTIONAL ACTIVITY
Game
Play *Give me one* (see p. T89) with the jobs.

WB page 116

1 Complete the words.

- Students complete the jobs with the missing letters.

2 Look and write.

- Students look at the pictures and complete the sentences with the correct job.

Lesson 2

Lesson aims
To review the vocabulary of Lesson 1 with a chant; to present the new structure.
Target language
What do you want to be? I want to be (a movie star).
Recycled language
Jobs
Materials
Multi-ROM, Flashcards (Jobs), A4 paper

Starting the lesson
- Play *Run and get it* (see p. T88) to review jobs.

SB page 39

Presentation
- Choose one of the jobs from the main illustration and say, *I want to be a (ballet dancer).* Point to a student and ask, *And you? What do you want to be?* Student answers. Ask more students. If necessary, help with new vocabulary.

3 Chant.
- Focus students' attention on the chant. Then play T48 for students to listen and follow the words. Play it again, pausing after each line for students to repeat.
- Play the chant once more for students to join in. If necessary, use the flashcards to help prompt the words.

Extra!
- Draw a word map with the class. Draw a circle and write *Jobs* in it. Brainstorm with the class words for jobs that they have learned in this lesson and for others that they have chosen for themselves. Write them on the board. Students copy the map into their notebooks.

Presentation
- Draw students' attention to the question and answers in the *Look!* box. Write them on the board, so that all students can follow your explanation. Ask them to pay attention to the differences between the questions and answers, the affirmative and the negative forms. Help them come up with a simple rule.
- Then point out the use of *a* or *an* with the jobs. Give some examples using *an*: *I want to be an engineer*; *I want to be an architect*, etc. Explain the difference in the use of *a*/*an*. Ask students to copy the examples into their notebooks.

4 Match. Then listen and check.
- Tell students to match the sentences to the characters.
- When they have finished, play T49. Students listen and check.

T49

Man What do you want to be, Cathy?
Cathy I want to be a ballet dancer. I love dancing!
Man What do you want to be, Di?
Di I want to be a farmer. I love animals!
Man And what about you, Al?
Al I like playing basketball. I want to be a basketball player.
Man And you, Ben? What do you want to be?
Ben I want to be a police officer.

5 Ask and answer.
- Divide the class into pairs (see ideas for dividing students on pp. XII and XIII). When you have their full attention, focus on the language in the speech bubbles (you can read the dialogue with another student).
- Ask students to choose one of the occupations in the main illustration. Then they take turns asking and answering about the occupations. As a follow-up, ask students to copy the dialogue into their notebooks.
- Alternatively, you can play *Conversation relay* (see p. T89) with the dialogue.

Game
- Write three or four words on the board using the vocabulary from this unit and from the previous ones. Students identify and circle the odd one out (e.g., *farmer – firefighter –* ***cooking*** *– movie star*).
- Students can continue playing in pairs, thinking of other lists of words and taking turns playing the game.

Ending the lesson
- Divide students into three groups. Play the chant (T48) again. Group A sings the questions, Group B sings the affirmative sentences, and Group C sings the negative sentences. You can create a mime to go along with the chant.

OPTIONAL ACTIVITIES
Games
Play *Pass the secret* (see p. T90) using vocabulary of the unit.
Play *Picture relay* (see p. T90) using vocabulary of the unit.

6 Listen and sing.

T50

Teacher, farmer, builder, doctor,
What does he want to be?
Teacher, farmer, builder, doctor,
Just a minute! Let me see…

Does he want to be a teacher?
No, no, no.
No, no, no, he doesn't.
Does he want to be a farmer?
No, no, no.
No, no, no, he doesn't.
Does he want to be a builder?
No, no, no.
No, no, no, he doesn't.
Does he want to be a doctor?
No, no, no.
Yes, yes, yes, he does.
He wants to be a doctor.
Chorus

LOOK!

Does he **want to be** a builder?
Yes, he **does**./No, he **doesn't**.

7 Play the game.

1	✗	✗	✓	✗
2	✗	✗	✗	✓
3	✗	✓	✗	✗
4	✓	✗	✗	✗

Does she want to be a teacher?

Number 2.

Yes, she does.

Workbook page 117, Activities 3 and 4.

Lesson 3

Lesson aims
To extend the unit vocabulary set; to practice the vocabulary with a song.

Target language
builder, doctor, teacher; Does (he) want to be a (builder)? Yes, (he) does./No, (he) doesn't.

Recycled language
Jobs

Materials
Multi-ROM, Flashcards (Jobs), spinners

Starting the lesson

- Play *Flashcard act out* (see p. T88) to review jobs.

SB page 40

Presentation

- Focus students' attention on the pictures of jobs. Introduce the new vocabulary. Point to each picture in turn and say, for instance, *He's a builder. Do you want to be a builder?*

6 Listen and sing.

- Play T50. Students listen and follow the words in their books. Create a mime to go with the different jobs, then play the song again for students to join in with the words and the mime.
- Divide the class into two groups (see ideas for group formation on pp. XII and XIII). Group A sings the questions, and Group B the answers. They sing the last line as a class. Then switch groups.

Extra!

- Show a flashcard, but say an incorrect sentence (e.g., show the *firefighter* and say, *I want to be a ballet dancer*). Students say, *No.* Ask them to make a correct sentence about the picture (e.g., *I want to be a ballet dancer*).
- Continue with other jobs, sometimes saying the right sentence for the flashcard, sometimes the wrong sentence.

Presentation

- Focus students' attention on the question and answers in the *Look!* box and write them on the board. Point out the use of *does* in questions and the use of *does/doesn't* in short answers.
- Ask questions about other students, or about the characters in Activity 4 (p. 39). Write the examples on the board. Use different colors (or underline/circle items in the sentences) to help students understand the structure. Students copy the examples into their notebooks.

7 Play the game.

- Divide the class into pairs (see ideas for dividing students on pp. XII and XIII). Focus on the chart and elicit the jobs from students.
- Draw students' attention to the language in the speech bubbles and explain (L1) that they are going to play a guessing game. Student A chooses one of the girls in the chart (Number 1). Student B asks questions to guess who she is, e.g., *Does (she) want to be a (doctor)? (No, she doesn't).* When Student B guesses, it is his/her turn to choose a girl.
- If necessary, monitor pairs to help with language use. As a follow-up, students can write the dialogues in their notebooks.

Extra!

- Students vote for their favorite job among the ones presented in Lessons 1 and 3. You can draw a pie chart or another graph on the board with the results. Invite some students to explain their choices. Point out that all jobs are equally important.

Ending the lesson

- Play *Lexical groups* (see p. T90).

OPTIONAL ACTIVITY

Spin and mime

Divide the class into small groups. Give each group a spinner. Stick the six flashcards on the board and number them from 1 to 6. One student in the group spins the spinner without letting the others see the number. He/she then acts out the occupation that corresponds to the number on the spinner. The other students in the group guesss, e.g., *He/She wants to be a (builder)* or *You want to be a (builder).*

WB page 117

3 Unscramble the words. Then complete the sentences.

- Students unscramble the words and use them to complete the sentences.

4 Unscramble and write questions.

- Students rearrange the words to make questions.

Lesson 4

Lesson aims
To develop reading, writing and speaking skills.
Recycled language
Jobs; *I want to be (a basketball player).*
Materials
Multi-ROM, Unit 5 mini cards, scissors, A4 paper

Starting the lesson

- Sing the chant from Lesson 2 (T48).

SB page 41

8 Read and match.

- Point to one of the photographs from 1 to 4 and ask, for instance, *Is she (a firefighter)?*
- Students read the notes and match each child to the correct photo (1 to 4). Check as a class.

9 Look at Activity 8. Listen and answer.

- Tell (L1) the class that you are going to play a recording about the children in Activity 8. They listen and say who is speaking.
- Play T51 once. Students just listen.
- Play the recording again. Stop after each question. Students answer.

	T51
1	
Emma	I can sing and dance. I want to be a movie star.
Woman	Who is it?
2	
Tim	I'm strong. I like climbing. I like helping people. I don't want to be an athlete. I want to be a firefighter.
Woman	Who is it?
3	
Bob	I like running. I can jump and I can catch a ball. I'm very tall. I want to be a basketball player.
Woman	Who is it?
4	
Mary	I like music. I can dance and I can jump. I want to be a ballet dancer.
Woman	Who is it?

10 Go to p. 81 and play the game.

- Divide the class into pairs (see ideas for dividing students on pp. XII and XIII). Ask them to cut out the mini cards on p. 81. When they have cut all the cards, say a job represented in the cards (*teacher*), and students then hold it up. Continue with the other images.
- Focus on the illustration and the language in the speech bubble. Tell students (L1) that the children are playing a game and that the class will do the same with their cards. They put them face down on their desks. Student A turns over two cards and makes a sentence about each one (e.g, *I want to be a ballet dancer*). If they are a pair, he/she keeps the cards; if they aren't, he/she puts the cards face down. Then it is Student B's turn.
- Monitor pairs to help with language use. As a follow-up, students can write the sentences in their notebooks.

Writing practice

- Write a description for a new job on the board, leaving gaps for students to complete with their own suggestions. Alternatively, you may supply a choice of words. E.g., *Teachers work in a ____. They go to school in the ____ and in the ____. They have a busy ____. At night they're ______, but they like _____ (teacher, students/lessons, school, morning, afternoon, day, tired, teaching).*
- Students copy the text into their notebooks and fill in the gaps. Check as a class.
- Then it is students' turn to write a text about one of the jobs in the unit. While students work, circulate helping with additional vocabulary if necessary. When they have finished, they can illustrate their work with drawings. Invite some students to read their texts to the class.

Tell the class to find out the English words for the jobs of their family members. Students share their findings in the following class.

Ending the lesson

- Divide the class into pairs to play *What's missing?* (see p. T88) using their mini cards.

OPTIONAL ACTIVITY
Game
Play *Picture dictation* (see p. T90) using the language and vocabulary of this unit.

WB page 118

5 Look, think and write.

- Students look at the example, then write similar sentences about the other two children.

8 Read and match.

9 Look at Activity 8. Listen and answer.

T51

1 Emma, 2 Tim, 3 Bob, 4 Mary

10 Go to page 81 and play the game.

11 T52 **Listen and read. Then act.**

STORY

NOW GO TO FILM STUDIO ISLAND.

Workbook page 118, Activities 6 and 7.

Lesson 5

Lesson aims
To consolidate the unit language with a story.
Recycled language
Jobs; *I love (dancing). What do you want to be? I want to be a (farmer). He wants to be (Madley Kool).*
Materials
Multi-ROM, Flashcards (Jobs)

Starting the lesson

- Students play *Memory game* (see p. T88) using the mini cards.

SB page 42

Presentation

11 Listen and read. Then act.

- Remind students of the story in the previous units. Then draw their attention to the picture and ask, for instance, *What kind of movie is it? (A musical.)*
- Before listening to the story, ask the following questions for the corresponding frames:

1 What is Ruby thinking? [Open discussion.]
2 *(Pointing to the thought bubble.)* Does Sam want to be a dancer? [No.]
3 *(Pointing to the thought bubble.)* Does Jenny want to be a basketball player? [No.]
4 Who's Jenny talking to? [Cleo.]
5 What is John doing? [Open discussion.]
6 What is John thinking about? [Open discussion.]

- Play T52, and students follow the story in their books. Play it again, pausing after each line for students to repeat.
- Next, to check students' understanding of the story, ask the following questions:

1 What does Ruby want to be? [A dancer.]
2 What does Sam like? [Jumping.]
3 What does Jenny want to be? [A farmer.]
4 What does Cleo want to be? [A detective.]
5 What is John thinking? [About a movie trailer with his name on.]
6 Who does he want to be? [Madley Kool.]

- Ask the class (L1) to predict what is going to happen in the next episode of the story.
- Divide students into three groups and assign a character to each. Students read their parts as a class from their seats. This may encourage shyer students to take part in the acting later on.
- Invite three students to take the parts of the characters in the story. Ask the volunteers to go to the front of the class to act out the story. Encourage tone of voice and expressions to match those in the pictures. Alternatively, you could have other students read the lines while those three students act it out.

Game

- Divide the class into two groups (see ideas for group formation on pp. XII and XIII). Retell the story making some deliberate mistakes. Every time groups spot a mistake, students put up their hands and correct it.

Students can now go online to Film Studio Island and enjoy the fun and games, at home or at the school computer lab. Ask them to find the 'hanger' that Cleo is holding in one of the pages of the unit (p. 43). Then tell students they should find the hanger on Film Studio Island (it is on the sign on the front of the Costume Studio). When students click on the hanger, they are taken to a supplementary language game based on the vocabulary in Unit 5.

Ending the lesson

- Divide students into small groups. Then ask students to rewrite the story, replacing the jobs and the movie star and adding new elements. When they have finished, groups read their new stories. The class votes for the best story.

OPTIONAL ACTIVITY
Flashcard game
Play *Hot seat* (see p. T88).

WB page 118

6 Match.

- Students look at the pictures, then match them with their corresponding jobs.

7 Look at the code on p. 94 and write the message.

- Students replace the letters with the correct letters in the wheel on p. 94 and write the sentence.

Lesson 6

Lesson aims
To integrate other areas of the curriculum into the English class; to develop the cross-curricular topic through a short project.
Cross-curricular focus
Physical education – I want to be a champion.
Values
Discuss the importance of discipline to achieve aims in life.
Target language
champion, go shopping, medal, Olympic Games
Recycled language
Days of the week, Sports, Telling the time; *afternoon, breakfast, lunch, morning, shoes, watching TV*
Materials
Multi-ROM, A4 paper, pictures of famous champions, Unit 5 mini cards

Starting the lesson

- Divide the class into two groups (see ideas for group formation on pp. XII and XIII). Group A writes a job on a piece of paper and gives it to one student from Group B. This student comes to the board and mimes it (e.g., *a doctor*). Group B guesses what it is.

SB page 43

Presentation

- Stick the pictures of famous champions on the board (some suggestions are Gustavo Borges – swimming; Jade Barbosa – gymnastics; and Giba – volleyball). Then ask (L1) what these athletes have in common (they are from Brazil, they went to the Olympic Games, they are champions). Introduce the words *champion* and *medal* (e.g., *Gustavo Borges has a gold medal. He's a champion*).
- Introduce *Olympic Games.* Ask (L1) where the last Games were held and what the class knows about them.

12 Listen, read and match.

- Direct students' attention to the the title of the article. Tell them to cover the text with a piece of paper and predict (L1) what the text is about.
- With books closed, play T52 once. Students check their predictions.
- Then tell students to open their books. They read and match the texts to the pictures. Explain (L1) that they don't need to understand every word in the text to match it to the pictures.
- Now play T52 again, pausing after each text to check answers.
- Clarify vocabulary. Then ask a few comprehension questions (e.g., *What does Naomi want to be? Is she a swimmer/runner? How many medals does she want to win? What time does she go swimming? What does she do in the afternoon? What does she do on Sundays?*).

13 Ask and answer.

- Divide the class into pairs (see ideas for dividing students on pp. XII and XIII). Focus on the cues. Explain (L1) that students should imagine they are training to be sports champions. They use them to ask and answer questions about each other. Before students start working in pairs, elicit all the questions and demonstrate the activity with one of them.
- If necessary, circulate, helping students with language. As a follow-up, you can ask them to write the questions in their notebooks and answer them.

Values

- Ask (L1) the class if they think Naomi will become an Olympic champion and why. Then discuss the importance of discipline. Focus on her timetable and diet and why she needs that.
- Ask what sportspeople students admire and what they know about them.

Mini project

- Tell the class that they are going to do a class survey. Explain (L1) what a survey is.
- Give each student an A4 sheet of paper. Draw a two-column grid on the board. Write *NAMES* on top of the first column and *JOBS* on top of the second. Students copy on their sheets.
- Students write five names of classmates in the *NAMES* column. Then they ask these students, *What do you want to be?*, and write their answers in the *JOBS* column. If necessary, help students with additional vocabulary.
- Collect the results on the board. Help the class write a report, e.g., *In our class, (number) students want to be (ballet dancers).*

FOR THE NEXT LESSON

- Ask students to bring a picture of a famous person they admire for the next lesson.

Ending the lesson

- Play *Make a sentence* (see p. T88) using the language and vocabulary of the unit.

OPTIONAL ACTIVITY
Mini card game
Play *Quick peek* (see p. T88).

WB page 119

8 Complete the article with words from the box.

- Students complete the text with the words in the box.

9 Read and circle.

- Students read the questions and look for the answers in Activity 8. Then they circle the corresponding pictures.

12 T53 **Listen, read and match.**

I WANT TO BE A CHAMPION!

1 Naomi Johnson wants to be a champion. She wants to win three medals at the next Olympic Games.

2 At 6 o'clock in the morning Naomi goes swimming. She swims for two hours and then she has a big breakfast. Then she goes running and at 12 o'clock, she has lunch. In the afternoon, she goes swimming again.

3 Sundays are a special day. Naomi doesn't go swimming. She likes watching TV and she goes shopping. She loves shoes!

a

b

c

13 **Ask and answer.**
Answers will vary.

1 What/want to be?
2 What time/play/go/do ...?
3 What/eat for breakfast?
4 What/do after lunch?
5 What/do on Sundays?

What do you want to be?

I want to be a firefighter.

MINI PROJECT
Do a class survey. Ask 'What do you want to be?'

Wider World

My hero

1 Listen and read. T54

1

Hi! I'm Alejandro. I'm from Spain and I love playing basketball. My favorite basketball player is Pau Gasol. He's cool! He's from Barcelona but he plays in the US. I want to be a famous basketball player.

Pau Gasol

Alina Somova

2

My name is Elena. I'm from Russia and I want to be a ballet dancer. I love dancing. I have ballet lessons every day. My favorite ballet dancer is Alina Somova. She's from Russia and she's a great dancer.

2 Look, find and say.

Who wants to be...

a) a ballet dancer? Elena

b) a movie star? Kate

c) a basketball player? Alejandro

d) a soccer player? Santiago

Workbook page 120, Activities 10 and 11.

Lionel Messi

3

I'm Santiago. I'm from Argentina. I like playing soccer. My favorite team is Boca Juniors. There are a lot of good soccer players from Argentina. My favorite is Lionel Messi. He can run very fast and he scores a lot of goals.

4

Hello! I'm Kate. I'm from Ireland. I like watching movies. I have singing and dancing lessons at school. I want to be a movie star. My favorite movie star is Emma Watson.

Emma Watson

3 Read and answer. *True* or *false*?

1 Alejandro wants to be a soccer player. False
2 Pau Gasol is from the US. False
3 Elena has ballet lessons every day. True
4 Santiago doesn't have a favorite soccer team. False
5 Kate likes Emma Watson. True

4 Tell your friend about your favorite famous person.

Answers will vary.

1 What does he/she do?
2 Where is he/she from?
3 What can he/she do?

Wider World

Lesson aims
To personalize the unit language; to learn about famous people; to provide an opportunity for self-evaluation.

Recycled language
Activities, Jobs; *I want to be (a famous basketball player). My favorite (ballet dancer) is (Alina Somova). I have (singing and dancing) lessons.*

Materials
Multi-ROM, Flashcards (Jobs), a map of the world, A4 paper, kraft paper, glue, pictures of famous people, Unit 5 mini cards

Special note: The activities from the *Wider World* lesson can be done in one or two classes, depending on the use of the *Pairwork*, *Extra!*, *Game* and *Optional activities* sections. The Workbook activities can also be assigned for homework in different classes.

Starting the lesson

- Play *Can you actions* by asking questions related to the jobs in the unit (e.g., *Can you swim/make movies/play basketball?* and so on).
- Write on the board: *TTRNSAAOU* (*astronaut*), *OORCTD* (*doctor*), *FFGHTRREEII* (*firefighter*), *AERRMF* (*farmer*), *UEIRDLB* (*builder*), *AAEELLTBDRCN* (*ballet dancer*). Divide the class into pairs (see ideas for dividing students on p. 00) and ask students to unscramble these words for jobs.

SB pages 44-45

Presentation

1 Listen and read.

- Focus students' attention on the large photos of famous people. Tell students to look for the jobs those people do and where they are from in the texts.
- Invite some students to come to the board and write the famous people's names, the places they are from and their jobs. Students find the countries/cities on the map.
- Tell students (L1) they are going to listen to four children talking about their role models. Ask students to follow the text as they listen to the recording. Play T54. If necessary, clarify vocabulary.

Extra!

- Work with shadow reading. Play T54 again. Students read the words while trying to stay at the same speed and rhythm as the recording. As students keep reading, you can turn the sound down some times.

2 Look, find and say

- Focus on the questions. Students reread the texts, find the information and make notes in their notebooks.
- Ask individual students to share the answers with the class.

Extra!

- Describe yourself as if you were a famous person, e.g., *I'm from the USA. I'm famous. I have long hair. I'm a good actress. I have six children. (Angelina Jolie.)*
- You can ask students to write a short paragraph, pretending to be a famous person, in their notebooks. Invite some students to read their descriptions for the class to guess who they are.

Pairwork

- Divide the class into pairs. They draw a picture of an imaginary character and write about what he/she wants to be, using Activity 12 on p. 42 as a model (e.g., *He/She likes making movies. He/She wants to be famous*).
- When they have finished, invite some pairs to show their work to the class and read their profiles.

③ Read and answer. *True* or *false*?

- Focus students' attention on the pictures from Activity 1. Ask them (L1) what they remember about the children and their role models. Students read the text again to decide if the sentences are true or false.
- Check as a class. Students correct the false sentences in their notebooks.

Extra!
- Ask students to close their books. Read the texts from Activity 1 again, making intentional mistakes. When students spot a mistake, they stand up, clap their hands and correct you.

Think!
- Write the task on the board: *Your friend wants to be a teacher. What personal qualities or skills does he/she need to be a good teacher?*
- Divide students into small groups. Encourage them to discuss the question and think of the characteristics of a good teacher. If necessary, help with additional vocabulary. Groups prepare a list and share it with the class.

Game
- Divide the class into two groups (see ideas for group formation on pp. XII and XIII) and play *Hangman* (see p. xx) to practice spelling the vocabulary learned in this unit.

④ Tell your friend about your favorite famous person.

- Brainstorm with students names of other famous athletes, movie stars and so on that students admire.
- Divide students into pairs. Then focus on the questions. Students use them to make a description of their favorite famous person. Demonstrate the activity before students start working in pairs. Invite students to ask each question. You can write your answers on the board as a model, e.g., *She's a singer and a movie star. She's from the USA. Her most famous role is Hannah Montana. (Miley Cyrus.)*
- If necessary, circulate helping with additional vocabulary.

Writing practice
- Students write a short profile of the famous person they described in Activity 4. If time allows, you can take students to the computer lab and have them find additional information on their favorite famous person.
- When students have finished, collect their texts and make a big poster on a large sheet of kraft paper. Students stick the photos next to the descriptions. Put the poster on the classroom wall.

Picture dictionary
- Divide the class into pairs. Direct students' attention to p. 141. Focus on the pictures in the Jobs section. Students read the words under the pictures carefully. Then they cover the words and take turns saying all the words in the correct order.

Ending the lesson
- Divide the class into two teams. Team A mimes a job from the lesson, and Team B has to guess which famous person does it. Then they switch roles.
- Students play *Memory buzz* (see p. T88) using the mini cards.

OPTIONAL ACTIVITY

Flashcard game

Play *I spy* (see p. T90) with the flashcards and the pictures of famous people.

WB pages 120-121

⑩ Look and write

- Students look at the pictures and write the correct job next to them.

⑪ Read and complete. Use the words in the box.

- Students read and complete the sentences with the appropriate word from the box.

⑫ What do you do want to be? Draw a picture.

- Students think about what they want to be when they grow up and draw and color a scene related to that.

⑬ Write about what you want to be.

- Students write a file for the picture by completing the sentences.

Self-assessment:
- Students choose and color the appropriate number of stars depending on how well they think they have completed the unit. Discuss with students what they have learned, what they can do now, which activities they liked best and which ones were difficult.

6 Rainforest

1 T55 **Listen, point and say.**

2 T56 **Listen and say the missing word.** Waterfall.

Workbook page 122, Activities 1 and 2.

3 Chant.

T57

Where's the snake?
It's behind Sam.
Where's the bird?
It's in front of Cleo.
Where's the crocodile?
It's under the bridge.
Where's the fish?
It's next to John.

LOOK!

in front of
behind
next to

4 Listen and circle the correct words.

T58

1 There's a crocodile *in* / *next to* the river.
2 It's *in front of* / *under* the bridge.
3 It's *next to* / *behind* you.
4 There's a snake *behind* / *next to* you.
5 There's a bird *next to* / *in front of* me!

5 Ask and answer.

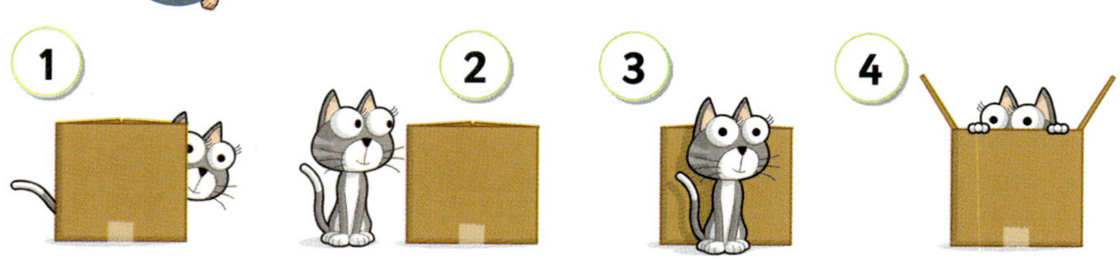

Number 1.
Where's Cleo?

She's behind
the box.

Lesson 1

Lesson aims
To present and practice new vocabulary.
Values
The importance of respecting small animals and plants.
Target language
bridge, mountain, rainforest, river, valley, waterfall
Recycled language
Animals, Colors, Nature, Numbers; *flowers, pond, rock; big, small; I'm swimming.*
Materials
Multi-ROM, Flashcards (The natural world), a map of the world or a globe, reference books, construction paper, scissors, colored pencils, masking tape

Starting the lesson

- Brainstorm with the class names of wild animals they have learned so far. Then focus students' attention on the title of the unit. Ask, *What's a rainforest? What can you see in a rainforest?* Ask if any of the animals from the brainstorm live in the rainforest.
- Point out that the characters are now on a new movie set: a rainforest set (make it clear it is not a real rainforest).

SB page 46

Presentation

- Present the vocabulary using the flashcards. Hold up each flashcard in turn and say the words for students to repeat. Hold up the flashcards again, this time asking individual students to say the words.
- Then show the cards in random order and ask, *What is it?*

1 Listen, point and say.

- Draw students' attention to the pictures at the bottom of the page. Then play T55, pausing after each word to give students time to find the picture. Play it again, pausing after each word, and students repeat them.
- Ask students, *What's number (three)?* They look at the images and answer. If you want to make the activity more challenging, ask students to close their books and try to say the nature vocabulary from memory. Students can continue in pairs.

Game

- Play *Pass the secret* (see p. T90) using a flashcard from the lesson. A student chooses a flashcard and whispers the word to another student. They go on passing the secret word around the class. The last student tells you the word, and you draw it on the board. The first student shows the flashcard to the class to check.

2 Listen and say the missing word.

- Now focus on the main illustration. Point to the characters and ask, *Who's this?* Ask students to name the different animals in the illustration.
- Instruct students to pay close attention to the main illustration. Play T56 once up to *What's missing?*. Give students time to locate the different natural elements in the illustration and find out which item is missing (*waterfall*). Play T56 again to the end.
- Play it again, pausing after each line for students to repeat. Encourage tone of voice and expressions to match those in the pictures.
- Ask a few comprehension questions (e.g., *Is Madley Kool in the rainforest? Is there a mountain in the rainforest? What can you see in the river?*).

T56

Jenny	Where are we?
Sam	Wow! It's a rainforest. Phew! It's hot.
Jenny	Where's Madley Kool? Is he here?
Sam	I can't see him. Wow! Look at that mountain and the beautiful valley! Hey!
Sam	Hey! Look at Ruby! She's on the bridge. And look who's in the river!
Ruby	Help!
Narrator	What's missing?
Children	Waterfall!

Ending the lesson

- Play *Hangman* (see p. T89) to practice the spelling of the new words.

OPTIONAL ACTIVITIES
Poster – natural places around the world
Bring a large map and reference books to the class or, if conditions permit, use the Internet. Tell students to look for names of rivers, mountains, waterfalls, etc. Students write the names and draw a picture on pieces of construction paper. They locate the places on a world map and stick the cards in the correct place.
Flashcard game
Play *Memory buzz* (see p. T88) using the nature words.

WB page 122

1 Look and write.

- Students look at the picture, then label its parts using the words in the box.

2 Unscramble and write the sentences.

- Students look at the pictures and at the scrambled words. Then they unscramble the words to write sentences.

Lesson 2

Lesson aims
To review the vocabulary of Lesson 1 with a chant; to practice the new structure.
Target language
behind, in front of, next to; Where's (the snake)? It's (behind Sam).
Recycled language
Animals, Nature; *in, on, under; box*
Materials
Multi-ROM, Flashcards (The natural world), a cardboard box, toy animals

Starting the lesson

- Review the vocabulary from Lesson 1. Hold up the flashcards and ask students to come to the front and write the words on the board.
- Bring a large box and put it where it is visible to all the class. Take different toy animals that students know the names of in English. Then review prepositions *in*, *on* and *under* by asking students, *Where's the (animal)?*

SB page 47

Presentation

- Taking advantage of the class layout, point to a student and say, for instance, *(Name) is in front of (name).* Repeat with a few more students.
- Then ask, *Where's (name)?* Students answer, *He/She's in front of (name).* Repeat with *behind* and *next to*.
- You can use the toy animals again, this time to practice the new prepositions. Students come to your table and place the toys in different positions. They ask the class, for instance, *Where's the (cat)?* The class answers.

3 Chant.

- Focus students' attention on the chant. Then play T57 for them to listen and follow the words. Play it again, pausing after each line for students to repeat.
- Play the chant once more for students to join in. If necessary, use mime to help prompt the words.

Presentation

- Draw students' attention to the words in the *Look!* box and match the prepositions to the correct picture on the left.
- Elicit other example sentences and write them on the board. Then students draw pictures and write sentences in their notebooks to illustrate the prepositions (e.g., *The cat is in front of the house*). When they have finished, invite some students to show their pictures to the class and say the sentences.

4 Listen and circle the correct words.

- Focus students' attention on the sentences. Clarify that *it*, in sentences 2 and 3, refers to the crocodile. Then play T58. Tell students to circle the correct words.
- Ask questions to check the answers, e.g., *Where's the (snake)?*

Ruby	Look! There's a crocodile in the river. It's under the bridge! Help!	**T58**
Sam	Watch out, John! There's a fish in the river. It's next to you!	
Jenny	Sam! Watch out! There's a snake behind you!	
Sam	Aaargh!	
Cleo	And there's a bird in front of me!	

5 Ask and answer.

- Divide the class into pairs (see ideas for dividing students on pp. XII and XIII). When you have their full attention, focus on the language in the speech bubbles (you can read the dialogue with another student). Then students take turns asking questions about Cleo.
- Monitor pairs to help with the pronunciation and language use. At the end of the activity, you can ask some pairs to perform the dialogues for the class.
- As a follow-up, students can write the sentences about Cleo in their notebooks.

Ending the lesson

- On the board write the first letter and spaces for the missing letters of one the prepositions, e.g., *b _ _ _ _ _ (behind)*. Students call out letters in order to guess the word.

OPTIONAL ACTIVITIES
Game
Play *Picture dictation* (see p. T90) using the unit vocabulary and language.
Young writers
Tell the class to focus on the picture on SB p. 47. Ask the class to suggest new verses for the chant. Write questions and answers on the board and chant the new lines as a class (e.g., *Where's Ruby? She's on the bridge. Where's Sam? He's in front of the snake*).

WB page 123

3 Read, look and circle.

- Students look at the pictures and the sentences, then choose the correct option and circle it.

4 Look and write. Use the words in the box.

- Students look at the picture and the sentences, then complete the sentences using the words in the box and the elements in the picture.

6 Listen and sing.

SONG

Animals live all around us,
All around you and me.
Animals live in the forest,
The mountains and the sea.

Monkeys live in the forest
And they can swing in the trees.
They have long arms and curly tails
And they can swing in the trees.
Chorus
Eagles live in the mountains
And they can fly in the sky.
They have sharp claws and silent wings
And they can fly in the sky.
Chorus
Whales live in the sea
And they can swim and sing.
They have strong tails and tiny eyes
And they can swim and sing.
Chorus

LOOK!

They have…
curly/strong tails.
silent wings.
tiny eyes.

7 Look at Activity 6. Ask and answer.

They have curly tails.

Monkeys.

Workbook page 124, Activities 5 and 6.

Lesson 3

Lesson aims
To extend the unit vocabulary set; to practice the vocabulary with a song.
Target language
forest, sky; eagles, whales; fly, swing; curly tails, sharp claws, silent wings, strong tails, tiny
Recycled language
Actions, Animals, Body parts; sea
Materials
Multi-ROM, Flashcards (Animals and The natural world), poster board, colored pencils and markers

Starting the lesson
- Play *I spy* (see p. T90) to review natural features and animals.

SB page 48

Presentation
- Focus students' attention on the picture. Point to the monkey and ask questions (e.g., *How many legs does it have? Does it have long arms?*). Introduce *swing.*
- Point to the whale and ask, *Is it a fish? No, it's a whale. Look! It has a strong tail.* Then point to the eyes and say, *Look at the eyes. Are they big or small? They're very small. They're tiny.*
- Point to the eagles and ask, *Are these birds? Yes, they're eagles.* Introduce *claws* and *wings.*

6 Listen and sing.
- Play T59. Students listen and follow the words in their books. Create the mime to go with the actions in the song (*swing, fly, swim* and *sing*), then play it again for students to join in with the words and the mime.
- Divide the class into three groups (see ideas for group formation on pp. XII and XIII). Group A sings the verse about monkeys, Group B the verse about eagles, and Group C the verse about whales. Switch groups and sing the song again so that all the class has a chance to sing the whole song.

Presentation
- Draw students' attention to the sentences in the *Look!* box and write them on the board. Point out that *curly* describe the monkeys' tails, *tiny* describes the whales' eyes and *silent* describes the eagles' wings. Give other examples from the song.
- Write some animals that students have learned on the board, then elicit adjectives to describe them (e.g., *tall giraffes, fat elephants, angry lions*, etc.). Students copy the examples into their notebooks.

7 Look at Activity 6. Ask and answer.
- Divide the class into pairs (see ideas for dividing students on pp. XII and XIII). Students look at the picture and the song. Student A describes an animal, and Student B guesses which animal it is.
- For extra practice, students may also make sentences about the color and size, e.g., *They're very big. They can swim. (Whales.) They're brown. They can fly. (Eagles.)* As a follow-up, ask students to write the sentences in their notebooks.

Game
- Divide the class into pairs. Students draw a picture of an animal they like. When they have finished, they take turns asking and answering questions to guess the animal. They can only ask Yes/No questions (e.g., *Is it big? Does it have four legs? Can it fly?*).

Ending the lesson
- Play *Charades* (see p. T89) to review what animals can do.

OPTIONAL ACTIVITIES
Flashcard game
Play *Hot seat* (see p. T88).
Make a rainforest poster
Divide the class into pairs. They draw their rainforest poster including animals of their choice. Display their work around the room and invite groups to describe them to the class, e.g., *There are birds in the trees. They can fly. The (hippos) are in the water. They can swim. They like swimming and they eat grass.*

WB page 124

5 Find and write the words.
- Students look at the pictures and the scrambled letters. Then they unscramble the letters and write them on the lines provided.

6 Read and complete.
- Students read the texts, then complete the descriptions with the words in the box.

Lesson 4

Lesson aims
To develop reading, listening and speaking skills.
Target language
Prepositions; *hippo*; *jaws*; *river bed*
Recycled language
Animals, Nature; boat, cool, sharp teeth
Materials
Multi-ROM, Unit 6 mini cards, scissors, pictures of a waterfall and a hippo, a map of the world or a globe, A4 paper, colored pencils and markers

Starting the lesson

- Give each student a noun phrase (adjective + noun) from the song (*long arms*, *curly tails*, *sharp claws*, *silent wings*, *strong tails* and *tiny eyes*). Play the song again (T59). Students stand up and turn around when they hear their collocation.

SB page 49

Presentation

- Focus on the picture of a waterfall you brought to class. Ask, *What's this?* Students answer. Now show the picture of the hippo. Ask, *What's this? Where do hippos live? Are there hippos in Brazil?* Do not confirm answers yet.

8 Look and read.

- Focus students' attention on the text. Ask what it is. Explain (L1) it is a diary someone has written while on vacation.
- Students read and look for names of places: Victoria Falls and Zambezi River. Bring a map of the world or a globe. Ask, *Where's the Zambezi River? And the Victoria Falls?* Help students locate these places (*In Africa*).
- Tell students to read the text and find information about hippos. When they have finished, ask questions (e.g., *Are hippos big or small? Do they swim?*)
- Then ask other questions about the text (e.g., *How do you go to the Victoria Falls? What animals can you see in the Zambezi River?*). Students read and answer.

9 Listen and answer. *True* or *false*?

- Explain (L1) that students will listen to some sentences about the text and that they need to decide if they are true or false.
- Play T60 once. Students just listen. Then play it again, pausing after each sentence so that students have time to write their answers in the boxes.
- Ask students to correct the false sentences.

T60
1 Victoria Falls is a small waterfall.
2 A lot of animals live next to the waterfalls.
3 Hippos have big jaws.
4 Hippos have long legs.
5 Hippos can swim.

Game

- Divide the class into two teams (see ideas for group formation on pp. XII and XIII) and explain the activity (L1). Students look carefully at the picture in Lesson 1 for a minute and close their books. Then students from each team take turns saying what there is in the picture (e.g., *There's a crocodile under the bridge*). Ask them to give as many details as possible. Give a point for each correct sentence.

10 Go to p. 83 and play the game.

- Students cut out the mini cards. When they have finished, say a word represented in the card (*bridge*), and students then hold up the card. Continue with the other cards.
- Explain the game (L1): Students put one set of cards face up on the table and try to memorize their position. Then they turn them all face down and take turns describing where the cards are using *next to* and *under*. Students turn the cards over as they speak to check whether they are right or wrong.
- Monitor pairs to help with language use.

Students draw a wild animal and tell their family about it in English. Remind students of the language they can use in their description.

Ending the lesson

- Students play *Quick peek* (see p. T88) using the mini cards.

OPTIONAL ACTIVITY
Imaginary animals
Give each student an A4 sheet of paper and ask them to create a new animal for the rainforest. They draw the animal and write a description. When they have finished, students ask each other questions about the new animals, e.g., *Is it big or small? What color is it? Does it have (four) legs? Does it have wings? Can it (swim)?* Display their work around the class.

8 Look and read.

Victoria Falls

Today I'm at Victoria Falls. There are a lot of big waterfalls here. They are on the Zambezi River.

It's cool! There are elephants, giraffes, monkeys, crocodiles and hippos.

Hippo is short for hippopotamus. Do you know that 'hippopotamus' means 'river horse'?

Look! You can see a hippo in the river. Hippos are very big and strong. They have big jaws with a lot of big, sharp teeth. They have short legs and big feet.

They can swim. They move their feet on the river bed like ballet dancers and walk in the water!

9 Listen and answer. *True* or *false*?

T60

1 False
2 True
3 True
4 False
5 True

10 Go to page 83 and play the game.

11 T61 **Listen and read. Then act.**

STORY

NOW GO TO FILM STUDIO ISLAND.

Lesson 5

Lesson aims
To consolidate the unit language with a story.
Target language
spider
Recycled language
Animals, Prepositions of place; *movie, star*
Materials
Multi-ROM, Unit 6 mini cards, speech bubbles with the lines of the story

Starting the lesson

- Students play *What's missing?* (see p. T88) with the mini cards.

SB page 50

Presentation

11 Listen and read. Then act.

- Remind students of the story in the previous units and ask, for instance, *Where are the children? (On a movie set.)* Then draw their attention to the frames and ask, *What animals can you see? Who's this?*
- Use the picture to introduce *spider.*
- Before listening to the story, ask the following questions for the corresponding frames. Try to ask and discuss them in English:
  1 *(Pointing to the leopard.)* What is this? [You may introduce the word *leopard*.]
  2 Is Ruby happy? [No, she's angry.]
  3 *(Pointing to the snake.)* What's this? [A snake.]
  4 Does Ruby like spiders? [No, she doesn't.]
  5 What can the children see? [A city.]
  6 Where's Cleo? What she's doing? [She's on a building. Open discussion.]
- Play T61, and students follow the story in their books. Play it again, pausing after each line for students to repeat.
- Next, to check students' understanding of the story, ask the following questions:
  1 What's the leopard doing? [It's scaring Ruby.]
  2 Is it a real leopard? [No, it's Jenny.]
  3 Is it a real snake? [No.]
  4 Is it a real spider? How do you know? [One can see John's hand holding the spider.]
  5 What's the name of the city? [New York.]
  6 Do you know the name of the movie? [Tell the class that the name of the film is *King Kong*.]
- Ask the class (L1) to predict what is going to happen in the next episode of the story. Will the children find Madley Kool?
- Divide students into four groups and assign a character to each (Ruby, Sam, John and Cleo). Students read their parts as a class from their seats. This may encourage shyer students to take part in the acting later on.
- Invite four students to take the parts of the characters in the story. Ask the volunteers to go to the front of the class to act out the story. Encourage tone of voice and expressions to match those in the pictures. Alternatively, you could have other students read the lines while those four students act it out.

Extra!

- Divide the class into two groups (see ideas for forming groups on pp. XII and XIII) and ask students to close their books. Retell the story making some deliberate mistakes. Every time one group spots a mistake, students put up their hands and correct it.

Students can now go online to Film Studio Island and enjoy the fun and games, at home or at the school computer lab. Ask them to find the 'guitar' that Cleo is holding in one of the pages of the unit (p. 48). Then tell students they should find the guitar on Film Studio Island (it is the guitar case leaning against the cabinet inside the Dino Park Studio). When students click on the guitar, they are taken to a supplementary language game based on the vocabulary in Unit 6.

Ending the lesson

- Prepare speech bubbles with the lines of the story and hand them out to different students. Play T61 again. When their line is playing, students jump up and go to the front of the classroom. They arrange themselves in order and hold up their speech bubbles.

OPTIONAL ACTIVITY
Flashcard game
Play *Race to touch* (see p. T88) using the language and vocabulary of this unit.

Lesson 6

Lesson aims
To integrate other areas of the curriculum into the English class; to develop the cross-curricular topic through a short project.
Cross-curricular focus
Geography – the Amazon Rainforest
Values
Discuss the importance of protecting the Rainforest and the animals in it.
Target language
humming bird, tapir; run through; nectar pretty
Recycled language
Animals, Food, Nature, Weather
Materials
Multi-ROM, A3 paper, a map of the world, Flashcards (The natural world), Unit 6 mini cards, colored pencils and markers

Starting the lesson

- Play *Flashcard act out* (see p. T88) with the flashcards and the mini cards.

SB page 51

Presentation

- Bring a map of the world or a globe to the class. Focus on the title of the article. Ask, *Where's the Amazon rainforest?* Then locate it on the map. Say, *It's in South America.*
- Focus on the pictures. Introduce *tapir* and *humming bird.* Ask students (L1) what they know about the animals in the text. Write students' predictions on the board.

12 Listen and read.

- Play T62 once. Students follow in their books and check their predictions. If necessary, clarify vocabulary.
- Play it again. Ask comprehension questions (e.g., *Is the Amazon long or short? Where do parrots live?*).

13 Read and answer.

- Focus students' attention on the questions. Students read the article again and answer them in their notebooks. Then ask individual students to read the answers.

14 Describe one of the animals in Activity 12. Ask your friend to guess.

- Divide the class into pairs (see ideas for dividing students on pp. XII and XIII). Demonstrate the activity by describing one or two animals from Lesson 3.
- Then students take turns describing an animal from the text in Activity 12 (e.g., *It's big. It has four legs. It lives next to the river. It eats fruit*). The other student guesses which animal it is.

Values

- Talk with students (L1) about the importance of being respectful with nature. Then ask students why it is important to look after the rainforest. Discuss the importance of small and big animals, insects, trees and flowers.

Think!

- Write the task on the board: *How long is the Amazon river? In what ways is it important for the people and animals that live in the Amazon Rainforest? How can you find out?*
- Divide students into small groups. Encourage them to discuss the questions and think of possible answers. Write students' ideas on the board, and ask them to explain them.
- Take students to the school library or to the computer lab to look up information on books or online to confirm their ideas. They can also do this as homework. If students search online, take the opportunity to discuss the relevance/reliability of the sources they quote. Encourage students to suggest several possible sources and how to judge their reliability.

Mini project

- Divide the class into pairs and ask students to find names of other animals that live in the rainforest. Bring reference books to the class or use the Internet. On the board, write the animals that students found.
- Pairs choose two animals and work together looking for information about them. Then they make a mini poster on an A3 sheet of paper with pictures or drawings and a written description.
- Display the posters on the classroom walls and ask some pairs to describe their animals.

Ending the lesson

- Students play *Lexical groups* (see p. T90) to review wild animals the class have learned so far.

OPTIONAL ACTIVITY
Game
Play *Bingo* (see p. T89) with animal, nature and weather words.

SB pages 125-126

7 Look, think and complete.

- Students look at the picture and the descriptions, then complete the texts with the words in the box.

8 Find, circle and write eight words from Unit 6.

- Students find words from the unit in the word search. Then they list the words according to their first letter, as in the example.

9 Complete the crossword.

- Students look at the pictures and complete the crossword.

12 Listen and read.

GEOGRAPHY

The Amazon Rainforest

It's hot and wet in the Amazon rainforest and there are a lot of tall trees. The Amazon river runs through the rainforest. It's very long.
A lot of animals live in the rainforest and the river. Look!

humming bird

These birds are very small. They drink nectar from flowers. They like red, orange and yellow flowers.

parrot

These birds have very long tails. They have pretty colors.

tapir

These animals have short necks. They live next to the river. They eat leaves and fruit. They love bananas.

13 Read and answer.

1 What's the weather like in the rainforest?
2 Do parrots have short tails?
3 Where do tapirs live?
4 What do tapirs eat?
5 What color flowers do humming birds like?

1 It's hot and wet. / 2 No. / 3 Next to the river. / 4 They eat leaves and fruit. / 5 They like red, orange and yellow.

14 Describe one of the animals in Activity 12. Ask your friend to guess.

Answers will vary.

MINI PROJECT
Find out about two more animals that live in the rainforest.

SCHOOL

1 Read and find.

1 He likes animals. He's in a car.
2 They eat fish. They're in a tree.
3 She can dance. She's behind the waterfall.
4 He wants to be a champion. He's next to the river.
5 It has a tail. It's black. It's in a tree.
6 He likes building. He's under the bridge.
7 They don't have legs. They're in the river.
8 It has strong jaws. It's long. It's next to a house.

2 Talk to a classmate.

He likes animals. He's in a car.

Farmer!

Review Units 5 and 6

Lesson aims
To review the language of Units 5 and 6; to personalize language; to provide an opportunity for self-evaluation.
Recycled language
Vocabulary and structures from Units 5 and 6
Materials
Flashcards (Jobs and The natural world), Unit 5 and Unit 6 mini cards, A4 paper, two boxes, real toys
Special note: The activities from the *Review* lesson can be done in one or two classes, depending on the use of the *Pairwork*, *Extra!*, *Game* and *Optional activities* sections. The Workbook activities can also be assigned for homework in different classes.

Starting the lesson

- Tell students (L1) that you are going to draw an animal and that they have to help. Ask a student, *Does it have a curly tail?* Students answer, *No, it doesn't. It has (long arms)*. Ask another student, *Can it climb?* Continue and draw the animal according to their answers.

SB pages 52-53

Game

- Play a different *Bingo* with the mini cards from Units 5 and 6. Instead of drawing pictures on a grid, tell the class to choose six cards to play and put them face up in front of them.
- Pick a card and ask a student to say what it is. The students who have that card put it face down on their tables. Continue with the remaining cards until a student has all the mini cards turned face down on the table and calls out, *Bingo!*

Pairwork

- Divide the class into pairs (see ideas for dividing students into pairs on pp. XII and XIII). On an A4 sheet of paper, they draw a scene of a rainforest and include an animal they like (e.g., a monkey). They write a description of the animal and the scene. Encourage students to use language from Unit 6 and from previous units.
- When they have finished, invite some pairs to read their description to the class without saying which animal it is. The class guesses the animal. Display the posters around the class.

1 Read and find.

- Focus students' attention on the picture. Explore it with students, eliciting as much language as possible. Then focus on the eight sentences. Explain (L1) that they are descriptions of people and animals in the picture.
- Students read the sentences and circle the items in the picture. Ask individual students to read the sentences, and the class then points to the items.

Extra!

- Divide the class into pairs. Student A describes an animal or person in the picture (e.g., *She's cleaning the house*). Student B says where the animal or person is, or he/she identifies the item.
- Tell the class to write down the clues and the items they find in their notebooks. Then group pairs in small groups of four students. Each pair reads their new clues to the other pair, who guesses the animal or person described.
- Circulate, helping with language use. When they have finished, ask some pairs to share their work with the class.

Pairwork

- Students work in pairs. Student A describes a job (e.g., *He likes dancing*). Student B guesses the job (*He's a ballet dancer*). Then it is Student B's turn to describe a job.

Group work

- Divide students into two teams. Call one student from Team A to the board and ask, *What do you want to be?* The student mimes the job (e.g., *tennis player*).
- The class guesses what job it is.
- Divide the class into two teams and turn this activity into a class competition.

Ending the lesson

- Divide the class into two groups. One student from each group leaves the classroom for a moment, or turns his/her back, or closes his/her eyes.
- Hide a flashcard somewhere in the classroom (e.g., in a bag, on the floor behind the curtain, etc.).
- The two students come back to ask [*yes – no*] questions to locate it: *Is it on the desk? Is it near the desk? Is it in the drawer? Is it under the chair?* And so on.
- When a student finally finds it, invite students to play the game in pairs using their mini cards.

OPTIONAL ACTIVITIES

Game

Play *Picture guess* (see p. T88) using the vocabulary of this unit.

Vocabulary tic-tac-toe

Divide the class into two teams and draw a basic tic-tac-toe grid on the board with vocabulary from this unit. Each word is missing one, two or three letters (depending on the level of difficulty you want to have in the game). One student from each team is called and must fill in the missing letter(s) and say the word aloud. The team with three correct words in a row wins.

Prepositions race

Divide the class into two teams and tell them to stand in two lines at one end of the room. Put two big boxes on the floor at the other end of the room. Put some toys or flashcards on the floor in front of the first student of each line. Say, for instance, *Put the crocodile behind the box.* Blow a whistle or clap your hands to start. Students get the correct flashcard or toy and run to the other end of the room to carry out your orders and run back to their lines. The first student to get back to the line gets a point for the team. If he/she gets the wrong item, or puts it in the wrong place, the team gets no points.

SB pages 126-127

10 Look, think and write.

- Students look at the picture, then use the words on the left to write sentences about the parrots.

11 Read and draw the animals.

- Students draw the listed animals in the illustration of the rainforest.

12 Write about your picture. Use words in the box.

- Using the prepositions in the box, students write sentences describing where the animals are in the illustration from Activity 11.

Self-assessment

- Students choose and color the appropriate number of stars depending on how well they think they have completed the unit. Discuss with students what they have learned, what they can do now, which activities they liked best and which ones were difficult.

7 Feelings

1 Listen, point and say. T63

1 tired

2 thirsty

3 hungry

4 angry

5 thrilled

6 happy

2 Listen and say the missing word. T64 Tired.

Workbook page 128, Activities 1 and 2.

3 Chant.

Why is she smiling?
Because she's happy.
Why is she crying?
Because she's sad.
Why is he drinking?
Because he's thirsty.
Why is he eating?
Because he's hungry.
Why is he shouting?
Because he's angry.
Why is she laughing?
Because it's funny!

LOOK!

Why is she smiling? **Because** she's happy.

4 Listen and answer. *True* or *false*?

1 Sam is laughing.
2 John is drinking.
3 Jenny is smiling.
4 Favolina is crying.

1 False / 2 True / 3 True / 4 False

5 Look at the chant. Ask and answer.

Number 1.
Why is she smiling?

Because she's happy.

Workbook page 129, Activities 3 and 4.

7 Feelings

Lesson 1

Lesson aims
To present and practice new vocabulary.
Target language
farm, thrilled
Recycled language
angry, happy, hungry, sad, scared, thirsty, tired; I'm (happy). He's (angry).
Materials
Multi-ROM, Flashcards (Feelings), a soft ball or bean toss

Starting the lesson

- Play *Ball/bean toss* (see p. T88) to review vocabulary from previous units.

SB page 54

Presentation

- Use the flashcards to teach and review the vocabulary. Hold them up in turn and say the words. Students repeat. Then hold up the flashcards again, asking individual students to say the words.
- Focus on the main illustration, point to the characters, and students say their feelings.

1 Listen, point and say.

- Draw students' attention to the pictures at the bottom of the page. Then play T63, pausing after each word to give students time to find the pictures. Play it again, pausing after each word, and students repeat them.
- Ask students, *What's number (three)?* They look at the images and answer. If you want to make the activity more challenging, ask students to close their books and try to say the words from memory.

Extra!

- Begin to draw a face showing a feeling or an object associated with a feeling (e.g., a sandwich, to mean *hungry*). Draw very slowly. Students guess.

Group work

- Draw a word map with the class. Draw a circle and write *Feelings* in it. Brainstorm with the class words for feelings that they have learned in this lesson. Write them on the board. Students copy the map into their notebooks.

2 Listen and say the missing word.

- Now focus on the main illustration. Point to the characters and ask, *Where are the children now?* Introduce *farm.* Explain (L1) that the children are on a different movie set and that the movie takes place in the countryside.
- Tell students (L1) that they are going to listen to the characters talking about what they and other people in the main illustration are feeling, but that one of the feelings from Activity 1 will be missing.
- Instruct them to pay close attention to the main illustration. Play T64 once up to *What's missing?*. Give students time to locate the people in the illustration and find out which feeling word was not mentioned (*tired*). Play T64 again to the end for students to check if they were right.
- Play it again, pausing after each line for students to repeat. Encourage tone of voice and expressions to match those in the pictures.

T64

Ruby	Where are we?
Jenny	There's a house, and there are some horses. It's a farm. I'm happy! I like horses. You're a good horse.
Sam	I'm hungry. Wow, there's cake! I like cake! Yum!
Ruby	Look, Sam!
Sam	Is it Madley Kool?
Ruby	No, no! Look! It's Favolina Jolly! Oooh! I'm thrilled!
Sam	She's sad.
Ruby	She's a movie star! I love her movies.
John	I'm thirsty. Oh, no!
Jenny	Cleo's scared! Oh dear!
Director	Cut! Grrrr!
John	Oops! He's angry.
Narrator	What's missing?
Children	Tired!

Extra!

- Tell the class to look at the picture carefully for a minute or two. Then they close their books. Ask, for instance, *Who's (thirsty)?* Students answer.

Ending the lesson

- Divide the class into pairs (see ideas for dividing students into pairs on pp. XII and XIII). They take turns choosing a character from the main illustration. They mime what the characters are doing. Their partners guess who it is.

OPTIONAL ACTIVITY
Game
Play *Give me one* (see p. T89) with the vocabulary from this lesson.

WB page 128

1 Look and write.

- Students look at the pictures and write sentences using the words from the box.

2 Draw how you and your friend are feeling. Then write.

- Students draw how they are feeling in one of the silhouettes. Then they choose a friend and draw him/her in the other. When they have finished, they complete the sentences.

Lesson 2

Lesson aims
To review the vocabulary of Lesson 1 with a chant; to present the new structure.

Target language
crying, laughing, shouting, smiling; funny; Why is she (smiling)? Because she's (happy). Why are you (laughing)? Because it's (funny).

Recycled language
Feelings

Materials
Multi-ROM, Flashcards (Feelings)

Starting the lesson

- Play *Spelling bee* (see p. T89) to review the spelling of vocabulary from Lesson 1.

SB page 55

Presentation

- Use the flashcards or the pictures on p. 54. Show the *hungry* picture. Ask, *Why is he eating?* Make an appropriate gesture to make the meaning of *Why* clear. Students answer (L1). Repeat for *thirsty*.
- Show a picture again and ask, *Why is he (smiling)?* Point to the face and imitate the gesture to make meaning clear. Students answer (L1). Say, *Because he's happy.* Then point to a student and ask, *And you?* Encourage the student to smile too.
- Continue with the other actions (*crying*, *laughing* and *shouting*), using the pictures on p. 55. Introduce *funny*.

3 Chant.

- Focus students' attention on the chant. Then play T65 for students to listen and follow the words. Play it again, pausing after each line for students to repeat.
- Play the chant once more for students to join in.

Presentation

- Draw students' attention to the question and answer in the *Look!* box. Write them on the board, so that all students can follow your explanation. Ask them to pay attention to the different words used in the question and in the answer – *Why* and *Because*. Help students come up with a simple rule (e.g., *Use* Why *in questions and* Because *in answers*). Students copy the rule into their notebooks.

Extra!

- Ask a student to mime an action (e.g., *crying*). Turn to him/her and ask, for instance, *Why are you (crying)?* Help the student with the answer *Because I'm (sad)*. Write this exchange on the board and practice it with the class, replacing the actions.

4 Listen and answer. *True* or *false*?

- Tell students (L1) that they will listen to the rest of the conversation among the characters in the main illustration.
- Draw students' attention to the true or false statements. Then play T66. If necessary, you can play it again two or three times. Check answers by asking individual students to read the sentences. Students can correct the false sentences in their notebooks.

Director	What's happening? Who is that boy?	T66
Ruby	It's Sam.	
Director	Why is he eating my cake?	
Ruby	Because he's hungry.	
Sam	Sorry!	
Ruby	And that's John. He's drinking because he's thirsty.	
Director	Hmm. What's your name?	
Jenny	I'm Jenny.	
Director	Why are you smiling?	
Jenny	Because I'm happy! I love horses.	
Director	Why are you laughing, Favolina?	
Favolina	I'm laughing because it's funny!	

5 Look at the chant. Ask and answer.

- Divide the class into pairs. Students take turns asking and answering questions about the pictures in Activity 3. You can write prompts on the board to help students remember the language, or simply ask them to refer to the *Look!* box.
- As a follow-up, students can write the exchanges in their notebooks.

Ending the lesson

- Divide the class into two groups and sing the chant again (T65). Group A chants the questions, and Group B chants the answers. Then groups switch roles.

OPTIONAL ACTIVITY
Flashcard game
Play *Hot seat* (see p. T88).

WB page 129

3 Look and write. Use words in the box.

- Students look at the picture, then complete the sentences using the words in the box.

4 Look at Activity 3. Read and match.

- Students look at the picture in Activity 3. Then they read the questions and match them with the appropriate answers.

6 T67 Listen and sing.

SONG

What makes you feel happy?
What makes you feel happy?
Sunny days.
Sunny days and holidays
Make me feel happy.

What makes you cry?
What makes you cry?
Sad movies.
Sad movies and long goodbyes
Make me cry.

What makes you feel scared?
What makes you feel scared?
Big storms.
Big storms and green monsters
Make me feel scared.

What makes you laugh?
What makes you laugh?
My friends.
My friends and naughty monkeys
Make me laugh.

7 Ask and answer.

feel scared feel happy
feel sad feel angry
laugh cry thrilled

What makes you feel scared?

Storms make me feel scared.

LOOK!

What **makes** you **cry**?
Sad movies **make** me **cry**.
What **makes** you **feel happy**?
Ice cream **makes** me **feel happy**.

Workbook page 130, Activities 5 and 6.

Lesson 3

Lesson aims
To extend the vocabulary set; to practice the vocabulary with a song.
Values
The importance of caring for others.
Target language
naughty; What makes you (feel happy)? (Sunny days) make me (feel happy.)
Recycled language
Animals, Feelings, Weather
Materials
Multi-ROM, Flashcards (Animals, Free time, The natural world, Weather and others), spinners

Starting the lesson

- Play *I spy* (see p. T90) to review feelings. Say, *I spy with my little eye a feeling beginning with...*

SB page 56

Presentation

- Bring a variety of flashcards to the class (e.g., weather conditions, nature, animals and others). Show a flashcard of something you really like (e.g., the sea), look very happy and say, *The sea makes me feel happy. What about you?*
- Show a picture of something scary (e.g., a storm) and say, *Storms make me feel scared.* Make appropriate gestures to make meaning clear. Continue with other feelings.

6 Listen and sing.

- Play T67. Students listen and follow the words in their books. Create mime to go with the feelings and actions in the song (*feel happy, cry, feel scared* and *laugh*), then play T67 again for students to join in with the words and mime.
- Divide the class into four groups and assign a verse of the song to each group.

Presentation

- Draw students' attention to the questions and answers in the *Look!* box and write them on the board. Point out that we use *makes you/me feel* + a feeling adjective (e.g., *happy, sad, angry*) and that we use *makes you/me* + an action verb (e.g., *cry, laugh*).
- Ask students the questions and write the questions and answers on the board. Students copy into their notebooks.

7 Ask and answer.

- Divide the class into pairs (see ideas for dividing students on pp. XII and XIII). Students take turns asking and answering questions using the words and the phrases in the box.
- Circulate, helping with language use and additional vocabulary. As a follow-up, ask students to write the questions and answers in their notebooks.

Extra!

- Review some of the vocabulary that students have learned so far. Draw word maps on the board for different lexical categories (e.g., nature, sports, activities, animals, etc.) and elicit words from students. Use the flashcards to help them remember.
- Ask students to choose a flashcard and tell the class (e.g., *Mountains make me feel happy; Hippos make me feel scared*).

Values

- Talk about (L1) things that make people sad at school (e.g., being laughed at, not being allowed to join in a game, etc.). What can students do to avoid making people sad? (Think before they say something rude, be careful not to hurt people by playing too roughly, etc.) How can they help if someone else in their class is feeling sad? (Be friendly, be a good listener, etc.)

Ending the lesson

- Tell the class that they are going to write new verses for the song with new things that make them happy, sad, scared, etc. Ask students to contribute lines similar to the ones in the original song in Activity 6. Copy them on the board. With the help of students, choose the new lines and make a new song. Sing as a class.

OPTIONAL ACTIVITY
Spinner game
Divide the class into small groups. Give each group a spinner (or a die). Stick the feelings flashcards on the board and number them from 1 to 6. One student in each group spins the spinner, hiding it from the rest. He/She acts out the feeling. The other students in the group guesses, e.g., *He/She feels (happy).*

WB page 130

5 Read the answers and complete the questions. Use the words in the box.

- Students read the questions and answers and then complete the questions using the words in the box.

6 Look, think and write.

- Students look at the pictures. Then they focus on the example and write similar sentences about each picture.

Lesson 4

Lesson aims
To develop reading, listening, writing and speaking skills.
Recycled language
Feelings; *because*
Materials
Multi-ROM, Unit 7 mini cards, scissors, Flashcards (Animals, Free time, Weather and others)

Starting the lesson

- Play *Flashcard act out* (see p. T88) to review vocabulary.

SB page 57

Presentation

- Focus students' attention on the article. Explain (L1) that it was taken from a website. Point to the boy in the picture and ask, *What's his name? (Ricky.) Is he famous? (Yes, he is.)* Ask the class (L1) if they have visited any websites of their favorite singers or actors.

8 Look and read.

- Point to the picture of Ricky. Ask, *What makes Ricky feel happy?* Students read the text and find the answer.
- Then point to Sam and ask, *What makes Sam feel sad?* Students read the text and find the answer. If necessary, clarify vocabulary.

9 Listen and circle.

- Explain (L1) that students will listen to some questions about the text. Play T68, and students just listen to the questions. Then play it again, pausing after each question, so that students have time to find and circle the answers in the text.
- Play the questions once more and ask students to help you write them on the board. Check as a class and ask individual students to write the answers. Students copy into their notebooks.

T68

1 Which two things make Ricky feel happy?
2 Which two things make Sam laugh?
3 What makes Sam feel sad?
4 What makes Ricky feel sad?

Presentation

- In the text in Activity 8, focus students' attention on the sentences with *because*. Write them on the board. Give a few other examples (e.g., *Snakes make me feel scared because they're dangerous*).
- Ask students to give other examples using *because* and the vocabulary of the unit. Write their sentences on the board. Students copy into their notebooks.

11 Go to p. 85 and play the game.

- Students cut out the mini cards. When they have finished, say a word represented in the card (*thrilled*), and students then hold up the card. Continue with the other cards.
- Divide students into pairs and explain the game (L1): Students shuffle their cards and put them in a pile in front of them.
- Each student turns over the top card from his/her face-down pile and describes it by saying, for instance, *I'm (happy)*. When the two cards on the top of the piles are the same, students say, *Snap!*. They them describe the card. The student who calls *Snap!* first scores a point. Students continue playing.

Writing practice

- Give each student an A4 sheet of paper. Ask them to imagine that they have a website or blog and that they will write a text about what makes them feel happy, sad, scared, etc. Explain that it will be similar to Ricky's text.
- They can write isolated sentences or a paragraph. Encourage them to explain their feelings using *because*. Circulate, helping with language use and additional vocabulary. When they have finished, display their work on the classroom walls.

Extra!

- Students play *Memory game* (see p. T88) using their mini cards. To make the activity more challenging, they can use sets of mini cards from other units to play the game.

Students tell their families what makes them feel happy. They also ask their family members what make them feel happy. Ask students to teach the song to their family members.

Ending the lesson

- Play *Hangman* (see p. T89) to review the vocabulary of this unit.

OPTIONAL ACTIVITY
Mini card game
Play *Memory game* (see p. T88) using the mini cards.

WB page 131

7 Read and match.

- Students read the sentences and match the halves.

8 Look and read.

Ricky Fansite!

Dear Ricky,
What makes you feel happy?
Sam

Hi Sam,
Good question. Playing the guitar makes me feel happy. Also, my friends make me feel happy because they make me laugh. We go skateboarding and play computer games. What makes you laugh?
Ricky

Funny movies make me laugh. My brother makes me laugh because he can make funny faces. But it makes me feel sad when he doesn't want to play soccer with me. What makes you feel sad?
Sam

Winter makes me feel sad because it's cold. But I love summer. Sunny days make me feel happy.
Ricky

9 T68 Listen and circle.

10 Go to page 85 and play the game.

11 T69 **Listen and read. Then act.**

STORY

NOW GO TO FILM STUDIO ISLAND.

Workbook page 131, Activities 8 and 9.

Lesson 5

Lesson aims
To consolidate the unit language with a story.
Target language
always, diver; They're six meters long.
Recycled language
Feelings; *shark; Do they have (sharp claws)? They have (very sharp teeth).*
Materials
Multi-ROM, Unit 7 mini cards, A3 paper, reference books, scissors, glue, colored pencils and markers

Starting the lesson

- Students play *Memory buzz* (see p. T88) using the mini cards.

SB page 58

12 Listen and read. Then act.

- Remind students of the story in the previous units and ask, for instance, *Where are the children? (On a movie set.)* Then draw their attention to the frames and ask, *What animal can you see? Who's this?*
- Before listening to the story, ask the following questions for the corresponding frames. Try to ask and discuss them in English:
  1 *(Pointing to the sign.)* What are Great Whites? [Open discussion.]
  2 Is the movie about monsters? [Open discussion.]
  3 Is the shark scared of the children? [No, it isn't.]
  4 *(Pointing to the diver.)* Who is this? [Introduce diver.]
  5 What does the shark want to do? [Eat the assistant.]
  6 *(Pointing to the faces.)* Do the children understand the message? [Open discussion.]
- Play T69, and students follow the story in their books. Play it again, pausing after each line for students to repeat.
- Next, to check students' understanding of the story, ask the following questions:
  1 Where are the children going? [To another movie set.]
  2 What are great white sharks? [They live in the sea. They're six meters long and they're always hungry.]
  3 What do sharks have? [They have sharp teeth.]
  4 Why does Ruby feel scared? [Because she doesn't like sharks.]
  5 What's the diver doing? [He's writing.]
  6 What does the message say? Can you spell it? [It says HELP backwards.]
- Ask the class (L1) to predict what is going to happen in the next episode of the story. Will the children find Madley Kool?
- Divide students into two groups and assign a character to each. Students read their parts as a class from their seats. This may encourage shyer students to take part in the acting later on.
- Invite students to take the parts of the characters in the story. Ask the volunteers to go to the front of the class to act out the story. Encourage tone of voice and expressions to match those in the pictures. Alternatively, you could have other students read the lines while the volunteers act it out.

Ending the lesson

- Divide the class into two groups (see ideas for group formation on pp. XII and XIII). Retell the story making some deliberate mistakes. Every time one group spots a mistake, students put up their hands and correct it.

Students can now go online to Film Studio Island and enjoy the fun and games, at home or at the school computer lab. Ask them to find the 'camera' that Cleo is holding in one of the pages of the unit (p. 61). Then tell students they should find the camera on Film Studio Island (it is just inside the Wild West Studio). When students click on the camera, they are taken to a supplementary language game based on the vocabulary in Unit 7.

OPTIONAL ACTIVITY
Predators
Tell students to look for information about predators. Explain the word *predator*. Brainstorm other predators and give their names in English. Bring reference books to the class or use the Internet. Divide the class into small groups and ask them to choose a predator and find information about it. Then they make a mini poster with the information and include pictures drawn by them, or downloaded from the Internet.

WB page 131

8 Read and number.

- Students read the bubbles and the information on the fact file. Then they number each piece of information to a point on Ruby's board.

9 Look, think and write.

- Students look at the text about sea animals, then complete it with the missing words and phrases.

Lesson 6

Lesson aims
To integrate other areas of the curriculum into the English class; to develop the cross-curricular topic through a short project.
Cross-curricular focus
Music – movie posters and music
Recycled language
Feelings
Materials
Multi-ROM, A3 sheets, colored pencils and markers

Starting the lesson

- Sing the song in Lesson 3 again (T67).

SB page 59

Presentation

- Ask students if they like music and what kind of music they like. Write words for types of music on the board (e.g., *rock*, *pop*). Then ask, *Who's your favorite singer? What's your favorite group?* Students vote for their favorite singer/group.

12 Listen to the music. How does it make you feel?

- Tell the class that you are going to play some music. They listen and say how it makes them feel. Then play T70. Pause after each piece and ask several students, *How does it make you feel?* Students answer.
- Tell students that you are going to play the recording again, but that this time they should write words in their notebooks (in English or L1) that the music inspires in them. Pause after each piece of music to give students time to write. If necessary, help with additional vocabulary.

T70
1 (recording of scary, horror music)
2 (recording of upbeat, high energy music)
3 (recording of sad, mournful music)
4 (recording of comedy music)

13 Read and match.

- Focus students' attention on the posters and explain that they are posters of movies. Point to each poster, and students then predict what kind of movie it is. Write students' ideas on the board.
- Next, students read the descriptions and match them to the correct poster. Check answers. Ask students which words in the text helped them in the exercise.

14 Look at the Activity 13. Ask and answer.

- Divide the class into pairs. Then focus students' attention on the question and answer in the example. Read them and ask students to repeat after you to practice pronunciation.
- Students ask each other how the movies make them feel. If necessary, monitor pairs to help with language use and additional vocabulary.
- Explain that music is very important in movies and that there are movies that have become very famous because of their music. Ask if they remember a song or a piece of music from a film.

Think!

- Write the task on the board. Students copy it into their notebooks:
- *Write down:*
  - *a song that makes you feel happy.*
  - *a movie that makes you laugh.*
  - *a movie character that makes you feel scared.*
- Give students some time to write the song and movies individually. Then ask students (L1) how they can find out who else in the classroom feels the same way they do about the same song/movies. Write their ideas on the board (e.g., ask questions, have the teacher ask everyone in class, pass the notebooks around the class, etc.) Students choose how they would like to do it and do the task.

Mini project

- Divide students into small groups. Give each group an A3 sheet of paper. Explain that they are going to create a movie poster and write a description of the movie, similar to the texts in Activity 13.
- Students choose a type of movie and its title and discuss the design for the poster. Then they use colored pencils and markers to decorate it. They also write a short text describing the poster and how it makes them feel.
- Circulate, helping students with language use and additional vocabulary. When they have finished, display their work around the class.

OPTIONAL ACTIVITY
Young movie makers
Divide the class into groups. Play a piece of music and tell students that they are movie directors and that they are going to make a movie. They have to imagine the story for the movie and choose the movie stars who are going to take part in it. Provide a skeleton on the board for students to describe their ideas (e.g., *Our movie is about... It happens in ... The stars are...*).

WB page 132

10 Read and circle.

- Students look at the movie scenes and the sentences, then circle the correct word.

11 Look and circle. Draw and write the one that is missing.

- Students look at the faces and circle the words that describe what each child is feeling. Then they write the feeling adjective that is missing and draw the appropriate facial features.

12 T70 **Listen to the music. How does it make you feel?**

Answers will vary.

13 **Read and match.**

1

2

3

4

a It's the end of the movie. They are at the train station. They're friends and they're saying goodbye. It makes me feel sad. It makes me cry.

b There are a lot of people. The music is great. They're learning to dance. It makes me feel happy. I want to sing and dance, too.

c There are two boys. They have a lot of fun. It's funny. It makes me laugh.

d It has a big, green monster. The monster has sharp teeth and long hair. It makes me feel scared.

14 **Look at Activity 13. Ask and answer.**

How does number 3 make you feel?

It makes me feel sad.

Workbook page 132, Activities 10 and 11.

Wider World

It makes me feel happy.

1 T71 **Listen and read.**

1

I'm Zhi. I'm from China. Chinese New Year makes me feel happy because it's fun. It's in January or February and it's called the Spring Festival. There are dragons and pretty lanterns. We clean our houses, then we visit friends and family. I love my friends and family. They make me feel happy.

2

Do you like my dress? I'm Ola. I'm from Poland. Dancing makes me feel happy because it's good exercise. I dance at a traditional dance school. Here I am with my friends. We're wearing traditional dresses and hats.

2 **Read and answer.**

1. When is Chinese New Year?
2. Why does Ola like dancing?
3. What is Ola wearing?
4. Is Mark scared of fireworks?
5. How does Victoria's choir go to other schools?

1 It's in January or February. / 2 Because it makes her feel happy. / 3 A traditional hat and dress. / 4 No, he isn't. / 5 They go by bus or train.

3

My name's Mark. I'm from the United Kingdom. Bonfire Night makes me feel happy. It's every year in November. I go to watch fireworks at the park with my brother and my mom and dad. In the photo we're wearing hats and scarves because it's cold. I'm not scared of fireworks.

4

Hi! I'm Victoria. I go to a music school and I sing in the African Children's Choir. At school we have singing and dancing lessons every day. We go by bus and train to other schools and sing in concerts. Singing in the choir makes me feel happy because I love music.

3 

Listen and say the name.

1 Ola, 2 Mark, 3 Zhi, 4 Victoria, 5 Ola

4 

Talk about what makes you feel happy.

Answers will vary.

1 What or when is it?
2 What do you do?
3 What do you wear?

Workbook page 133, Activities 12 and 13.

7

Wider World

Lesson aims
To learn about festivals in other countries; to personalize the language from Unit 7; to provide an opportunity for self-evaluation.
Target language
choir, dragon, fireworks, lantern, traditional dress
Recycled language
Feelings
Materials
Flashcards (Feelings), a bag or a box, a map of the world or a globe, A4 paper
Special note: The activities from the *Wider World* lesson can be done in one or two classes, depending on the use of the *Pairwork, Extra!, Game* and *Optional activities* sections. The Workbook activities can also be assigned for homework in different classes.

Starting the lesson

- Remind students of the chant in Lesson 2 (T65). Then divide the class into two groups and sing the chant. Group A chants the questions, and Group B the answers.

SB pages 60-61

1 Listen and read.

- Draw students' attention to the photos and the texts. Ask students to find out the children's names and where they are from. Then write the names and the countries on the board.
- Display the world map on the board, or show the globe to students. Invite some students to come to the board to find the countries on the map.
- Tell students (L1) they are going to listen to four children talking about activities that make them feel happy. Ask them to follow the text as they listen to the recording. Play T71. If necessary, clarify vocabulary.

Background information:

Bonfire Night – The night of November 5th, when people in the UK light fireworks and burn a figure of a man on a fire. This is done in memory of the time when Guy Fawkes tried to destroy the English Parliament in London in 1605, although for most people this connection is no longer important. Formerly, most families used to have their own bonfires and fireworks, but it is now more common for people to go to large, organized firework shows in parks.

Chinese New Year – It is celebrated on the first day of the lunar month in January or February. There are festivities in lots of countries, and each new year is named after one of the twelve animals of the Chinese zodiac.
(Source: *Longman Dictionary of English Language and Culture*, 1998)

Extra!

- Brainstorm with the class names of festivals in Brazil. Write them on the board. Ask students what they do on these occasions and when they are celebrated.
- Ask students to help you write about one of these festivals, as if they were another child in Activity 1. Elicit information and language from students and write the text on the board. Students copy it into their notebooks.

2 Read and answer.

- Focus students' attention on the questions and, if necessary, clarify vocabulary. Students read the texts in Activity 1 again and answer the questions in their notebooks.

3 Listen and say the name.

- Explain (L1) that students will listen to five sentences about the children in Activity 1 and that they should say who the children are.
- Play T72 once. Students just listen. Then play the recording again, pausing after each speaker to allow students time to think and decide. Alternatively, students write the children's names in their notebooks.

T72
1 She goes to a dance school.
2 He's wearing a hat in the photo.
3 She's happy because she's with her family.
4 She loves music.
5 She's wearing a traditional white and red dress in the photo.

Extra!

- Work with shadow reading. Play T71 again. Students read the words while trying to stay at the same speed and rhythm as the recording. As students keep reading, you can turn the sound down occasionally.

Group work

- Divide the class into small groups or pairs. Give each of them an A4 sheet of paper and tell them to make a word snake (similar to the one on p. 132) using words that they like from this unit.
- When they have finished, they exchange sheets with other groups and find the words.

Picture Dictionary

- Divide the class into pairs. Direct students' attention to p. 142. Focus on the pictures in the Feelings section. Students read the words under the pictures carefully. Then they cover the words and take turns saying all the words in the correct order.

Pairwork

- Divide the class into pairs. They write a sentence about one of the children in Activity 1, similar to the ones they have heard in Activity 3.
- Then they read their sentence to the class. The class guesses who the sentence refers to.

Extra!

- Ask students to close their books. On the board, write the names of the children, the countries and the key vocabulary (*lantern* and *dragon*, *traditional dress*, *fireworks* and *choir*) from Activity 1. Organize the language into three columns.
- Invite a student to come to the board. Then play T71 again. The student draws lines matching the three columns (e.g., *Zhi – China – lantern and dragon*). Continue with the other children, inviting other students to come to the board.

4 Talk about what makes you feel happy with your friend.

- Divide the class into small groups. Focus students' attention on the questions. Tell them to use the questions as a guide to think about what makes them feel happy.
- Students talk about it. Circulate to help with additional vocabulary as necessary. To wrap up the activity, you can ask the groups what they talked about, using the same questions. Alternatively, you can turn it into a writing activity by asking students to answer the questions in their notebooks.

Ending the lesson

- Play a guessing game. Say a sentence about one of the festivals in this lesson, e.g., *It's in January or February. It is called the Spring Festival. You can see dragons and lanterns.* (Chinese New Year.) *It's in England. It's in November. There are fireworks.* (Bonfire Night.) Include descriptions about festivals in Brazil and about other special dates students have learned about (Halloween, Easter, Christmas, etc.). Students guess which one it is.
- Put the flashcards in a bag or box. Pick one and begin to take it out very slowly. The class guesses what picture it is and makes a sentence using the words (e.g., *Storms make me feel scared. I'm eating because I'm hungry*). The first student to make a correct guess takes your role. Alternatively, you can begin the sentence, and then students complete it.

OPTIONAL ACTIVITIES

Games

Play *Jumping the line* (see p. T88) using the vocabulary of Unit 7.

Play *Bingo* (see p. T89) to review the vocabulary of feelings, hobbies and months.

Guessing game

Students make a list of things that make them happy, scared or sad. Divide the class into pairs. Students try to guess what each other has written. Student A says, for instance, *Spiders make you feel scared.* Student B then says, *Yes/No.*

WB page 133

12 What makes you feel happy and scared? Draw pictures.

- Students draw things that make them feel happy, or scared, in the correct frame.

13 Write about your pictures.

- Students complete the sentences with what makes them feel happy or scared.

Self-assessment

- Students choose and color the appropriate number of stars depending on how well they think they have completed the unit. Discuss with students what they have learned, what they can do now, which activities they liked best and which ones were difficult.

8 By the sea

1 T73 **Listen, point and say.**

2 T74 **Listen and say the missing word.**

Surfing.

Workbook pages 134 and 135, Activities 1, 2 and 3.

3 T75 Chant.

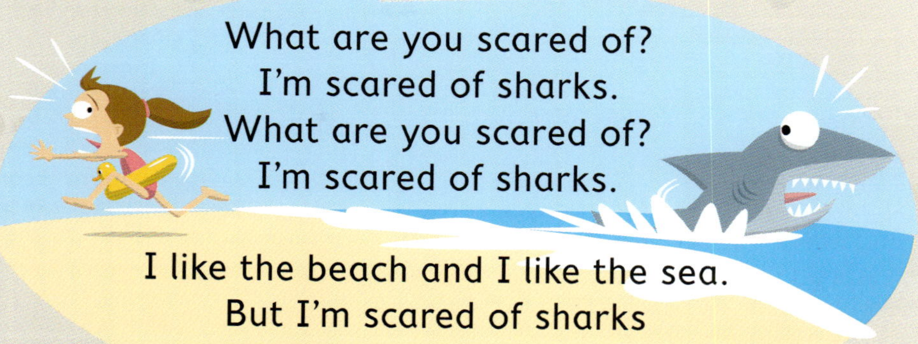

What are you scared of?
I'm scared of sharks.
What are you scared of?
I'm scared of sharks.

I like the beach and I like the sea.
But I'm scared of sharks
And they're scared of me!

LOOK!

What **are** you **scared of**?
I'**m scared of** sharks.

4 T76 Listen and answer the questions.

1 What are you scared of, Ruby?
2 What are you scared of, Jenny?
3 What are you scared of, Sam?

1 I'm scared of horses.
2 I'm scared of sharks.
3 I'm scared of sharks.

5 Ask six friends.

8 By the sea

Lesson 1

Lesson aims
To present and practice new vocabulary.
Target language
fishing, horseback riding, sailing, snorkelling, surfing
Recycled language
Free-time activities, Sports; *beach, present, sea; (She)'s (snorkelling).*
Materials
Multi-ROM, Flashcards (By the sea), A4 paper

Starting the lesson

- Play *Teacher says* (see p. T89) to review free-time activities and sports.

SB page 62

Presentation

- Present the vocabulary using the flashcards. Hold up each flashcard in turn and say the words for students to repeat. Hold up the flashcards again, this time asking individual students to say the words.
- Then show the cards in random order and ask, *What is it?*

1 Listen, point and say.

- Draw students' attention to the pictures at the bottom of the page. Then play T73, pausing after each word to give students time to find the picture. Play it again, pausing after each activity, and students repeat them.
- Ask students, *What's number (three)?* They look at the images and answer. If you want to make the activity more challenging, ask students to close their books and try to say the vocabulary from memory. Students can continue in pairs.

2 Listen and say the missing word.

- Now focus on the main illustration. Point to the characters and ask, *Who's this?* Ask students to name the different activities in the illustration. Point to the director and the assistant and explain (L1) who they are.
- Tell students (L1) that they are going to listen to the director and the assistant talking about the different activities, but that one of the items from Activity 1 will be missing.
- Instruct students to pay close attention to the main illustration. Play T74 once up to *What's missing?* Give students time to locate the different activities in the illustration and find out which item is missing (*surfing*). Play it again to the end.
- Play T74 again, pausing after each line for students to repeat. Encourage tone of voice and expressions to match those in the pictures.

T74

Director OK. Are we ready? Is everyone on the beach?
Assistant Yes, sir. On the beach or in the sea, sir.
Director This is Madley Kool's big scene. Is he ready?
Assistant Errr...
Director Good! Let's start. What's everyone doing? Where's Joe?
Assistant He's sailing.
Director OK. What's Julian doing?
Assistant He's fishing.
Director Right. What's Jane doing?
Assistant She's snorkelling.
Director Right. And James?
Assistant He's... err, he's horseback riding.
Director He's WHAT? And why is James horseback riding?
Assistant Because he's scared of sharks.
Narrator What's missing?
Children Surfing!

Pairwork

- Review the use of *be* + action + *-ing*. Show some flashcards to students and ask, *What's (he) doing? (He)'s (surfing).* Write some examples on the board and highlight the structure.
- Divide students into pairs (see ideas for dividing the class on pp. XII and XIII). Student A makes a sentence about one of the characters. Student B points to the person in the main illustration.

Ending the lesson

- Divide the class into pairs. Student A chooses one of the activities from the main illustration and mimes it. Student B guesses who it is.

OPTIONAL ACTIVITY
Guess the action
Draw an object (e.g., fishing rod), and the class then guesses the activity.

WB page 134-135

1 Match

- Students match the words to the pictures.

2 Look and complete.

- Students look at the descriptions of the two pictures and then complete them with the correct words from the lesson.

3 Look, read and complete.

- Students look at the pictures and then complete the questions and the answers accordingly.

Lesson 2

Lesson aims
To review the vocabulary of Lesson 1 with a chant; to present the new structure.
Target language
What are you scared of? I'm scared of (sharks).
Recycled language
Animals
Materials
Multi-ROM, Flashcards (By the sea), pictures of snakes, spiders and other wild animals, A4 paper

Starting the lesson
- Play *Aye, aye, Captain!* (see p. T89) to review the vocabulary of Lesson 1.

SB page 63

Presentation
- Show students some pictures of animals that people are usually scared of. Then say, *I'm scared of (spiders).*
- Point to a student and ask, *What are you scared of?* Continue with a few more students. If necessary, help with additional vocabulary.

3 Chant.
- Focus students' attention on the chant. Then play T75 for students to listen and follow the words. Play it again, pausing after each line for students to repeat.
- Play the chant once more for students to join in. If necessary, use mime to help prompt the words.

Presentation
- Draw students' attention to the question and answer in the *Look!* box. Point out that we use *of* at the end of the question.
- Elicit some example sentences and write them on the board. Students copy into their notebooks.

4 Listen and answer.
- Focus students' attention on the sentences. Tell students (L1) that they are going to listen to the characters talking about things they are scared of.
- Play T76 a few times. Students write the answers in their notebooks. Check as a class.

T76

Ruby I'm scared!
Jenny What are you scared of, Ruby?
Ruby I'm scared of horses. I don't like horses.
Jenny Don't worry, Ruby. I'm scared of sharks, and they're filming a shark!
John I am not scared of sharks.
Sam You are!
John I am not.
Sam You're scared of crocodiles.
John I don't like crocodiles, but I am not scared of crocodiles. Or sharks!
Sam I am.
John You're scared of sharks, Sam?
Sam Yes, I am.
Cleo Madley Kool is scared of sharks.

Practice
- Ask students to help you rebuild the dialogue. Play T76, pausing after each exchange.
- Ask questions to help students remember, e.g., *Who's that?* Students answer, for instance, *Ruby.* Continue until you write the entire dialogue on the board.
- When you have finished, divide the class into groups and assign a character to each group. They read their parts from their seats.

5 Ask six friends.
- Draw students' attention to the boy and girl and to what they are saying. You can ask a boy and a girl to read the dialogue.
- Give each student an A4 sheet of paper. They write down the names of six friends for the activity.
- When they have finished, they stand up and circulate around the room, asking their friends, *What are you scared of?* Students write down the answers. Help them with additional vocabulary.
- Ask students to report back to the class, saying, for instance, (*Name*) *is scared of* (*spiders*). Keep track of the results on the board and see what things students are most scared of.

Ending the lesson
- Write the first letter and spaces for the missing letters of one of the vocabulary words, e.g., *s* _ _ _ _ _ _ _ _ _ _ (*snorkelling*). Students call out letters in order to guess the word.

OPTIONAL ACTIVITY
Game
Play *Picture dictation* (see p. T90) using the unit vocabulary and language.

WB page 135

4 Look, think and write.
- Students look at the pictures and then classify them into the correct category.

6 Listen and sing. T77

SONG

What are you fond of?
I'm fond of these:
Movie stars and fishing,
Pasta and cheese.

What are you bored with?
I'm bored with these:
Dancing and toy cars,
Watching TV.

What am I scared of?
I'm scared of these:
Lions and crocodiles
Spiders and bees.
Anything else, you ask?
I'm terrified of sharks!

LOOK!

I'm **scared of** lions.
I'm **bored with** watching TV.
I'm **fond of** fishing.
I'm **terrified of** sharks.

7 Make sentences.

soccer   swimming   spiders
reading   surfing   crocodiles
cooking   horseback riding

fond of   bored with
scared of   terrified of

Workbook page 136, Activity 5.

Lesson 3

Lesson aims
To extend the vocabulary set; to practice the vocabulary with a song.
Target language
I'm bored with, fond of, terrified of
Recycled language
Animals, Free-time activities; *I'm scared of (lions).*
Materials
Multi-ROM, Flashcards (By the sea), homemade cards (adjectives and prepositions)

Starting the lesson

- Play *The ball* (see p. T88) with the flashcards. Students make sentences using *be* + action + *-ing.*

SB page 64

Presentation

- Focus students' attention on the picture. Point to the different animals and ask, *What are these?* Point to the bees and ask, *Are these spiders?* Review *bees.* Say, *I'm scared of spiders.*
- Then say, for instance, *I like reading very, very, very much! I'm fond of reading. And you?* Invite students to say what things they are fond of. Continue giving examples for *bored* and *terrified.* Mime to make the meaning clear.

6 Listen and sing.

- Play T77. Students listen and follow the words in their books. If necessary, clarify vocabulary. Then create a mime to go with the items in the song and play it again for students to join in with the words and the mime.
- Divide the class into three groups. Group A sings the verse with *fond of*, Group B the verse with *bored with*, and Group C the verse with *scared of.* All the groups sing the two last lines. Switch groups and sing the song again so that all the groups have a chance to sing the whole song.

Presentation

- Draw students' attention to the sentences in the *Look!* box and write them on the board. Point out the use of *scared, bored, fond* and *terrified* with the prepositions. Give other examples from the song.
- Ask students to give more examples. Write them on the board. Students copy them into their notebooks.
- Prepare eight cards. Write the adjectives *scared, bored, fond* and *terrified* on four separate pieces of card. Then write the corresponding prepositions on another four.
- Shuffle the cards and place them face down on your table. Ask individual students to come to the board and pick a card. They put it up on the board and match the adjectives to the prepositions.

7 Make sentences.

- Divide the class into pairs (see ideas for dividing students on pp. XII and XIII). Draw students' attention to the boy and girl in the example, then explain the activity. Students take turns asking and answering questions using the words and phrases in the box. Student A says an activity, and Student B says how he/she feels about it. Then they switch roles.

At home, students ask their family what they are fond of and bored with. Students make a mini poster with drawings or printed pictures showing some of the things that their family mentions. Students show their work and read their sentences in the next lesson.

Ending the lesson

- Divide the class into small groups. Then write the activities from Activity 7 on the board and ask students to copy them into their notebooks. Students ask the other members of their group if they like each activity, by saying, *Do you like (cooking)?* Each group determines most popular activity in their group. On the board, collect results from each group to find out the class' favorite activity.

OPTIONAL ACTIVITY
Young songwriters
Divide the class into small groups of three. Tell them to write a new verse for the song with new things that they are bored with, fond of, etc. When they have finished, collect the writings and make new songs. Groups sing their songs.

WB page 136

5 Look, read and complete. Use the words in the boxes.

- Students look at the four faces that show different feelings and read the labels. Whenever they come across one of the faces in the text, they write the corresponding word. They also focus on the words in the box, and use them when appropriate.

Lesson 4

Lesson aims
To develop reading, listening, writing and speaking skills.
Target language
dolphins; rock climbing
Recycled language
Free-time activities
Materials
Multi-ROM, Unit 8 mini cards, scissors, postcard templates, pictures of people swimming with dolphins and of a person rock climbing.

Starting the lesson

- Sing the song in Lesson 3 (T77) in groups.

SB page 65

Presentation

- Ask students where they like to go on vacation (e.g., to the sea, to the mountains).
- Brainstorm things they can do in each place. List them on the board and vote for the most popular.
- Then show the pictures for dolphins and rock climbing. Ask students where they can do these activities. Have students repeat *swimming with the dolphins* and *rock climbing* several times.

8 Look and read.

- Focus students' attention on the picture. Ask, *What place is this? Where do you think it is? Is it in Brazil? What's the weather like? How does it make you feel?*
- Ask students to read the postcard and find one thing Tom is scared of. Then ask other questions about the text (e.g., *Who is he writing to? What does he like doing? Does he like dolphins? What does his father like doing? What is his mother bored with?*).

9 Listen and answer.

- Explain (L1) that students are going to listen to some questions about the text and that they are going to answer them in their notebooks.
- Play T78 once. Students just listen. Then play it again, pausing after each sentence so that students have time to write the answers.
- Ask students to correct the false sentences.

T78

1 What's the weather like?
2 What does Tom like doing?
3 What does dad like doing?
4 What is mom doing?

10 Go to p. 87 and play the game.

- Students cut out the mini cards. When they have finished, say an activity represented in one of the cards (*dancing*), and students hold up the card. Continue with the other cards.
- Explain the game (L1): Students put one set of cards in a pile face down on the table. Student A turns one card over and says the activity (e.g., *Surfing*). Student B then says a sentence using the activity (e.g., *I like surfing in the* summer). Then it is Student B's turn to get a card.
- Encourage students to come up with different kinds of sentences, using *I (don't) like...*, *I'm* (verb + *-ing*) and other structures they have learned. Monitor pairs to help with language use. As a follow-up, you can ask students to write sentences using the mini cards in their notebooks.

Writing Practice

- Tell the class to imagine that they are on vacation in a very nice place and that they are going to write a postcard to a family member or friend. Draw their attention to Tom's postcard, pointing out the use of language, the greetings and the address.
- They can write the texts in the notebook, or on postcard-sized templates (pieces of blank poster board the size of a postcard). They can illustrate the text with drawings if they wish.
- Circulate, helping with language use and additional vocabulary. When they have finished, ask a few students to read their postcards.

Ending the lesson

- Students play *Quick peek* (see p. T88) with the mini cards.

OPTIONAL ACTIVITIES
Game
Play *Question chain* (see p. T90) using the unit language and vocabulary.
Play *Lexical groups* (see p. T90) using the vocabulary learned so far.

8 Look and read.

Dear Grandma and Grandpa,
I'm having fun here on vacation. It's hot and sunny and there are a lot of things to do. I like swimming with the dolphins in the sea. Dolphins are cool. They make me feel happy.
Dad likes horseback riding on the beach. Not me. I'm scared of horses! Mom is bored with the beach. Today she's rock climbing.
Lots of love,
Tom

Mr and Mrs Smith
22 The Street
London
NW18 9TF
UK

9 Listen and answer.

T78

1 It's hot and sunny. / 2 He likes swimming with the dolphins. / 3 He likes horseback riding on the beach. / 4 She's rock climbing.

10 Go to page 87 and play the game.

11 T79 **Listen and read. Then act.**

STORY

NOW GO TO FILM STUDIO ISLAND.

Workbook page 137, Activity 6.

Lesson 5

Lesson aims
To consolidate the unit language with a story.
Target language
crazy about
Recycled language
What's Cleo doing? I'm not really scared of sharks.
Materials
Multi-ROM, Unit 8 mini cards, a picture of a food item, speech bubbles with the lines of the story, A4 paper, colored pencils and markers

Starting the lesson

- Students play *What's missing?* (see p. T88) with the mini cards.

SB page 66

Presentation

- Use a picture of a food item you really like to introduce *crazy about*. Show the picture and say, for instance, *I like chocolate ice cream very, very much. I'm crazy about chocolate ice cream.* Ask students to give examples using other food items, activities or famous people.

11 Listen and read. Then act.

- Remind students of the story in the previous units and ask, for instance, *Where are the children? (On a movie set.)* Then draw their attention to the frames and ask questions about what is happening and who the characters are (e.g., *What animals can you see? Who's this?*).
- Before listening to the story, ask the following questions for the corresponding frames. Try to ask and discuss them in English:
  1 What's Cleo doing? [Open discussion.]
  2 What's the shark doing? [Going away.]
  3 What's Cleo doing? [Open discusstion.]
  4 Who's the diver? [Madley Kool.]
  5 Is the director happy? [No.]
  6 What's Madley doing? [He is acting.]
- Play T79, and students then follow the story in their books. Play it again, pausing after each line for students to repeat.
- Next, to check students' understanding of the story, ask the following questions:
  1 Is Cleo a hero? [Yes.]
  2 What's Cleo doing? [She's entering the tank.]
  3 What's Cleo doing? [She's opening the diver's helmet.]
  4 Is Madley Kool scared of sharks? [He pretends he is not scared.]
  5 What's the director saying? ['Madley Kool! It's your scene. Now!']
  6 Why is Cleo happy? [Because the children are crazy about Madley Kool.]
- Divide students into seven groups and assign a character to each. Students read their parts as a class from their seats. This may encourage shyer students to take part in the acting later on.
- Invite seven students to take the parts of the characters in the story. Ask the volunteers to go to the front of the class to act out the story. Encourage tone of voice and expressions to match those in the pictures.

Game

- Divide the class into two groups (see ideas for group formation on pp. XII and XIII). Ask them to close their books. Retell the story making some deliberate mistakes. Every time one group spots a mistake, students put up their hands and correct it.

Students can now go online to Film Studio Island and enjoy the fun and games, at home or at the school computer lab. Ask them to find the 'crab' that Cleo is holding in one of the pages of the unit (p. 67). Then tell students they should find the crab on Film Studio Island (it is in front of the Coconut Shack on the beach). When students click on the crab, they are taken to a supplementary language game based on the vocabulary in Unit 8.

Ending the lesson

- Prepare speech bubbles with the lines of the story and hand them out to different students. Play T79 again. When their line is playing, students jump up and go to the front of the classroom. They arrange themselves in order and hold up their speech bubbles.

OPTIONAL ACTIVITIES
My favorite character
Students draw their favorite character and write a short description. If necessary, help students with language and vocabulary.
Vote for your favorite episode
Ask, *Who likes episode (one)?* Count the number of votes. Determine what the class's favorite story is then read and listen to it again.

WB page 137

6 Read and complete.

- Students read the paragraph about Madley Kool, then complete the sentences with the words in the box.

Lesson 6

Lesson aims
To integrate other areas of the curriculum into the English class; to develop the cross-curricular topic through a short project

Cross-curricular focus
Science – save the reefs

Values
Discuss the importance of protecting the seas and sea life.

Target language
butterfly fish, coral reef, parrotfish, sea horses, sea snakes, starfish; global warming; dead, save

Materials
Multi-ROM, Flashcards (By the sea), A4 paper, a map of the world or a globe, reference books, pictures of the sea animals from the text, poster board, glue, scissors, colored pencils and markers

Starting the lesson

- Play *Flashcard act out* (see p. T89).

SB page 67

Presentation

- Bring a map of the world or a globe to the class. Focus students' attention on the title of the article. Ask, *What's a reef?* Encourage students to guess (L1). Use the pictures to introduce the different sea animals that can be found in coral reefs.
- Ask if they know where they can find reefs. Locate the Great Barrier Reef in Australia.
  Note: The Great Barrier Reef, off the northeast coast of Australia, is the largest coral reef in the world. It is around 2,000 km long.
  (Source: *Longman Dictionary of English Language and Culture*, 1998).

12 Listen and read.

- Tell the class you are going to listen to and read a text about coral reefs.
- Play T80 once, asking students to pay attention to the sea animals mentioned in the text. Then play it again, pausing after the questions at the end of the paragraph. Discuss the questions with students.

13 Read and answer.

- Focus students' attention on the questions. Tell the class to read the article again and answer the questions in their notebooks.

Values

- Ask (L1) students if they know what global warming (an increase in the Earth's average temperature) is and what causes it (exhaust fumes from cars, the use of fossil fuels like coal and oil, forest fires, etc).
- Talk with the class about what they can do to help prevent global warming. Write some of these ideas on the board (e.g., walk or use public transportation instead of using cars, take shorter showers, recycle paper, metal and plastic, etc.).

14 Talk to your friend.

- Divide the class into pairs (see ideas for dividing students on pp. XII and XIII). Students discuss the questions. Bring reference books to the class or have students use the Internet to look for more information.
- Alternatively, you can have a whole-class discussion or have students discuss the questions in small groups. You can also ask them to answer the questions in their notebooks.

Think!

- Write the task on the board: *Coral reefs need sunlight and warm temperatures. Name two places where coral reefs can't survive.*
- Divide students into small groups. Encourage them to discuss the task and think of possible answers. Write students' ideas on the board, and ask them to explain them.
- Take students to the school library or to the computer lab to look up information on books or online to confirm their hypotheses. They can also do this as homework. If students search online, take the opportunity to discuss the relevance/reliability of the sources they quote. Encourage them to suggest several possible sources and how to judge their reliability.

Mini project

- Divide the class into small groups. Elicit from students animals that live in coral reefs. Then ask students to look for further information on these animals on reference books or, if conditions permit, take the class to the computer lab to use the Internet.
- They choose three animals. On poster board, they stick or draw pictures of the animals and write some information about them. When they have finished, display their posters around the classroom.

Ending the lesson

- Divide the class into pairs and ask them to write two *True or false?* sentences about the coral reef text. Collect all the sentences and solve as a class.

OPTIONAL ACTIVITY
Game
Play *Category tag* (see p. T89) with sea/land animals, nature, activities, etc.

WB page 137

7 Read. Then match.

- Students read the passage about penguins, then match the questions to the corresponding answers.

12 T80 **Listen and read.**

Save the Reefs!

You can find coral reefs in the sea where it's hot and sunny. They are called the rainforest of the sea because a lot of fish and sea animals live on them. There are seahorses, sea snakes, starfish, butterfly fish, parrotfish and many more. There are a lot of pretty colors in the reef. How does this coral reef make you feel?

Now look at this coral reef. It's white and there are no fish or sea animals on it. The sea is too hot because of global warming and the coral is dead. Fish don't like dead coral. How does this coral reef make you feel?

Please help us save the coral reefs.

13 **Read and answer the questions.**

1 Where can you find coral reefs? In the sea.
2 Why are coral reefs called the rainforests of the sea?
3 What are some sea animals that live on a coral reef? Name three. Seahorses, sea snakes, starfish, butterfly fish, parrotfish.
4 Look at the second picture. Why is the coral white?

2 Because a lot of fish and sea animals live on them. / 4 Because the coral is dead.

14 **Talk to your friend.**
Answers will vary.

1 Which places are in danger in your country?
2 Which animals live there?

Review Units 1 to 8

1 T81 Listen, look and say. Then match.

They're sailing.

She's snorkeling.

They're horseback riding.

They're fishing.

He's surfing.

2 T82 Listen to the interviews and answer. *True* or *false*?

Claire, Australia

Ryan, Wales

1 Claire goes swimming with her friends. True
2 She's fond of snorkeling. False
3 Claire isn't scared of sharks. True
4 She wants to be a ballet dancer. False
5 Ryan likes surfing. False
6 He has music lessons on Saturdays in the afternoon. False
7 Ryan doesn't like soccer. True
8 He wants to be a doctor. True

Workbook page 138, Activities 8 and 9.

3 Talk about the pictures. Use the words in the boxes.

drinking	crying	shouting
smiling	eating	laughing

hungry	thirsty	happy
angry	funny	sad

Why is she shouting?

Because she's angry.

4 Do the quiz.

1 Does Madley Kool like skiing?
2 Where does Will live?
3 What do hippos eat?
4 Can elephants jump?
5 What's the weather like in Brazil in the fall?
6 What is a hurricane?
7 What does Sam do on Saturdays?
8 What time does Fifi have her ballet class?
9 What does Jenny want to be?
10 Can Naomi Johnson swim for two hours?
11 Where do whales live?
12 What's the weather like in a rainforest?
13 Who is Favolina Jolly?
14 What makes Ricky feel sad?
15 What is Ruby scared of?
16 Can you find coral reefs in the mountains?

5 Listen and check your answers.

T83

Answers are in the Teacher Book.

Review Units 1 to 8

Lesson aims
To review the language of units 1 to 8; to personalize language; to provide an opportunity for self-evaluation.
Recycled language
Vocabulary and structures from Units 1 to 8.
Materials
Units 1-8 mini cards, Flashcards (Units 1-8), A4 paper, Worksheet 8

Starting the lesson

- Play *Pass the secret* (see p. T90) using the vocabulary from previous units.
- Play *Category writing* (see p. T89) to review vocabulary from previous units.

SB pages 68-69

1 Listen, look and say. Then match.

- Ask students what they like doing in their free time or when they are on vacation. List the answers on the board.
- Then focus students' attention on the pictures. Tell them that they are going to hear a recording of the activities in the pictures.
- Play T81. Give students time to point and say the words. Play the recording again. Ask some students to say the activities to the class. Students them match the pictures to the words.

T81

1 [sound of a person reeling in a large fish and boy saying 'Wow!']
2 [sound of waves breaking on the beach and boy saying 'Whoa!']
3 [sounds of horses' hooves and birds singing]
4 [sound of a person splashing around, breathing through the snorkel]
5 [sounds of sea and rope being pulled through a metal ring]

2 Listen to the interviews and answer *true* or *false*.

- Focus students' attention on the two pictures. Ask where the children are from. Use a world map or a globe to help students locate the countries.
- Explain that students are going to listen to the children talking about themselves. Students have to decide if the sentences are true or false.
- Focus on Claire first. Ask the class to read the sentences carefully. If necessary, clarify vocabulary. Then play T82 once for students to listen. Play the recording again. Students listen and write *true* or *false*.
- Repeat the procedure with Ryan's interview. As a follow-up, students can correct the false statements in their notebooks.

T82

Reporter	Claire, what do you like doing in your free time?
Claire	I like going to the beach. I live near the sea. On the weekend I go swimming with my friends. We have lunch on the beach, stay there all afternoon and go home in the evening. It's great.
Reporter	Do you have swimming classes?
Claire	No, I don't. I have surfing classes on Saturdays with my brother. He's twelve. He goes snorkelling too. But I don't like snorkelling.
Reporter	Are you scared of sharks?
Claire	No, I'm not scared of sharks. There aren't any sharks near the beach.
Reporter	What do you want to be?
Claire	I want to be a firefighter.
Reporter	What do you like doing in your free time?
Ryan	I like riding horses, skateboarding and playing computer games with my friends.
Reporter	What do you do on Saturdays?
Ryan	I have music classes in the morning. I play the guitar. On sunny days I go to the park in the afternoon. I go skateboarding there with my friends. On rainy days we play computer games at my house.
Reporter	Do you like soccer?
Ryan	No, I don't. My brother talks about soccer all the time. I'm bored with soccer.
Reporter	What do you want to be?
Ryan	Well, my dad is a doctor. He works hard and on the weekend he's tired, but it makes him feel happy. I want to be a doctor, too.

Game

- Play *Bingo* (see p. T89) using the vocabulary from previous units.

3 Talk about the pictures. Use words from the boxes.

- Divide the class into pairs. Draw students' attention to the pictures and the words in the boxes. Then point out the language in the speech bubbles. You can demonstrate the dialogue with another student before they start working in pairs.
- Monitor pairs, helping with vocabulary and language use. As a follow-up, you can ask students to write the questions and answers in their notebooks.

4 Do the quiz.

- Students work in pairs. Focus on the questions in the quiz, clarifying vocabulary if necessary. Explain that they need to look at previous units to find the answers and that they should write them in their notebooks.

5 Listen and check your answers.

- When they have finished answering the quiz, play T83, pausing after each question and answer so that students have time to check their work.

T82

1 Does Madley Kool like skiing?
Yes, he does.
2 Where does Will live?
He lives in a lighthouse.
3 What do hippos eat?
They eat grass.
4 Can elephants jump?
No, they can't.
5 What's the weather like in Brazil in the fall?
It's windy.
6 What is a hurricane?
It's a big storm.
7 What does Sam do on Saturdays?
He goes skateboarding.
8 What time does Fifi have her ballet class?
She has her ballet class at ten o'clock.
9 What does Jenny want to be?
She wants to be a farmer.
10 Can Naomi Johnson swim for two hours?
Yes, she can.
11 Where do whales live?
They live in the sea.
12 What's the weather like in a rainforest?
It's hot and wet.
13 Who is Favolina Jolly?
She's a movie star.
14 What makes Ricky feel sad?
Winter makes Ricky feel sad.
15 What is Ruby scared of?
Ruby is scared of horses.
16 Can you find coral reefs in the mountains?
No, you can't. You can find coral reefs in the sea.

Now students can do Worksheet 8.

Ending the lesson

- Students play different games (see pp. 88-89) with the mini cards from several units. Ask them which language topics or lexical categories they liked best and why.

OPTIONAL ACTIVITY

Flashcard Game

Play *Hot seat* (see p. T88).

WB pages 138-139

8 Find the odd one out.

- Students look at each word list and find the odd one out.

9 Read and complete. Use the words in the box.

- Students read the passage about Elizabeth and complete it using the words in the box.

10 What do you like doing on vacation? Draw a picture.

- Students draw and color their favorite vacation activities.

11 Write about what you like doing on vacation.

- Students write a description about what they like doing on vacation.

Self-assessment

- Students choose and color the appropriate number of stars depending on how well they think they have completed the unit. Discuss with students what they have learned, what they can do now, which activities they liked best and which ones were difficult.

Mother's Day

1 T84 **Listen and read. Then answer the questions.**

Today is Sunday and it's Mother's Day. This is breakfast in bed for my mom. It's a treat because she makes breakfast for me and my dad every day. My mom likes toast and tea for breakfast. Today she has a rose and some presents, too. My present for Mom is a box of chocolates!

1 Which day is Mother's Day? Sunday.
2 Where is Mom having breakfast? In bed.
3 What is Mom having for breakfast? Toast and tea.
4 What's in the box? Chocolates.

2 T85 **Listen and sing.**

When I'm happy, when I'm sad,
You're always there.
When I'm good, when I'm bad,
You really care.

When I'm hungry, when I'm scared,
You know what to do.
So today's the day to say
A big THANK YOU!
Happy Mother's Day!

Mother's Day

Lesson aims
To learn about Mother's Day celebrations.
Target language
Mother's Day, box of chocolates, tea, rose; care (verb)
Recycled language
always, breakfast, present, toast, treat, present
Materials
Multi-ROM, a calendar, A3 paper, markers, assorted items to decorate a poster, glue

Cultural note: Mother's Day in the United States

- On Mother's Day children give their mothers cards and presents. They also give them extra help, such as doing the cooking or cleaning. Some families like to go out for lunch on Mother's Day. It is always on the second Sunday in May. It is traditional in some areas to eat a special cake on Mother's Day.

Starting the lesson

- Put a calendar up on the board and ask students (L1) when Mother's Day is celebrated in Brazil and how. Talk about special presents, meals or decorations.

SB page 70

Presentation

- Focus students' attention on the picture and use it to present the new vocabulary. Ask students to predict (L1) what they think the man and the boy in the picture are going to do with the things on the tray.

1 Listen and read. Then answer the questions.

- Tell the class that they are going to listen to a boy speaking about celebrating Mother's Day. Play T84. Students listen and follow in their books.
- Then ask students to read the text again and answer the questions in their notebooks.
- When they have finished, ask a few students to read the answers to the class. Tell them (L1) more about American Mother's Day celebrations (see above).

2 Listen and sing.

- Play T85. Students follow in their books. Explain the meaning of *You really care* and clarify any other vocabulary students have difficulty with.
- Play the song again a few times, and students join in until they can remember the song without help from the book.

Game

- Play a memory game. Say, *It's Mother's Day, and Mom has a rose.* Invite a student to add a present or food item to the sentence (e.g., *It's Mother's Day, and Mom has a rose and a book*). Continue around the class, with each student repeating the previous items and adding something new to the list. If someone makes a mistake, start playing again.

Ending the lesson

- Students plan the perfect day for their mothers. Alternatively, students can plan a perfect day for another family member (e.g., older sister, aunt or grandma).

OPTIONAL ACTIVITY

Make a *Dear Mom, I promise...* poster
Discuss (L1) with the class what makes mothers happy (e.g., that children clean their bedrooms, do their homework, treat others with respect etc.). Students write the heading *Dear Mom, I promise...* on an A4 sheet of paper. They write a promise on this mini poster and decorate it. Alternatively, students can make a poster dedicated to another family member. For instance, *Dear Grandma, I promise...*

Christmas

Lesson aims
To learn about Christmas celebrations.
Target language
dessert, ham, potatoes, snowman, tree, turkey, vegetables
Recycled language
dinner, lights, presents
Materials
Multi-ROM, a calendar, construction paper in different colors, colored pencils and markers

Cultural note: Christmas in the United States

- In the United States, families usually have dinner together on Christmas Eve (December 24th) or on Christmas day (December 25th). The traditional meal consists of roast turkey with vegetables and sauces, goose, duck or ham served with cranberry sauce and desserts, such as pie. The weather is very cold in most states at Christmas, so people generally have dinner indoors. After dinner, children hang up their stockings on the fireplace before they go to bed. In the following morning (December 25th), children get up to look for candy in their stockings and also find presents under the Christmas tree. The decoration in the houses generally includes holly and mistletoe along with Christmas trees decorated with tinsel, lights, popcorn strings and candy canes.

Starting the lesson

- Put a calendar up on the board and ask the class (L1) when Christmas is celebrated in Brazil and what people usually do. Talk about local traditions, food, presents and music.

SB page 71

Presentation

- Tell the class (L1) or elicit information about American Christmas traditions (see above). Focus students' attention on the photograph and use it to present the words.

1 Listen and read. Then answer the questions.

- Tell the class that they are going to listen to the girl in the photo (Grace) talk about Christmas traditions.
- Play T86. Students listen and follow in their books. Then ask students to read the text again and answer the questions in their notebooks.
- When they have finished, ask a few students to read the answers.

2 Listen and sing.

- Play T87. Students follow in their books. Clarify any other vocabulary students have difficulty with.
- Play the song again a few times, and students join in until they can remember the song without help from the book.
- Divide the class into four groups, and each group sings a verse. All the groups sing *On Christmas Day in the morning.*
- Write some new verses for the song (e.g., *And we are eating Christmas lunch. My grandma's wearing a hat,* etc.). Write them on the board and then add them to the song.

Ending the lesson

- Play the song again. Students move around the classroom. When you pause the song, all students must freeze. Point randomly to a student. He/she sings or says the next word in the song. If the student responds correctly, he/she points to another student to continue, then sits down on the floor. Each student who can correctly sing or say the next word in the song when called upon may sit down.

OPTIONAL ACTIVITY
Christmas cards
Give students a sheet of construction paper. They fold it in two and draw a Christmas design on the front. Write a message on the board: *Dear..., Merry Christmas! Best wishes from...* Students copy the message (with names) into their cards. Then they give the card to a friend.

Christmas

1 On Christmas morning. / 2 On Christmas. / 3 Turkey or ham, potatoes and vegetables. / 4 She has a brother.

1 T86 **Listen and read. Then answer the questions.**

Hi! I'm Grace. This is my family on Christmas Day. Every year for Christmas, we put presents under our Christmas tree. We open them on Christmas morning. In the afternoon I play with my presents. If it's snowy, my brother and I make a snowman in the front yard, or we stay inside and play board games. We always have a special dinner on Christmas. We eat turkey or ham, potatoes and vegetables. Then we have dessert. Yum!

1 When does Grace open her Christmas presents?
2 When do Grace and her family eat a special meal?
3 What do they eat?
4 Does Grace have any brothers or sisters?

2 T87 **Listen and sing.**

My dad is hanging Christmas lights.
On Christmas Day, On Christmas Day.
My dad is hanging Christmas lights.
On Christmas Day in the morning.

My mom is cooking Christmas lunch...
My sister's playing snowball games...
And we are singing a Christmas song...

Mini cards

Units 1-8

Mini cards

Units 1-8

Workbook

Welcome

Welcome

1 Read and write. Then match.

1 She's 9.
She has black hair.
She likes pink.
Her name is Ruby.

2 She's 11.
She has red hair.
She likes movies.
Her name is Jenny.

3 He's 8.
He has blond hair.
He likes skateboards.
His name is Sam.

4 He's 8.
He has red hair.
He has a sister.
His name is John.

2 Read and complete. Then draw yourself.
Answers will vary.

I'm ________. I have ________ hair.
I like ________________.
My ________________________.

3 Look and number.

March	3	September	9	June	6	December	12
May	5	November	11	February	2	April	4
January	1	August	8	October	10	July	7

Unit 1

1 Free time

1 Match.

2 Read and circle.

1 I like / don't like skateboarding.

2 I like / don't like riding my scooter.

3 I like / don't like computer games.

4 I like / don't like playing the guitar.

3 Read and ✓ or ✗.

Ruby likes cleaning and swimming. She doesn't like cooking.
She doesn't like playing soccer.
John likes cooking and playing soccer. He likes swimming.
He doesn't like cleaning.

Workbook

Unit 1

4 **Look and write.**
Use the words in the box.

Madley Kool   Cleo the cat   cooking   pizza   sunglasses   ~~black~~

1 He has short black hair.
2 He likes wearing sunglasses.
3 His favorite food is pizza.
4 He doesn't like cooking.
5 His best friend is Cleo the cat.
6 His name is Madley Kool.

5 **Look at the code and write the message.**

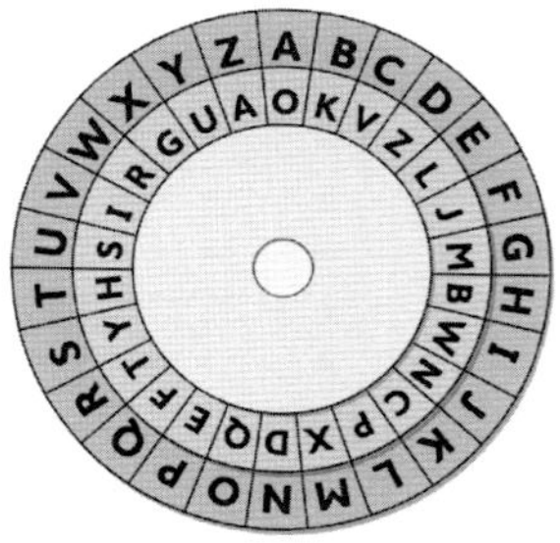

RBLTL WY XOZPLU CQQP?

Where is Madley Kool?

6 **Find out about Megan.**
Then write T (true) or F (false).

This is Megan.
She lives in a special house. It's a castle. Megan loves her house. It has twenty-one rooms and a big garden. She loves playing in the garden and likes reading outside. In the morning she can hear the birds but at night it's very quiet. She doesn't like cleaning her room, it's too big!

1 Megan likes reading in the castle. F
2 She doesn't like cleaning the castle. T
3 There are twelve rooms in the castle. F
4 Megan can hear birds at night. F
5 The castle is very big. T

7 **Read the text in Activity 6 again and complete.**

	Megan
house	castle
house description	twenty-one rooms big garden
what she likes	playing in the garden reading
what she doesn't like	cleaning her room

8 **Complete the puzzle.**

1 reading
2 skateboarding
3 playing
4 riding
5 swimming
6 cleaning
7 cooking

9 **Read, think and complete.**

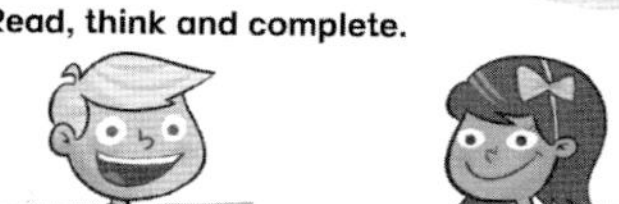

cooking ✓
reading ✓
watching TV ✗
playing soccer ✓
riding my bike ✓

playing computer games ✓
swimming ✓
skiing ✗
playing the guitar ✓
skateboarding ✗

He likes [1] cooking and [2] reading. He likes [3] playing soccer and [4] riding his [5] bike.
He doesn't like [6] watching TV.

She [7] likes playing computer games and swimming.
She [8] likes playing the guitar. She [9] doesn't like skiing or skateboarding.

10 **What do you like doing?**
Draw a picture.

I CAN DO IT!

11 **What do you like doing? Use the words in the box.**
Answers will vary.

in the morning   in the afternoon   at night

Workbook

Unit 2

2 Animals

1 Match.

2 Look and write.

1 It's a lion.
2 It's an elephant.
3 It's a monkey.
4 It's a hippo.
5 It's a crocodile.
6 It's a giraffe.

3 Read and write. Answers will vary.

	Fruit	Leaves	Grass	Insects	Meat
monkeys	✓	✗	✗	✓	✗
lions	✗	✗	✗	✗	✓
elephants	✓	✓	✓	✗	✗
crocodiles	✗	✗	✗	✓	✓

1 Do monkeys eat fruit?
Yes, they do.
2 Do lions eat ______________________?
3 Do elephants eat insects?
4 Do ______________ eat ______________?

4 Read and circle.

Monkeys

1 They live in *England* / *Africa*.
2 They eat fruit, leaves and *insects* / *meat*.
3 They can *run* / *fly*.
4 They like *playing* / *sleeping*.

5 Find, think and write the questions.

1 monkeys / Africa / live / do / in — Do monkeys live in Africa?
2 fruit / eat / they / Do — Do they eat fruit?
3 run / they / Can — Can they run?
4 like / What / they / do / doing — What do they like doing?

6 Write the animals in the correct columns. Add four more.

big	small
hippo	bird
giraffe	spider
elephant	mouse

2

7 Look at the code on page 94 and write the message.

BL WYD'H WD HBL NSDMPL.

He isn't in the jungle.

8 Read the text on page 19 again. Then complete the crossword.

1 Elephants say hello with their trunks.
2 Elephants can't jump.

				2 j	
	1 h			u	
	e			m	
3 s	l	e	e	p	
	l				6 d
4 s	o	c	c	e	r
					i
					n
	5 b	l	a	c	k

3 Giraffes can sleep standing up.
4 Elephants can play soccer.
5 Giraffes have long black tongues.
6 Giraffes don't drink every day.

Workbook

Unit 2

9 Find and write the words.

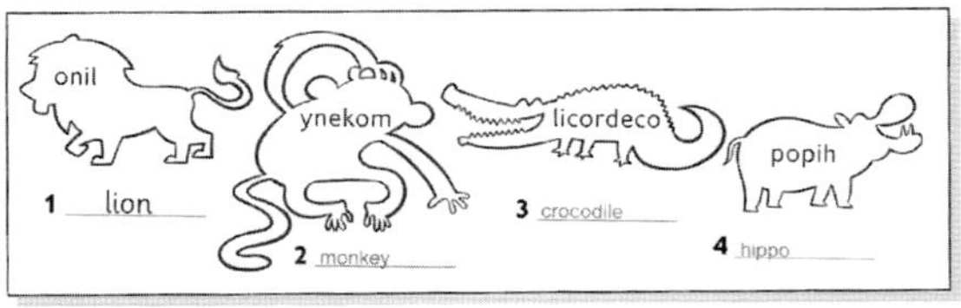

1 lion
2 monkey
3 crocodile
4 hippo

10 Write about monkeys. Use the words in the box.
Answers will vary.

~~fruit~~ trees long tails climb ski

1 Monkeys eat fruit.
2 ______
3 ______
4 ______
5 ______

11 Draw your favorite animal.

12 Write about your favorite animal.
Answers will vary.

It lives in ______ . It can ______ .

It eats ______ . It likes ______ .

Unit 3

3 Weather

1 Match.

sun
cloud
rain
snow
storm
wind

2 Look, read and complete.

Here, the [1] sun is hot.
Here, there's a [2] storm .
Here, there's a strong [3] wind .
Here, there's a lot of [4] rain and there's a big [5] cloud in the sky.
There's [6] snow here today. It's cold.

3 Look and write.

~~wet~~ sunny cloudy snowy ~~rainy~~ stormy windy

1 It's wet and rainy.

2 It's hot and sunny .

3 It's windy .

4 It's snowy . He's cold.

5 It's stormy .

6 It's cloudy .

4 Complete.

What's the weather like today?
Answers will vary.

It's ______ .

Workbook

Unit 3

5 Look and write. Use the words in the box.

~~spring~~ winter fall summer

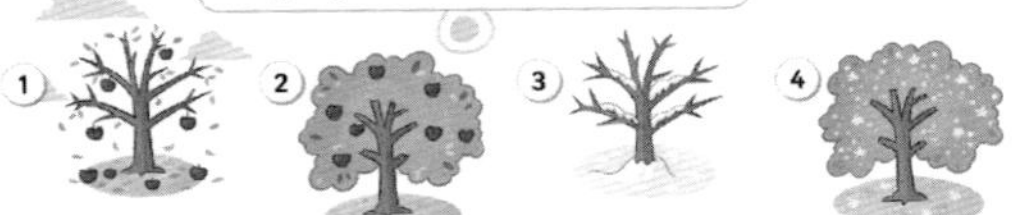

1 It's fall.
2 It's summer.
3 It's winter.
4 It's spring.

6 Look and write. Then match.

snows ~~rains~~ swim fly summer fall

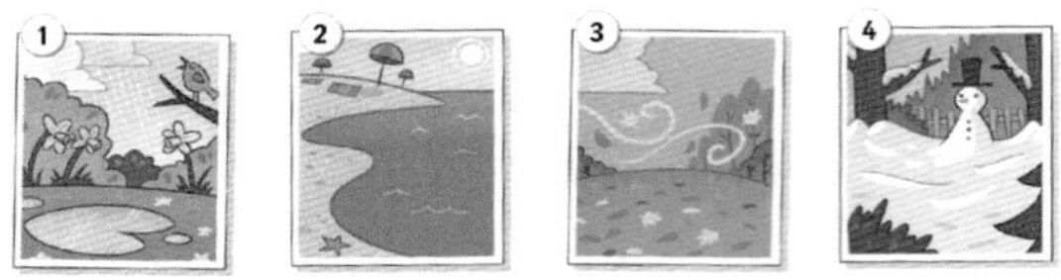

1 It rains in the spring.
2 The sun shines in the summer.
3 The wind blows in the fall.
4 It snows in the winter.

I play in the snow. [4]
[1] I splash in the rain.
I fly my kite. [3]
[2] I swim in the sea.

7 Think and write the words.

~~sunny~~ ~~kite~~ ~~coat~~ ~~birds~~
hot apples snow
windy sea
cold rains flowers

8 Look at the code on page 94 and write the message.

VOD UQS YRWX?

Can you swim?

9 Complete the crossword.

Across →

Down ↓

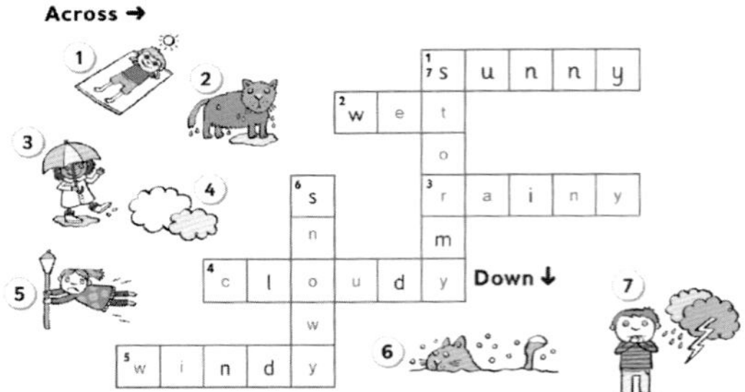

							1 7 s	u	n	n	y
					2 w	e	t				
							o				
				6 s			3 r	a	i	n	y
				n			m				
		4 c	l	o	u	d	y				
				w							
5 w	i	n	d	y							

10 Read the email. Then complete the answer.

Hi! How are you? It's winter here and it's really cold. I love winter. It's my favorite season. I like skiing and playing in the snow with my friends. What's your favorite season? I don't like spring, sometimes there are tornadoes. I don't like rain, but my little sister likes it.
Bye! :-)
Joe

Hi Joe,
It's [1] summer here and it's [2] hot. I [3] like the summer because I'm on vacation. In the summer I [4] go to the park and play [5] soccer with my friends. It's my [6] favorite season. I [7] don't like fall because it's cold and windy. I have a sister, too. She's thirteen.
Bye,
Claire

11 Draw your favorite season.

I CAN DO IT!

12 Write about your favorite season.
Answers will vary.

My favorite season is ______.
I like ______.
I ______.

Workbook

Unit 4

4 My week

1 Look and write.

have music lessons
go swimming
~~go skateboarding~~
have ballet lessons
do gymnastics
do karate

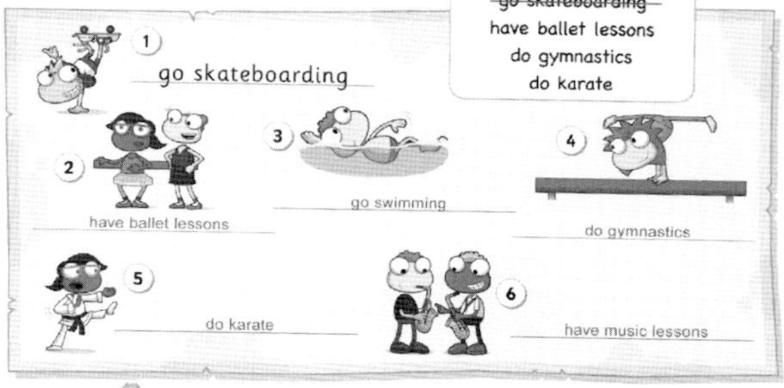

1 go skateboarding
2 have ballet lessons
3 go swimming
4 do gymnastics
5 do karate
6 have music lessons

2 Look, think and complete.

go have do

What do you do on Saturdays?

1 I do gymnastics.
2 I do karate.
3 I go swimming.
4 I go skateboarding.
5 I have ballet lessons.
6 I have music lessons.

3 Look at the calendar and write.

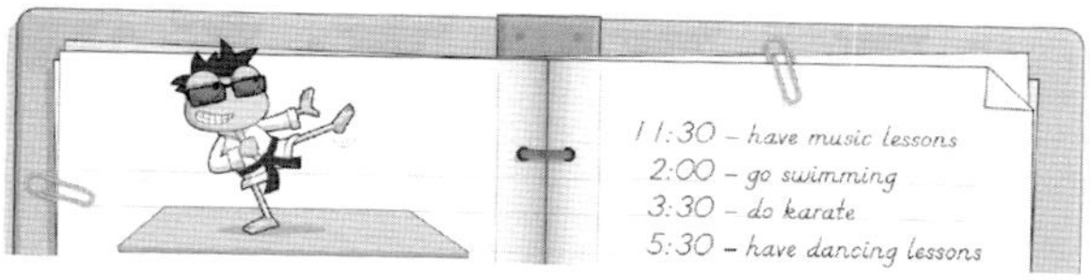

1 He has music lessons at eleven thirty.
2 He goes swimming at two o'clock.
3 He does karate at three thirty.
4 He has dancing lessons at five thirty.

4 How does he/she go to the park? Look, think and write.

1 He goes by bike.
2 She goes by bus.
3 She goes by car.
4 He walks.

5 Follow and write.

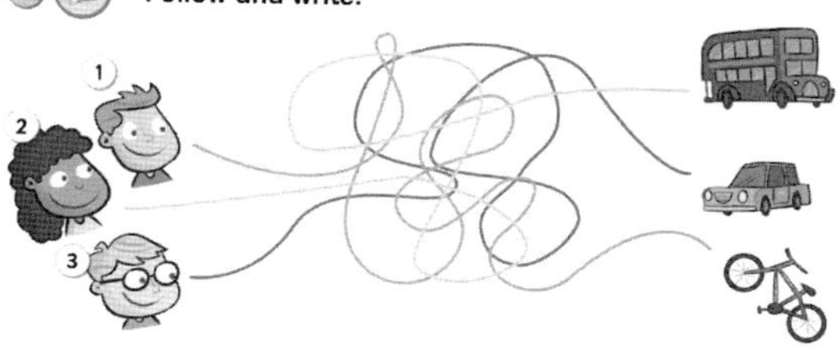

1 He goes to school by bike.
2 She goes to school by bus.
3 He goes to school by car.

6 Unscramble and write sentences.

1 lessons | has | Midge | music | 10 o'clock | at

Midge has music lessons at 10 o'clock.

2 does | thirty | eleven | She | gymnastics | at

She does gymnastics at eleven thirty.

3 o'clock | park | 2 | at | She | to | goes | the

She goes to the park at 2 o'clock.

4 swimming | at | She | four | goes | thirty

She goes swimming at four thirty.

4

7 Look and write.

1 I walk to school.
2 I go to school by train.
3 I go to school by bus.
4 I go to school by bike.

8 Look at the code on page 94 and write the message.

VOD XOZPLU CQQP YRWX?

Can Madley Kool swim?

Workbook

Unit 4

9 Complete the words and find the answer.

1 I have balle t lessons.
2 I have m u sic lessons.

3 I go skat e boarding.
4 I go s wimming.

5 I d o kar a te.
6 I do g y mnastics.

What day is it? T u e s d a y

10 Write about what you do on Mondays.

Monday

9	*school (boat)*	1	I go to school by boat at 9 o'clock.
11	*karate (the park)*	2	I do karate in the park at 11 o'clock.
2	*swimming (the river)*	3	I go swimming in the river at 2 o'clock.
4	*my friend's house*	4	I go to my friend's house at 4 o'clock.
8	*home (boat)*	5	I go home by boat at 8 o'clock.

11 What do you do on Saturdays? Draw a picture.

I CAN DO IT!

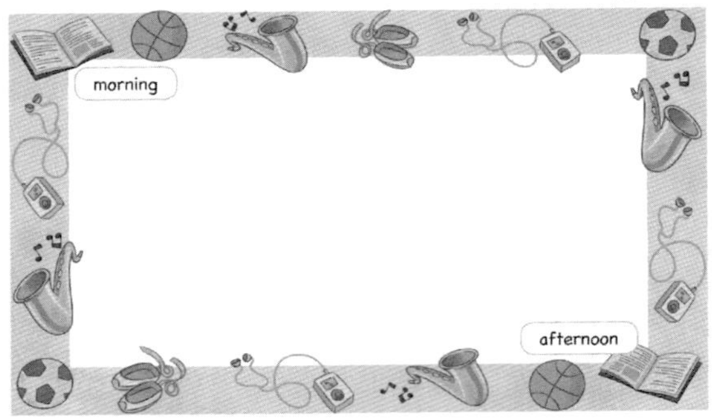

12 Write about what you do on Saturdays.
Answers will vary.

On Saturdays, in the morning, I ____________________

____________________.

In the afternoon, I ____________________

____________________.

Unit 5

5 Jobs

1 Complete the words. a e i o u

1 firefighter
2 basketball player
3 ballet dancer

4 police officer
5 farmer
6 movie star
7 astronaut

2 Look and write.

3 Unscramble the words. Then complete the sentences.

luberid erathec ~~tocrod~~ refram

1 She wants to be a doctor.
2 He wants to be a builder.

3 He wants to be a farmer.
4 She wants to be a teacher.

4 Unscramble and write questions.

1 he want Does to a farmer be
Does he want to be a farmer?

2 want be to teacher Does a she
Does she want to be a teacher?

3 a Does want be to he builder
Does he want to be a builder?

4 doctor she want Does to a be
Does she want to be a doctor?

Workbook

Unit 5

5 Look, think and write.

1 He has a hat.

He wants to be a builder.

2 He has a ball.

He wants to be a basketball player.

3 She has shoes.

She wants to be a ballet dancer.

6 Match.

movie star

farmer

builder

doctor

firefighter

detective

teacher

7 Look at the code on page 94 and write the message.

RBOH ZQ UQS RODH HQ KL?

What do you want to be?

8 Complete the article with words from the box.

playing morning ~~soccer~~ goes plays lunch

HE WANTS TO BE A CHAMPION!

Matthew wants to be a [1] soccer player. He [2] goes running at 7 o'clock in the [3] morning. He eats pasta and chicken for [4] lunch. After lunch he [5] plays soccer. He likes [6] playing computer games on Sundays.

9 Read and circle.

1 Hello, Matthew. What do you want to be? — I want to be a (soccer / basketball) player.

2 What time do you go running in the morning? — I go running at (clocks).

3 What do you eat for lunch? — I eat (pictures).

4 What do you do after lunch? — I (pictures).

5 What do you do on Sundays? — I (pictures) with my friends.

10 Look and write.

1	police officer	6	ballet dancer
2	basketball player	7	firefighter
3	doctor	8	builder
4	teacher	9	movie star
5	farmer	10	astronaut

11 Read and complete. Use the words in the box.

o'clock ~~farmer~~ tired morning
winter bed cows day

I want to be a [1] farmer. I want to have a lot of [2] cows. Farmers get up at five [3] o'clock in the [4] morning. They have a very busy [5] day. Then they go to [6] bed at night. Phew! They're [7] tired. It's fun in the summer, but it's difficult in the [8] winter.

12 What do you want to be? Draw a picture.

I CAN DO IT!

13 Write about what you want to be.

Answers will vary.

I like ______

I can ______

I want to be ______

Good ☆☆☆☆☆ Excellent

Workbook

Unit 6

6 Rainforest

1 Look and write.

~~rainforest~~ waterfall river
mountain valley bridge

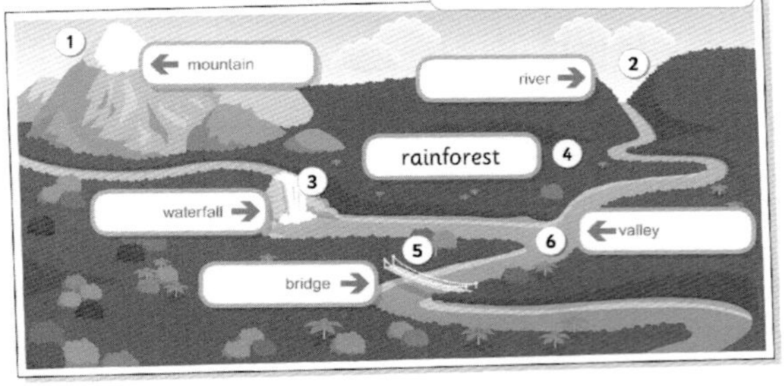

2 Unscramble and write sentences.

1 swimming | I'm | river | the | in
I'm swimming in the river.

2 mountain | a | climbing | I'm
I'm climbing a mountain.

3 a | I'm | walking | on | bridge
I'm walking on a bridge

4 valley | a | walking | I'm | in
I'm walking in a valley

3 Read, look and circle.

1 The monkey is *next to* / *in* the tree.
2 The snake is *in front of* / *next to* the tree.
3 The frog is *next to* / *behind* the tree.
4 The giraffe is *under* / *behind* the tree.

4 Look and write. Use the words in the box.

under on next to
~~in front of~~ behind

1 There's a cat in front of the TV.
2 There's a soccer ball under the table
3 There are skis next to the sofa
4 There's a crocodile behind the sofa
5 There's a hat on the chair

5 Find and write the words.

whales — monkeys — eagles

6 Read and complete.

strong eyes tails wings
~~arms~~ sharp

Monkeys live in the rainforest. They can climb trees. They have long [1] arms and curly [2] tails.

Eagles live in the mountains. They can fly very high. They have [3] sharp claws and silent [4] wings.

Whales live in the sea. They can swim and they can sing. They have [5] strong tails and tiny [6] eyes.

7 Look, think and complete.

eat tails ~~are~~ long live
claws legs

These animals [1] are big. They [2] live in the mountains. They have [3] long necks and short [4] legs. They have sharp [5] claws and curly [6] tails. They [7] eat leaves.

8 Find, circle and write eight words from Unit 6.

r	y	o	n	t	e	c	l	w	i
u	a	m	o	u	n	t	a	i	n
w	h	i	b	h	i	w	b	n	b
a	r	l	n	r	v	a	r	g	r
z	n	o	g	f	r	t	i	s	i
r	i	v	e	r	o	e	d	a	g
j	t	y	w	i	f	r	g	t	a
v	a	l	l	e	y	f	e	e	p
m	i	w	s	t	e	a	c	s	u
u	l	r	s	i	m	l	o	m	t
p	s	l	l	a	c	l	a	z	s
s	z	v	a	s	e	d	f	s	b

1 r ainforest
2 m ountain
3 w aterfall
4 b ridge
5 v alley
6 r iver
7 t ails
8 w ings

Workbook

Unit 6

9 Complete the crossword.

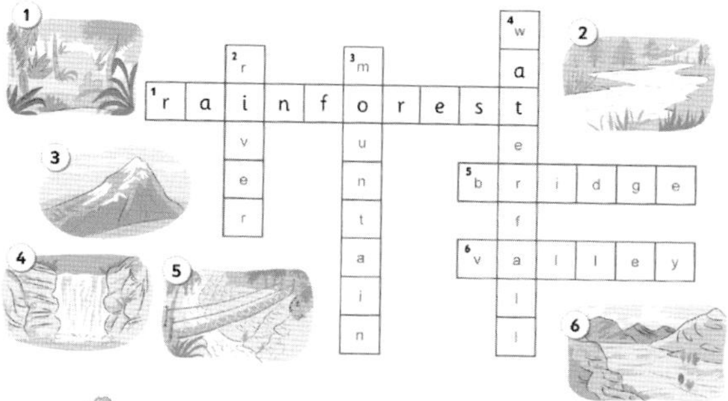

10 Look, think and write.

1 rainforest — They live in the rainforest.
2 long tails — They have long tails.
3 sharp claws — They have sharp claws.
4 fruit and insects — They eat fruit and insects.
5 pretty — They are pretty.

6 I CAN DO IT!

11 Read and draw the animals.

crocodile humming bird hippo
spider snake monkey

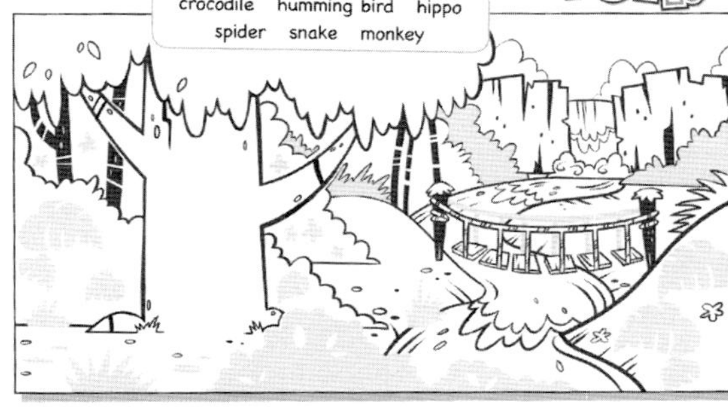

12 Write about your picture. Use the words in the box.

Answers will vary.

next to behind in front of under in on

1 The crocodile is ______________
2 The humming bird is ______________
3 The hippo is ______________
4 The spider is ______________
5 The snake is ______________
6 The monkey is ______________

Good ☆☆☆☆☆ Excellent

Unit 7

7 Feelings

1 Look and write.

tired thirsty angry scared
sad thrilled ~~hungry~~ happy

1 He's hungry.
2 She's tired.
3 She's thirsty.
4 He's happy.
5 He's angry.
6 She's scared.
7 She's sad.
8 He's thrilled.

2 Draw how you and your friend are feeling. Then write.

Answers will vary.

3 Look and write. Use the words in the box.

crying laughing ~~smiling~~
thirsty angry hungry

1 She's smiling.
2 He's hungry.
3 She's thirsty.
4 He's angry.
5 She's laughing.
6 He's crying.

4 Look at Activity 3. Read and match.

1 Why is she smiling?
2 Why is he eating?
3 Why is she drinking?
4 Why is he shouting?
5 Why is she laughing?
6 Why is he crying?

a Because he's hungry.
b Because it's funny.
c Because she's happy.
d Because he's sad.
e Because she's thirsty.
f Because he's angry.

Workbook

Unit 7

5 **Read the answers and complete the questions. Use the words in the box.**

hungry ~~thrilled~~ thirsty scared happy

1 Doing exercises makes me feel thrilled.
2 Spiders make me feel scared.
3 My friends make me feel happy.
4 Seeing drinks makes me thirsty.
5 Seeing food makes me hungry.

6 **Look, think and write.**
Answers will vary.

1 They make me feel scared.
2 They make me ______
3 They ______
4 They ______
5 They ______

7

7 **Read and match.**

1 Rainy days make me feel sad
2 Parties makes me feel thrilled
3 Reading books makes me feel happy
4 Spiders make me feel scared

a because I love stories.
b because I like the sun.
c because they're fun.
d because they're horrible.

8 **Read and number.**

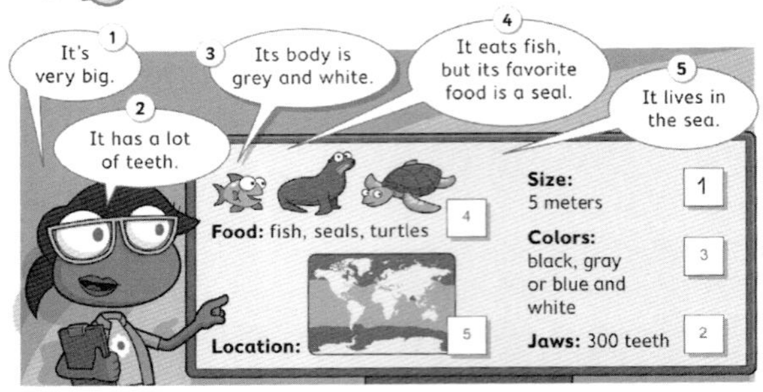

9 **Look, think and write.**

Small [1] fish are scared of [2] big fish.
Seals are [3] scared of great [4] white sharks.
Big [5] fish are scared of [6] seals.

10 **Read and circle.**

It makes me feel *happy* / *scared*. (circled: scared)

It makes me *cry* / *laugh*. (circled: laugh)

It makes me feel *sad* / *happy*. (circled: happy)

It makes me feel *sad* / *scared*. (circled: sad)

11 **Look and circle. Draw and write the one that is missing.**

tired

7

12 **What makes you feel happy and scared? Draw pictures.**

I CAN DO IT!

13 **Write about your pictures.**
Answers will vary.

______ me feel happy.
______ me feel scared.

Unit 8

8 By the sea

1 Match.

surfing
horseback riding
fishing
snorkeling
sailing

2 Look and complete.

Jenny is [1] sailing. Sam is [2] surfing, John is [3] horseback riding and Ruby is [4] fishing. Cleo is on the [5] beach.

Jenny is [6] fishing. Sam is [7] horseback riding, John is [8] sailing and Ruby is [9] surfing. Cleo is in the [10] sea.

3 Look, read and complete.

1 What's she doing?
She's watching TV.

2 What's she doing?
She's playing soccer.

3 What's he doing?
He's surfing

4 What's he doing?
He's snorkeling

5 What's she doing?
She's reading.

6 What's he doing?
He's fishing

4 Look, think and write. Answers will vary

What do you like? What are you scared of?

sharks the sea horses crocodiles storms doctors

I like	I don't like	I'm scared of

5 Look, read and complete. Use the words in the boxes.

~~bored with~~ fond of scared of terrified of

sunny walking watching ~~raining~~ plays tennis drinking bus

Lucy is [1] bored with the weather. It's [2] raining. She likes [3] sunny weather because she's [4] fond of tennis. She [5] plays tennis on Tuesdays. Today is Tuesday but it's raining.

Lucy is [6] walking to the tennis club. She doesn't go by [7] bus because she's [8] scared of buses. ZAP! A storm! Lucy is [9] terrified of storms. Poor Lucy!

Lucy is home again. She's [10] watching TV and she's [11] drinking some hot chocolate. She's happy. But there's a spider in the living room. Oh dear! Lucy is [12] terrified of spiders. This isn't a very good day!

8

6 Read and complete.

movie making acting saves people sharks man ~~movie star~~

Madley Kool is a great [1] movie star ! He likes [2] making adventure movies. His new [3] movie is **Great Whites**. In this movie, there are some big [4] sharks. Madley Kool plays a brave [5] man in the movie. He [6] saves a lot of [7] people from the sharks. But in real life, Madley Kool is scared of sharks. He says, 'I like [8] acting with people, but sharks are scary.'

7 Read. Then match.

PENGUINS
Adélie Penguins live in Antarctica. They live on the land and in the sea. They eat a lot of fish. In the winter they go swimming a lot because it is very cold on land. They can swim, but they can't fly. The penguins are black, white and red. They have long tails and they live for twenty years.

1 Do they live in Antarctica?
2 Do they eat fish?
3 Can they swim?
4 Can they fly?
5 Are they black and pink?
6 Do they have long tails?

a No, they aren't.
b Yes, they do.
c Yes, they can.
d Yes, they do.
e No, they can't.
f Yes, they do.

Workbook

Unit 8

8 Find the odd one out.

1 ~~insect~~ cleaning reading skiing
2 lion crocodile ~~cry~~ hippo
3 Tuesday ~~November~~ Friday Sunday
4 ~~scared~~ snowy wet rainy
5 astronaut ~~beach~~ basketball player builder
6 river waterfall ~~plane~~ rainforest
7 horseback riding sailing fishing ~~winter~~

9 Read and complete. Use the words in the box.

ballet dancer skateboarding of ~~fall~~ by like
and morning terrified Saturday o'clock

Hi, I'm Elizabeth. My favorite season is [1] fall and I love the pretty colors. The leaves on the trees are orange [2] and red. I [3] like horseback riding. I'm not scared [4] of horses but I am [5] terrified of spiders! I love my horse. I like ballet, too. I want to be a [6] ballet dancer. I have lessons on Mondays and Saturdays at school. My lessons start at eight [7] o'clock in the [8] morning. It's very early! I go [9] by bike because it isn't far away. On [10] Saturday afternoons I go to the park and go [11] skateboarding with my friends.

10 What do you like doing on vacation? Draw a picture.

I CAN DO IT! 8

11 Write about what you like doing on vacation.
Answers will vary.

On vacation I like ______________________

____

Good ☆☆☆☆☆ Excellent

Picture dictionary

Picture dictionary

Free time

swimming playing soccer cleaning reading

skiing cooking watching TV riding my bike

playing the guitar skateboarding playing computer games

Animals

elephant lion monkey giraffe crocodile hippo

insects fruit grass meat leaves

Weather and seasons

spring summer fall winter cold hot

sunny cloudy snowy rainy stormy windy wet

Picture dictionary

My week

get up, go to bed, go skateboarding, go swimming, go to school, go to the park, go to a party, do karate, do gymnastics, have ballet lessons, have music lessons

Jobs

firefighter, police officer, movie star, farmer, ballet dancer, basketball player, astronaut, teacher, builder, doctor

The natural world

waterfall, mountain, rainforest, river, bridge, valley, sea, eagle, whale

141

Feelings

tired, thirsty, hungry, angry, scared, thrilled, happy, sad, smiling, laughing, crying, shouting

By the sea

sailing, surfing, snorkeling, horseback riding, fishing, beach, coral reef

Christmas

turkey, Christmas tree, Christmas present, snowman, board game

Mother's Day

card, box of chocolates, tea, toast, rose

142

Game Bank

Playing games is an essential part of growing up and learning, as children experiment, discover, and interact with their environment. Not to include games in the language classroom would be to deprive children of an essential tool for understanding their world. The context provided by a game makes the foreign language immediately useful, making the reasons for speaking plausible even to reluctant children. They also allow for meaningful repetition because, although students can play a game several times, it never produces identical results.

However, it is essential that you are clear about what you expect from the children. Consider the children's active and passive language knowledge in relation to the response the game requires. The personal characteristics of the group are also important: whether they are very active and energetic or rather passive, if their attention span is short or long, what the boy-girl ratio is, as sometimes boys refuse to play on the same team as girls, or hold hands with them.

As regards the use of L1, there are times when an explanation in Portuguese can be helpful, especially when using a game which includes concepts and procedures the children have not yet learned, or when the procedure is somewhat complicated. If you start explaining a game in English and realize the class does not understand it, a short prompt in Portuguese will help you. If you stick to English regardless of the situation, children will become impatient and it might mean trouble for classroom management.

Flashcard Games

Flashcard Act Out: Choose one or more students to come to the front. Show a flashcard or whisper a word, and have the students act it out. This can be used with many topics (e.g., sports, actions, verbs, animals, etc.).

Hot Seat: A student sits with his/her back to the board or to the teacher. The teacher displays a flashcard. Other students describe what is on the card so that the student guesses what it is.

Jumping the Line: Put a piece of masking tape across the middle of the classroom floor. Designate one side as 'true' and the other as 'false'. Line up the students on the masking tape line, hold up a flashcard and say a word. If it matches the flashcard, students jump to the 'true' side, otherwise they jump to the 'false' side. Students who make a mistake miss a round.

Make a Sentence: Display the flashcards on the board and divide the class into two teams. One student from each team chooses a vocabulary item and uses it correctly in a sentence. Teams can repeat items, but they cannot repeat the sentence. Give a point for each correct sentence.

Memory Buzz: This game can be played mixing mini cards or flashcards of target vocabulary in any unit. Display flashcards around the room. Have the students sit in a circle and start building a sentence. Student A says, *In the classroom, I see a rock*. Student B says, *In the classroom, I see a rock and a map*. Student C says, *In the classroom I see a clock, a map and a chair,* etc. If played with mini cards, divide the class into small groups and proceed in the same way. For a variation, see 'Question Chain'.

Picture Guess: Have a student come up to the front and show him/her a flashcard. He/She draws it on the board. The first student to guess the picture gets a point. This can also be played in teams.

Race to Touch: Lay the flashcards on the floor at one end of the classroom, and have students line up in teams at the other end. Call out a flashcard and have the first student in each team race to grab the card. Those students then go to the back and the next students race to grab the next flashcard the teacher calls.

Run and Get It: Divide the class into two teams and have them stand in two lines facing each other. Assign each team member a number from one to four. Place a few flashcards in the middle of the two teams. Call a number and a flashcard (e.g., *Student three – rabbit*). The students assigned that number run into the center, touch the flashcard and shout the word. The student who touches and calls first can take the flashcard to his/her team.

The Ball: Pass a flashcard around a circle of students. Then ring a bell or blow a whistle. The student holding the flashcard answers a question or makes a sentence with it.

Mini card Games

Memory Game: Students work in pairs with two sets of mini cards spread out face down on the table. They take turns turning over two cards and saying the words on the cards. If the cards are a match, the student keeps the cards. If they are different, they are turned face down. The student with the most pairs is the winner.

Quick Peek: Divide the class into pairs. Student A takes a mini card and quickly shows it, so that Student B gets just a quick peek. If Student B guesses it correctly, he/she keeps it. If he/she doesn't, Student A keeps the card.

What's Missing? Students work in pairs. They scatter mini cards face up on the table. Student A closes his/her eyes and Student B takes away one card. Tell Student A to open his/her eyes and ask *What's missing?* Reward the student that guesses correctly.

TPR Games

Aye, Aye, Captain!: You are the captain. Give orders to the class. This is a useful activity to review actions, body parts, colors, numbers, and classroom objects. Say, *Jump three times, Touch your (head), Turn around,* etc. Children say *'Aye, aye, Captain!'* and carry out the order. Model a few times and then invite students to be the Captain.

Ball/Bean Toss: Say a day of the week (e.g., *Wednesday*). Throw a ball or bean toss to a student. He/She says the following day and throws the ball to another student. They go on until somebody makes a mistake. Play this game to practice any lexical set as a class or in groups.

Basketball: Ask a question to a student. If he/she answers correctly, he/she has a shot at the basket. If the student gets the ball in the basket, he/she wins two points. If he/she only hits the basket, he/she wins one point. The student who gets the most points is the winner. This can also be played in teams.

Category/Topic Tag: Choose a lexical category (e.g., family, face, animals, numbers or food). Students run around the room and you pretend to chase them in order to tag them. When you tag a student, he/she must name a word from the category. Set a time limit to answer. If the student answers correctly, he/she takes up your role. If he/she cannot answer, or says a word that has already been used, he/she sits out until the next round. This is a great game to play in the courtyard.

Teacher Says: Give students instructions, but tell them to follow the instructions only if they are preceded by *Teacher says*. If you say *Pick up a pencil*, students should do nothing, but if you say Teacher says pick up a pencil, students pick it up. They lose a point for doing an action when they shouldn't. Vary the speed of the instructions to make the game more interesting. You could also ask some students to give the instructions.

The Ball II: Throw a soft/paper ball to a student and ask a question. The student answers and throws the ball to another student, asking the same question (e.g., *Can you swim? Yes, I can./No, I can't*).

Team Games

Category Writing: Divide the classroom into two or three groups. Each group chooses their 'captain'. The teacher writes on the board a vocabulary category, like SPORTS or FOOD. Each group tells their captain to write down as many words as they can which belong to that category. They have one or two minutes to do that. Each group takes one point for each correct word. Pay close attention to spelling.

Charades: Divide the class into two groups. Write down vocabulary words in strips of paper. Choose a member from each group to come up to the front of the class. Take one of the strips of paper and show it to these two students. Next, ask them to face their groups, with their backs turned against each other. Without talking, students act out the vocabulary for the other members of the group to guess. Set a time limit of 60 seconds. The student who correctly guesses the vocabulary word wins the round and earns a point for his / her group. The group with the highest score wins the game.

Picture relay: Divide the students into two teams. Whisper a word to the first member of both teams and have them draw the word on the board as fast as possible. Their teams guess the word. Award points to the fastest team.

Spelling Bee: This can be done with the whole class or in two teams. The first player on Team A is given a word to spell. If correct, the team gets a point. If you do it as a class competition, line the students up and give them words one by one. When they make a mistake they sit down. The last student standing is the winner.

Miscellaneous Games

Bingo: it can be used with any topic. Ask students to draw the bingo grids. Then they write or draw in the boxes the vocabulary items you wish to review. The winner is the first student to cross out all the numbers/words on the grid. Don't use more than 6 – 8 squares, otherwise the game will take too long.

Conversation Relay: Line up the students in two teams and have the last one in each team tap the shoulder of the student in front and have a conversation (e.g., *What's your name?, How are you?*). The student who answers then follows the conversation with the student in front, and so on. When the conversations reach the front, the students at the front run to the back and continue the procedure. The first team to get all the students back in their original positions wins.

Give me one: Choose a word students have learned (e.g., giraffe). Then say, *Give me a G!* The class calls, *G!* Then call out the second letter of the word, e.g., *Give me an I*, and so on, until the word has been spelled out. Then ask, *What word is it?* The students answer. The first student to call the word correctly takes up your role. After two or three rounds, divide the class into two groups and play the game as a competition. This game can be played with any vocabulary set.

Hangman: Divide students into teams. Choose a word and write the appropriate number of spaces on the board. Students guess a letter one by one. If they guess correctly, write that letter in the space and give a point to the team. If the guess is incorrect, start drawing a hanging man and have the next team guess a letter.

I Spy: Say, *I spy with my little eye something beginning with G*. Students guess the object. You can also play the game to review colors (e.g., *I spy with my little eye something blue*).

Letter Mess: Write a selection of letters on the board. Explain to the class that they have to make up as many words as possible from the given letters within a time limit. Give one or two examples on the board before starting the game.

Lexical Groups: Say a family word, e.g., *father,* then point to a student. He/She says the corresponding pair (*mother*). This student points to another, who says, *father, mother, and sister*. Continue until all students have taken part in the chain. Keep a fast pace to maintain interest. This game can be used with any lexical set.

Question Chain: Students sit in a circle. Start by asking the student on the right a question (e.g., *What's your name?, Can you play football?, Do you like beans?, Are you wearing shorts?,* etc.), according to the type of question you want the class to practice. He/she answers and asks another question to the next student. Go on until somebody makes a mistake.

Pass the Secret: Tell the students to sit in a circle. Start the secret by whispering a simple sentence to the student next to you (e.g., *I have a yellow hat*). The students pass the secret around the circle. The last student says the secret out loud. Compare how close it is to the original secret. If necessary, write the original secret on the board.

Picture Dictation: Divide the class into pairs. Student A describes a picture to Student B, who draws it. Then, they switch roles. This game can be played with any lexical set.

Stop the bus: Write a letter on the board, and shout, Start the bus! Students write as many words beginning with this letter as they can think of. When you shout out, *Stop the bus!*, everyone stops writing. Students get one point for each word.

Tests Teaching Notes

Evaluation can be described as an attempt to analyze the learning that a child has achieved over a period of time as a result of the classroom teaching/learning situation. It plays an integral part in the teaching and learning process.

The evaluation material included in *Our Discovery Island* has been designed to assess students' progress with the aim of reinforcing the positive aspects and identifying areas for improvement.

There are five main reasons for evaluation:

Formative – to increase motivation by making evaluation a part of the continuous learning process.

Summative – to give students feedback on their progress or achievement at a particular point in time, often formally through tests.

Informative – to give students and parents feedback on progress or achievements.

Diagnostic – to monitor individual students' needs and help identify students who need special support.

Evaluative – to identify students' level of achievement and select or order students according to merit, to check effectiveness of teaching methods, teaching materials and teachers.

Our Discovery Island provides four photocopiable tests for use every two units. It also encourages self-evaluation at the end of each unit in the Workbook, giving students an important opportunity to express their own opinion of their progress.

Test – Units 1 and 2

Materials students will need for the test: pencil or pen

1 Listen to Katy and Dan. Then write (K) or (D).

- Ask students to look at the pictures. Explain (L1) that you are going to read a dialogue between Katy and Dan. Students listen and write (K) or (D) to identify what each of them like doing.

Teacher script

Katy Hi Dan! Do you like cleaning?
Dan Yes, I do, but I don' like cooking. And you?
Katy I like cooking! And I like reading. What do you like doing?
Dan I like swimming and watching TV. Do you like playing soccer?
Katy Yes!!!!, I do!!! And you?
Dan Well... (*a bit ashamed*) No... I don't.

Key
Dan watching TV, swimming, cleaning
Katy playing soccer (example given), reading, cooking

1.5/10 = 0.25 point for each correct answer.

2 Look at Activity 1 and write about Katy and Dan.

- Students write one sentence about Katy and another one about Dan, using the information from Activity 1.

Key – Possible answers:
Dan likes watching TV.
Katy likes playing soccer.

1/10 = 0.5 point for each correct answer.

3 Read. Then write (T) or (F).

- Focus students' attention on the sentences. Tell them to read the text and decide if they are true or false.

Key **1** T **2** F **3** T **4** F

2/10 = 0.5 point for each correct answer.

4 Write about you and your family.

- Ask students to write four sentences about them and some of their family members, saying what they like or don't like doing. In sentences 3 and 4, ask students to choose one of the family members listed and circle it.

Key – Possible answers:
1 I like skateboarding.
2 I don't like cleaning.
3 My dad/brother/grandpa likes reading.
4 My mom/sister/grandma doesn't like swimming.

2/10 = 0.5 point for each correct answer.

5 Listen and √ the correct food.

- Focus students' attention on the table. Explain that you are going to read a dialogue and they have to check the correct food.

Teacher script

Student	What do lions eat?
Teacher	They eat meat.
Student	And giraffes? Do giraffes eat meat?
Teacher	No, giraffes and elephants don't eat meat. They eat leaves. Elephants eat grass too.
Student	And monkeys? Do monkeys eat meat and fish?
Teacher	No, monkeys like fruit.

Key

elephant – grass/leaves; giraffe – grass/leaves; monkey – fruit; lion – meat

2/10 = 0.5 point for each correct answer.

6 Read, think and answer.

- Focus students' attention on the questions. Tell them to think about what they have learned about these animals and answer the questions.

Key

2 No, they don't.
3 No, they can't.
4 They like sleeping in the sun.
5 No, they don't.

2/10 = 0.5 point for each correct answer.

Test – Units 3 and 4

Materials students will need for the test: pencil or pen

1 Listen and number.

- Focus students' attention on the pictures of the weather. Explain that you are going to read three short dialogues and they have to number them in the correct order.

Teacher script:

1

Child What's the weather like today, dad?
Dad It's snowy and windy.
Child Ohhh! I can't play.

2

Child What's the weather like today, mom?
Mom It's wet and stormy.
Child Oh, I'm scared!

3

Child What's the weather like today?
Children It's hot and it's sunny. We're happy, let's play soccer!

Key 3,1, 2

1.5/10 = 0.5 point for each picture numbered correctly.

2 Listen. Then look at Activity 1 and write the weather.

- Read Script from Activity 1 again. Students look at the pictures from the previous activity and write sentences about the weather.

Key
1 windy.
2 wet / stormy.
3 hot / sunny.

2/10 = 0.4 point for each correct word.

3 Look. Then, read and complete.

- Students complete the sentences using the words in the box.

Key summer / hot / sunny / sea / swimming / eating

1.5/10 = 0.5 point for each correct answer.

4 Read and circle the correct answer.

- Ask students to read the text about Ron and circle the correct word in each pair.

Key
lowers / rains / spring / windy / likes / splashes / rain / season

2/10 = 0.5 point for each correct circled word.

5 What does Maria do on Saturdays? Listen and write.

- Focus students' attention on the picture. Tell them that you are going to read about the things Maria has to do on Saturday. Students listen and complete the diary. Read it a few times. Give students time to write the sentences.

Teacher script:
Today is Saturday and Maria has a busy day. She does gymnastics at 9 o'clock. At ten thirty she has music class. She loves music! At one o'clock she goes home. She goes swimming with her mother at three thirty and at five o'clock she goes skateboarding with her friends. At eight o'clock she has dinner and she goes to bed at nine o'clock.

Key
She has music class. / 1:00 / She goes swimming. / She goes skateboarding. / 8:00 / 9:00

1.5/10 = 0.5 point for each correct answer.

6 Now write how Maria goes to those places.

- Students read the sentences and look at the pictures of means of transportation. Then they follow the example and write complete sentences.

Key
2 She goes to music class by car.
3 She goes home by bus.
4 She goes swimming by bike.

1.5/10= 0.5 point for each correct sentence.

Test – Units 5 and 6

Materials students will need for the test: pencil or pen, colored pencil (optional)

1 Listen, look and circle. Then write.

- Focus students' attention to the pictures. Explain that you are going to read a dialogue and they have to identify the job each child wants to have in the future. Read it a few times so that students have time to circle the correct job for each child.

Teacher script

1
Suzy What do you want to be, Lucia?
Lucia I want to be a ballet dancer. I love dancing!
2
Mark What do you want to be, Suzy?
Suzy I love movies. I want to be a movie star.
3
Suzy And what about you, Mark? Do you want to be a movie star too?
Mark Oh, no! I like playing basketball. I want to be a basketball player. I want to play with the Lakers!!
4
Lucia And you, Willy? Do you want to be a basketball player too?
Mark Ha! Ha! No, Willy doesn't like basketball. He likes animals!!
Willy Yes, I like horses, and cows, and hens... I want to be a farmer.
Key movie star /basketball player / farmer

1.5/10 = 0.5 point for each correct answer.

2 Listen. Then write.

- Read Script from Activity 1 again. Repeat a few times so students have time to complete the sentences with the correct job.

Key
Suzy to be a movie star.
Mark want to be a basketball player.
Willy I want to be a farmer.

1.5/10 = 0.5 point for each correct answer.

3 Look at the table and write sentences.

- Tell the class to look at the table. Then they complete the sentences.

Key
Anihoa doesn't want to be a builder.
Daniela doesn't want to be a builder.
Daniela wants to be a firefighter.
Luka doesn't want to be a doctor.

2/10 = 0.5 point for each correct answer.

4 Look and complete. What does Harry want to be?

- Students use the word bank to complete the sentences about Harry.

Key
player / Spain / tennis classes / Tuesday / Friday / friends

1.5/10 = 0.25 point for each correct word.

5 Listen and draw.

- Tell the class that you are going to read a dialogue and they have to draw the things they hear in the correct places. Students may use colored pencil for this activity.

Teacher script
Sarah Daniel, do you have my skateboard?
Daniel Yes, it's next to the sofa. Hey, where are my books?
Sarah They're under the table.
Daniel ...and where's my basketball?
Sarah Mmm.... There!! It's behind you!
Sarah AGHHHH!!!!! LOOK! A SNAKE!!!!!
Daniel Where?
Sarah There!!! In front of you!!!!

Key
a skateboard next to the sofa, **books** under the table, **a basketball** behind the boy and **a snake** in front of the boy.

1/10 = 0.25 point for each correct drawing.

6 Look, read and complete.

- Focus students' attention on the text and the words in the box and tell them to complete the description.

Key jump / tiny / strong / sharp / meat

2.5/10 = 0.5 point for each correct answer.

Test – Units 7 and 8

Materials students will need for the test: pencil or pen

1 Listen, look and number.

- Focus students' attention on the pictures. Explain that you are going to read five short dialogues and students have to number each child to the feeling expressed by each of them in the dialogue. Read the dialogue a few times so that students have time to decide and number.

Teacher script

1

Adult Why are you angry, Naomi?
Naomi Where's my skateboard?? Do you have my skateboard? I can't find my skateboard!!!!!

2

Adult Hi, Benjamin. How are you?
Benjamin Hi. I'm veeery tired! Uffff...

3

Adult Laura, why are you happy?
Laura: Look!!! That's Madley Kool!! My favorite movie star!!! OOOHHHHH!!!

4

Adult voice Greg!!! Please!!!
Greg I'm hungry!!!

5

Emma HEEELPP!!!!!HELLPP!!!!!
Adult voice What's wrong, Emma? What happens?
Emma Look!!! A frog!!!I'm scared of frogs!!!

Key **2** tired **3** happy **4** hungry **5** scared

2/10 = 0.5 point for each correct number.

2 Look at Activity 1. Then write.

- Students choose two characters from Activity 1 and write one sentence for each, telling how they are feeling.

Key – Suggested answers:
Naomi is angry. / Benjamin is tired. / Laura is happy. / Greg is hungry. / Emma is scared.

1/10 = 0.5 point for each correct sentence.

3 Look, think and write.

- Focus students' attention on the picture and tell them to complete the sentences asking and answering about how the people are feeling.

Key
2 Why is he crying? Because he's sad.
3 Why is he shouting? Because he's angry.
4 Why is he eating? Because he's hungry.
5 Why is she drinking? Because she's thirsty.
6 Why is she smiling? Because she's happy.

2.5/10 = 0.25 point for each correct question/answer.

4 Complete the sentence about you.

- Ask students to think about what makes them feel happy, sad, tired, etc. Then students complete the sentence about themselves.

Key – Suggested answers:
Playing basketball makes me feel tired. / Sad movies make me cry.

1/10 = 0.5 point for each correct sentence.

5 Look, read and write.

- Focus students' attention on the pictures and the sentences. They complete with the missing words, using the pictures as a hint.

Key hot / fond of / river / bored with / scared of / terrified of

1.5/10 = 0.25 point for each correct answer.

6 Write about you.

- Students write four sentences about themselves.

Key – Suggested answers:
1 I'm fond of dancing.
2 I'm terrified of snakes.
3 I'm bored with tennis.
4 I'm scared of spiders.

2/10 = 0.5 point for each correct sentence.

Test – Units 1 And 2

NAME: ______________________ CLASS: __________

TEACHER: ______________________ SCORE: __________

1 Listen to Katy and Dan. Then write (K) or (D).

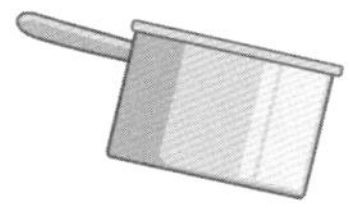
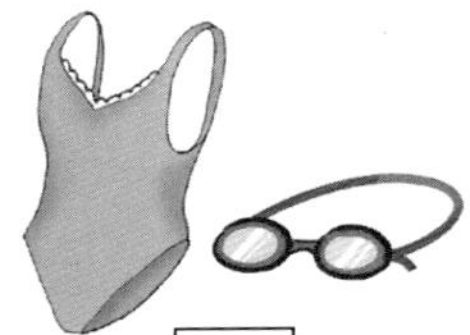

K | ☐ | ☐ | ☐ | ☐ | ☐

2 Look at Activity 1 and write about Katy and Dan.

Katy ______________________________

Dan ______________________________

3 Read. Then write (T) or (F).

Hi! I'm Jimmy. I like skateboarding and swimming. My dad doesn't like skateboarding. He likes skiing. My mom likes reading, and she likes watching TV. She likes riding her bike and my father likes riding his scooter. I have two brothers, Tim and Jerry. Tim likes playing the guitar and sleeping, he doesn't like playing soccer or swimming. Jerry likes skiing and playing soccer.

1 Jimmy likes swimming. ☐

2 Jimmy's mom likes playing soccer. ☐

3 She likes reading and watching TV. ☐

4 Tim likes playing soccer and swimming. ☐

4 Write about you and your family.

1 I like ______________________________

2 I don't like ______________________________

3 My dad / brother / grandpa likes ______________________________

4 My mom / sister / grandma doesn't like ______________________________

5 Listen and ✓ the correct food.

Elephant				
Giraffe				
Monkey				
Lion				

6 Read, think and answer.

1 Where do lions live?

They live in Africa.

2 Do crocodiles eat bananas?

____

3 Can elephants jump?

____

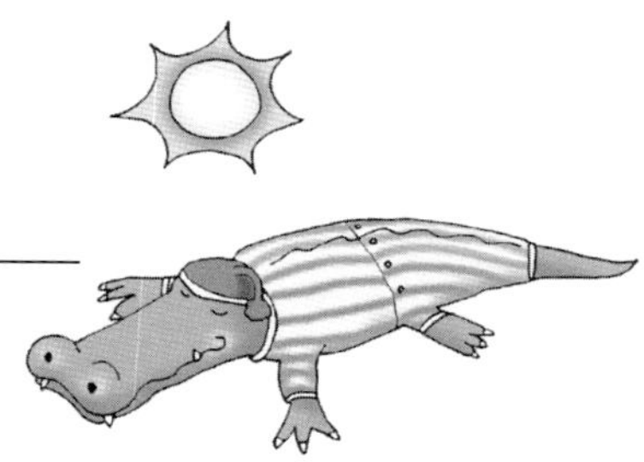

4 What do crocodiles like doing?

____

5 Do elephants like insects?

____

Test– Units 3 And 4

NAME: ______________________ CLASS: __________

TEACHER: ______________________ SCORE: __________

1 Listen and number.

2 Listen. Then look at Activity 1 and write the weather.

1 It's snowy and ____________.

2 It's ____________ and ____________.

3 It's ____________ and ____________.

3 Look. Then, read and complete.

hot sunny sea
swimming eating summer ~~season~~

My favorite season is ____________.

It's ____________ and ____________. I like going to the ____________ with my family. I like ____________ and ____________ ice-cream.

4 Read and circle the correct answer.

It's spring. There are a lot of ***birds*** **/ *clouds*** and ***flowers / snow*** in the trees. It ***snows / rains*** in the ***summer / spring*** and it's ***windy / snowy***. Ron ***likes / don't like*** the spring. He ***splashes / swims*** in the ***snow / rain***. Spring is Ron's favorite ***weather / season***.

5 What does Maria do on Saturdays? Listen and write.

Saturday	
9.00	She does gymnastics.
10.30	
	She goes home.
3.30	
5.00	
	She has dinner.
	She goes to bed.

6 Now write how Maria goes to those places.

1 Maria / gym / 

Maria goes to the gym by bus.

2 She / music lessons / 

____

3 She/ home / 

____

4 She / swimming / 

____

Test – Units 5 And 6

NAME: ______________________ **CLASS:** __________

TEACHER: ______________________ **SCORE:** __________

1 Listen, look and circle.

2 Listen. Then write.

Lucia I want to be a ballet dancer.

Suzy I want ______________________.

Mark I ______________________.

Willy ______________________.

3 Look at the table and write the sentences.

	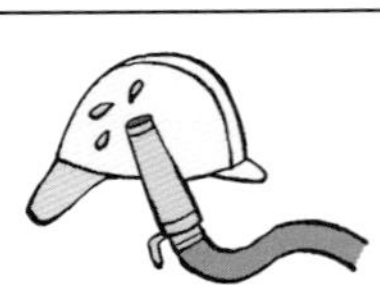	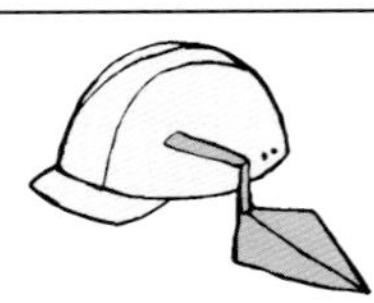	
Luka	✓		
Ahinoa			✓
Daniela	✓		

Luka wants to be a firefighter.

Ahinoa ______________________ builder

Daniela ______________________ builder

Daniela ______________________ firefighter.

Luka ______________________ a doctor.

4 Look and complete. What does Harry want to be?

Spain	~~playing tennis~~	player	
tennis classes	Tuesday	friends	Friday

Harry loves playing tennis.

His favorite __________ is Rafael Nadal. He's from __________.

He has __________ at three on __________ and __________.

He plays with his __________ on Saturday.

He wants to be a famous tennis player

5 Listen and draw.

6 Look, read and complete.

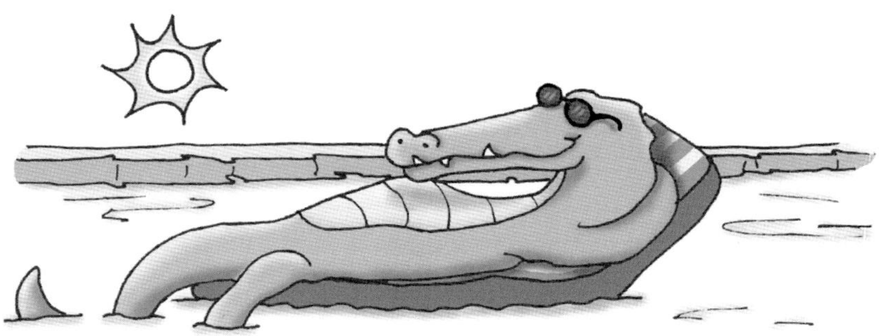

sharp	~~swim~~	tiny	strong	meat	jump

Crocodiles live next to rivers. They can swim, but they can't __________.

They have __________ eyes and a very __________ tail.

They have __________ teeth. They like sleeping in the sun and eating __________.

Test – Units 7 And 8

NAME: ______________________ CLASS: __________

TEACHER: ______________________ SCORE: __________

1 Listen, look and number.

1 Naomi | 2 Benjamin | 3 Laura | 4 Greg | 5 Emma

tired [ ] | hungry [ ] | happy [ ] | angry [1] | scared [ ]

2 Look at Activity 1. Then write.

____

____

3 Look, think and write.

WHY?

drinking eating
crying shouting
~~laughing~~ smiling

BECAUSE

angry ~~funny~~
sad thirsty
hungry happy

1 Why is he laughing?
Because it's funny.

2 Why ______________________?
Because ______________________.

3 ____?

____.

4 ____?

____.

5 ____?

____.

6 ____?

____.

4 Complete the sentence about you.

____________________ make/makes me feel ____________________.

5 Look, read and write

Jeremy is on vacation. He's in the 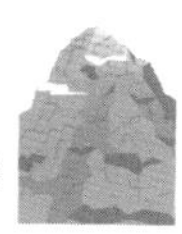 __mountains__ with his friends. It's 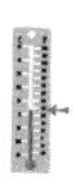 ____________ and sunny and there are lots of things to do. He's  ____________ swimming in the  ____________ and climbing, but he's  ____________ fishing. He has a problem. He's  ____________ spiders and  ____________ snakes!!

6 Write about you.

1 I'm fond of ____.

2 I'm terrified of ____.

3 I'm bored with ____.

4 I'm scared of ____.

Flashcards List

Flashcards		
cooking	do gymnastics	bridge
skiing	do karate	mountain
watching TV	go skateboarding	rainforest
skateboarding	go to a party	river
playing the guitar	go to school	valley
	go to the park	waterfall
crocodile	have music lessons	
elephant	have ballet lessons	tired
giraffe		angry
hippo	ballet dancer	
lion	basketball player	climbing
monkey	builder	fishing
	doctor	horseback riding
storm	farmer	sailing
	firefighter	snorkeling
	movie star	surfing
	police officer	

Spinner Template

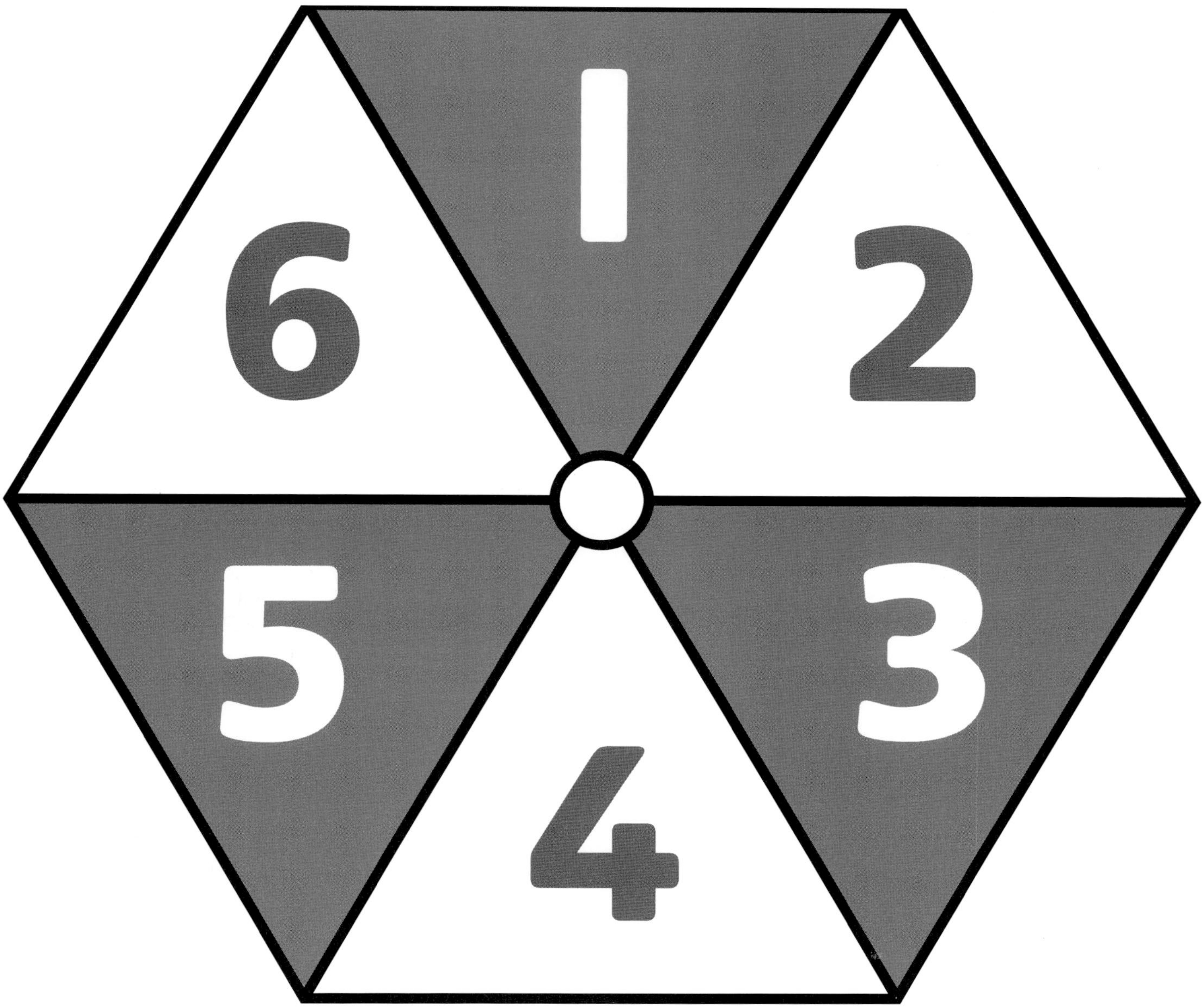